A DESCRIPTION

OR

BREIFE DECLARATION

OF ALL THE

ANCIENT MONUMENTS, RITES, AND CUSTOMES

BELONGINGE OR BEINGE WITHIN THE

MONASTICAL CHURCH OF DURHAM

BEFORE THE SUPPRESSION.

WRITTEN IN 1593.

**FACSIMILE REPRINT 1998
LLANERCH PUBLISHERS
FELINFACH**

ISBN 1 86143 074 4

LONDON: PRINTED BY J. B. NICHOLS AND SON,
25, PARLIAMENT-STREET, WESTMINSTER.

THE PUBLICATIONS

OF THE

SURTEES SOCIETY

ESTABLISHED IN THE YEAR

M.DCCC.XXXIV.

M.DCCC.XLII.

PREFACE.

In preparing the following pages for the press, four Manuscripts have been used, two as forming the text, and two as affording various readings.

I. *MS. Cosin.*—A Manuscript upon paper, of the quarto size, marked B. ii. 11, in the Episcopal Library of Durham founded by Bishop Cosin, and containing, 1. An Exposition of the Catechism. 2. Hegg's Legend of St. Cuthbert. 3. A discription or Briefe declaration of all the Ancient Monuments, Rites, and Customes, belonginge or beinge within the Monasticall Church of Durham before the Suppression, written 1593; and, 4. An Act for a publike Thanksgivinge to Allmightie God every yeare on the fift of November. Anno Jacobi Regis tertio. The book is in the same hand from beginning to end, and the period of its compilation is proved by the last article of its contents to be subsequent to the year 1606. It was probably written about the year 1620, or 1630, but certainly before the Usurpation. The title of the Legend of St. Cuthbert, "The History of the Church of Durham, written by Stephen Hegg," is inscribed by Bishop Cosin in the more distinct hand of his earlier life, tending to prove that the volume. belonged to him before his elevation to the See of Durham. In the absence of any earlier authority, this Manuscript constitutes the text of our pages to p. 20, with additions and various readings from the other sources hereafter specified.

II. A manuscript Roll, sixty-seven feet in length, and six inches in breadth, of which the writing occupies five inches and a quarter, and consisting of sixty-five pieces of paper stitched together with thread, belonging to Thomas Jefferson Hogg and John Hogg of Norton, in the county of Durham, Esqrs. who have very obligingly permitted the Society to make use of it for this publication. This Roll is written in a bold hand, at a period certainly not much later than the date which the compilation itself in the Cosin MS. purports to bear, the year 1593. The following memoranda occur at some of the joinings of the sheets *in dorso*, indicating probably that it was copied by more scribes than one, of whom these may be the names:—" 2nd. part Mr. Iles, following Mr. Iles." " 3rd part of the 2nd part, following Mr. Iles." "John Wright," " Thomas Wright." Of these persons no record has been found. It is much to be regretted that this Roll does not contain the whole of the original compilation. It commences only with the battle of Neville's Cross; but, as it is manifestly of higher date and authority than the Cosin MS. the latter is after p. 20 rejected as the basis of our text, and is afterwards only used for subsidiary purposes: the Roll, from the page referred to, to the end of the book, is our chief authority.

III. MS. Hunter, No. 45, upon paper, in quarto· This is a book of a very miscellaneous nature. It appears to have belonged originally to persons of the names of Gabriel Archer and John Archer of Malton, as a school book, and from them to have passed into the hands of Theophilus Brathwaite, who, as he himself says in a pedigree of the family of Radclyffe of Threshfield, in the county of York, which he recorded in one of its pages in the year 1655, " was borne at Nunburnholm, the tenth day of January 1595, and was baptized the 18th day following, his godfathers Mr. Mawburne of Holm in Spaldingmore, Mr. Longley near Pocklington, and Mrs. Percy of Harswell godmother;" and that on the 11th day of October, 1624, being then " of the city of Yorke, Esqr. one of the gentlemen sewers to his late Majesty of famous memory Kinge Charles," he married Annabella, eldest daughter of Charles Radclyffe of Threshfield, Esq. by whom he had three daughters. When the book came into Mr. Brathwaite's possession it contained much blank paper, which he has filled up with entries equally miscellaneous—pedigrees of the Sovereigns of Europe, of the Emperors of Rome, biographical notices of Archbishops of York, and what more concerns us, a *sparsim* transcript of numerous portions of the Record, which is printed in its entire state in the following pages, together with many very valuable additions, bringing it down to his own time. It is to be regretted that portions of the document are here wanting. They were probably contained in "the ould booke" to which he refers, (see p. 18 hereafter,) and of which nothing is now known. Of this manuscript we have made much use under the reference H. 45.

IV. MS. Hunter, No. 44, Tract 10, upon paper, in quarto. This is the latest of our MS. authorities, and appears to have been written subsequently to the Restoration. It has furnished a few various readings referred to under H. 44; but it alone contains an account of the painted windows which decorated the church of Durham at the time of its compilation. Appendix I. pp. 91—102.

The Society is under great obligation to the Dean and Chapter of Durham, and to the Trustees of Bishop Cosin's Library, for permission to make use of these manuscripts.

A note by Dr. Hunter, in the margin of MS. Cosin, (p. 46,) refers to another MS. in the possession of a Mrs. Milner, of which no trace has been found.

A considerable portion of the Record here presented to the Society and to the public, was published in a curtailed and modernized shape, by John Davies, of Kidwelly, in the year 1672, in a volume of the duodecimo size, under the following title: "The Ancient Rites and Monuments of the Monastical and Cathedral Church of Durham, collected out of Ancient Manuscripts about the time of the Suppression." In the Dedication, dated London, October 4, 1671, "to my much honoured friend, James Mickleton, of the Inner Temple, Esqr." Davies speaks of his obligations to " a famous native of Durham, his early friend and patron, John Hall," who was brother-in-law to Mickleton by marriage; and it is probable that from this person he received his manuscript. Hall was a poet, and died young; having been a contemporary of Davies at St. John's College, Cambridge. Of Davies himself, and his various writings, a full account is given by Wood (Athen. Oxon. ii. 902, second edition). His publication of the little volume now engaging our attention, brought upon him and his book the following unmerited attack from " a severe Calvinist, and afterwards a Bishop," whose name Wood has withheld. " Liber hic omnino apochryphus μυσαριάς et Legendæ putidæ plurimum, vero historiæ (praxi et cultu monachorum superstitioso exceptis) parum habet, adeo ut mirari subit, inscitiam ejus qui edidit, et negligentiam (veritati et ecclesiæ Anglicanæ damnosam) qui prœlo permisit.'

It seems evident, that Davies curtailed his manuscript, and modernized its spelling and language. The slightest comparison between his book and even the later of our two text authorities, the Cosin MS. will afford abundant proof of the defects of his edition, but the Norton roll establishes them in the most decided way. Old North-country words have been rejected; peculiar modes of expression of a local character have been generalized, and whole sentences have occasionally been so condensed as to convey an imperfect idea of their original character and meaning. That Davies took these liberties is the more to be regretted, as the manuscript from which he printed, although apparently in some respects less perfect than those above specified, seems to have contained matter not to be found in any of them; and the editor has not scrupled, upon a few occasions, to transcribe from Davies's book what could not elsewhere be found, using the reference *Dav.*

The above reason may suffice to justify the Surtees Society in apparently departing from one of its rules. This interesting Record of the Rites and Ceremonies of the Monastical Church of Durham, unique in its kind, and throwing so much light upon Benedictine and monastic observances, is now, for the first time, faithfully printed from the best authorities which can be found, with a collation of other existing manuscripts; and the garb which it assumes invests it with a new character. It must further be stated, that Davies's book, in its original state, is so exceedingly rare, that few people possess it, and that even in this respect alone a new edition was desirable.

We have said in its original state, for in the year 1733, Dr. Christopher Hunter made it the basis of a little volume, which he published under the following title:

"Durham Cathedral, as it was before the Dissolution of the Monastery, containing an account of the Rites, Customs, and Ceremonies used therein, together with the histories painted in the windows, and an appendix of various Antiquities, collected from several manuscripts.—Durham, printed by J. Ross for Mrs. Waghorn, 1733."

In the year 1743, Dr. Hunter professed to publish a second edition of the above book, but the title only was new. It runs as follows:

"The History of the Cathedral Church of Durham as it was before the Dissolution of the Monastery, containing an account of the Rites, Customs, and Ceremonies used therein, together with a particular description of the fine paintings in the windows; likewise the Translation of St. Cuthbert's body from Holy Island, with the various accidents that attended its interment here; with an appendix of divers Antiquities collected from the best manuscripts. Durham, printed for John Richardson, bookseller, at the Bible and Crown, price 2s."

Dr. Hunter's book contains a few corrections of Davies from MS. Cosin and H. 45, to which he seems to have had access, and also a few monumental inscriptions: but there is the same disregard of ancient phraseology, and a remarkable neglect of Brathwaite's additions to the latter of the above authorities. We have made one or two references to Dr. Hunter's edition. Of his appendix we shall have occasion to speak hereafter.

In the year 1767 Hunter's edition was reprinted by a bookseller in Durham of the name of Patrick Sanderson, with still further deviations from the original, and with numerous additional inaccuracies, the result of carelessness. Appended to Sanderson's edition is a Description of the County Palatine of Durham, occupying 135 pages, taken from the Magna Britannia. The title of Sanderson's Book, of which there was a large impression, is as follows :—

" The Antiquities of the Abbey or Cathedral Church of Durham, also a particular Description of the County Palatine of Durham, compiled from the best Authorities and Original Manuscripts, to which is added, The Succession of the Bishops, Deans, Archdeacons, and Prebend's, The Bishops Courts and his Officers, And the Castles and Mansion Houses of the Nobility and Gentry, with other Particulars. Newcastle-upon-Tyne. Printed by J. White and T. Saint, for P. Sanderson, at Mr. Pope's Head in Durham, MDCCLXVII."

In our Appendix (No. 1.) is printed from H. 44, the only manuscript in which it is contained, " A Description of the Histories in the Glass Windows of the Church of Durham."[1] This description is also printed by Hunter, and from the same authority: but here again the language is modernized, and there are great inaccuracies in his text. The compilation is ascribed by Hunter to Prior Wessington, upon no authority. In fact, some of the figures represented persons who flourished long after Wessington's death.

The memoranda and letter of Henry the Sixth (Appendix, p. 103) are also printed by Hunter, p. 167, but no authority is assigned. We have found them in a manuscript in the Library of Bishop Cosin, B. II. 2,[2]

---

[1] The reader will be pleased to consider the above as the proper title of the first Article in the Appendix, and not " A Description of the Glass Histories in the Windows."

[2] " Collectio Antiquitatum Ecclesiæ Dunelmensis, begun the 14th of November, 1660. A transcript of a manuscript which Mr. Greeke hath: ended 26 of November, 1660." This volume, which was transcribed at the instance of Bishop Cosin, and contains several directions to the copyist in his hand, consists chiefly of extracts from Simeon Dunelm. and Prior Wessington's Collections, relative to the Benedictines in the MS. D. and C. D. B. iii. 30, hereafter mentioned.

and have thought it right, by printing them entire, to supply Hunter's omissions.

Appendix III. p. 105—117. The reference to the authority for this portion of the Appendix is given in a note to p. 105. These inscriptions are now printed for the first time, curtailed, however, of much of the history which is appended to each in the manuscript, and which was probably equally omitted upon the picture. We have, however, printed at length such biographical notices as are appended to the Saints of Lindisfarne, or the Northern Counties, and from them the nature of the rest may be ascertained.

Appendix IV. p. 118—124. These inscriptions, probably upon panel beneath the figures represented, are to be found only in the MS. Cosin, B. ii. 2, above referred to. They were first printed, but inaccurately, by Dr. Hunter.

Appendix V. p. 125—128. A list of the dependants or livery men of the Church of Durham, in 1510, with their respective offices, from an entry in one of the Bursar's Books, together with the quantity of cloth which each received, according to his station.

Appendix VI. p. 129—138. An abstract of such Indulgences as are preserved in the Treasury, granted to those who promoted the building of the Nine Altars, who visited in devotion and with gifts the shrine of St. Cuthbert, the various altars and relics of the Church, or who in any way contributed to its benefit. These Indulgences afford many valuable dates; and it is interesting to observe how those dates confirm the character of existing architectural details.

At a MEETING of the COUNCIL of the SURTEES SOCIETY, held on the 6th day of September, 1844, it was

RESOLVED, That the RITES and MONUMENTS of the Cathedral CHURCH of DURHAM be published by the Society to be edited by the Secretary.

JAMES RAINE, *Secretary*.

The Surtees Society.

RULES, &c.

OF

THE SURTEES SOCIETY,

ESTABLISHED IN 1834,

In honour of the late Robert Surtees, of Mainsforth, Esquire, the Author of the History of the County Palatine of Durham, and in accordance with his pursuits and plans; having for its object the publication of inedited Manuscripts, illustrative of the intellectual, the moral, the religious, and the social condition of those parts of England and Scotland, included on the East between the Humber and the Frith of Forth, and on the West between the Mersey and the Clyde, a region which constituted the Ancient Kingdom of Northumberland.

THE SURTEES SOCIETY

I. Shall consist of an unlimited number of Members, out of whom shall be triennially elected a President, twelve Vice-Presidents,* two Treasurers, and a Secretary,† who shall constitute the Council. Of this number five, including the Secretary and one of the Treasurers, shall be capable of acting as a Meeting. The President shall be ineligible a second time until three years shall have elapsed from his departure from the office. The other Members of the Council shall be capable of being re-elected.

II. The Officers of the Society shall be elected at each Third Annual Meeting. Any vacancy which may occur in the Offices of Treasurer or Secretary shall be provisionally filled up by the Council.

III. Those gentlemen who have assented, or do now assent, to the general principle of its proposed Rules and Regulations, and have signified their wish to become Members, shall be deemed original Members of the Society. In the case of persons applied to previously to the 27th of May, by Mr. Raine, at the request of the preliminary Meeting of the 17th of April, and from whom no answer has been received, the list shall be left open till the 1st of July next.

---

* The number of Vice-Presidents was increased to twenty-four at the Anniversary in 1836.

† An Under-Secretary was added at the Anniversary in 1836; but since the lamented decease of Mr. Gordon, in 1837, no new appointment has been made.

IV. Subsequent Members shall be elected by Ballot at the Anniversary; each candidate having been proposed by a Member, in a letter, post-paid, addressed to the Secretary, two months before the day of meeting. The Members present at the Anniversary shall alone be entitled to vote. One black ball in ten shall exclude.

V. Each Member shall pay to the Treasurers an Annual Subscription of two guineas in advance. The sum so raised shall be expended in transcribing and publishing, in a closely-printed octavo form, such inedited Manuscripts as illustrate the intellectual, the moral, the religious, and the social condition of those parts of England and Scotland, included within the above lines of demarcation, from the earliest period to the time of the Restoration,—every thing, in short, which has a tendency to throw light upon the mind, the morals, or the habits of our ancestors. No apartments shall be hired, except for the Annual Meeting. No collection of Books or of any other nature shall be formed. The Subscriptions, and the money arising from the sale of Books under a subsequent Rule, shall be solely devoted to the transcribing of MSS., the expenses of the press, and other incidental expenses.

VI. The Council shall itself supply matter for the press for the first year. Afterwards it shall annually call upon twenty members, in alphabetical order, for notices of MSS. which they who are applied to would recommend to be printed. These notices shall be sent to the Secretary within a prescribed time, accompanied by the manuscript itself, or an analysis of its contents. But in no instance shall any Member be applied to by the Council a second time until each Member shall have had an opportunity of recommending a MS. or of waiving his turn.

VII. No MS. shall be sent to the press by the Council, without the sanction of a majority of the Members. In order to obtain this sanction, the Council shall, by their Secretary, transmit to each Member, upon a single sheet, a condensed printed account of the various analyses which have been submitted for consideration. This sheet each Member shall return to the Secretary, with a mark in the margin opposite to those MSS. of which he approves the publication. The Council may, if it think fit, point out, as a matter of opinion, such in particular as it approves. The votes of Members who return no answer, shall be at the disposal of the Council. When there is a deficiency of matter in any year, that deficiency shall be supplied by the Council.

VIII. The expense of transcribing for the press every MS. of which the publication is determined upon, under the above rules, shall be defrayed by the Society, if the Member by whom it is proposed should require it.

IX. No matter shall be printed in connection with any MS. save what is necessary for its illustration. A short biographical account of its Author, and brief Notes illustrative of his phraseology, and of the customs and manners and opinions of his time, will be permitted to a reasonable extent, with the modern names of the places which he mentions, and occasional notices of persons who occur in his writings. The Council shall have a discretionary power of rejecting any additions of the contributor which do not, in their opinion, come within these limitations.

X. The number of copies of each publication shall be regulated by the Council. Of these one shall be given to each Member, whose subscription is not in arrear. The rest, of which the Council shall in each case determine the number, shall be sold at the price it shall appoint. The money raised by sale to go to the general fund.

XI. The Armorial Bearings of Mr. Surtees, and some other characteristic decoration connecting the Society with his name, shall be used in each publication. These embellishments shall be determined upon by the Council.

XII. The selection of a Printer and Publisher shall be left to the Council.

XIII. A List of Officers and Members, with an account of the receipts, expenses, and general proceedings of the Society, shall be annually printed, of an uniform size with its publications, and transmitted to each Member.

XIV. An Anniversary shall be held in Durham, on the second Tuesday in July, in each year,* for the regulation of the affairs of the Society. The first Anniversary to be held on the second Tuesday in July 1835. The Council shall have the power of calling extraordinary Meetings.

XV. The Society shall be answerable for no expenses which may be incurred at the Anniversary Meetings, save the hire of a Room for the transaction of its business.

XVI. No alterations shall be made in these rules, except at an Anniversary Meeting. Three months' notice of the alterations proposed shall be submitted to each Member.

* The Anniversary was, in 1836, removed to the *fourth Thursday in September*.

PUBLICATIONS OF THE SOCIETY.

I. REGINALDI MONACHI DUNELMENSIS LIBELLUS DE ADMIRANDIS BEATI CUTHBERTI VIRTUTIBUS. 8vo. Price to Non-Members, £1 1s.

II. WILLS AND INVENTORIES, illustrative of the History, Manners, Language, Statistics, &c. &c. of the Northern Counties of England, from the Eleventh Century downwards. [Chiefly from the Registry at Durham.] 8vo. Price to Non-Members, £1 5s.

III. THE TOWNELEY MYSTERIES. 8vo. Price to Non-Members, £1 5s.

IV. TESTAMENTA EBORACENSIA, or Wills registered at YORK, illustrative of the History, Manners, Language, Statistics, &c. of the Province of York from the Year 1300 downwards. PART 1. 8vo. Price to Non-Members, £1 5s.

V. THE CHARTERS OF ENDOWMENT, INVENTORIES, AND ACCOUNT ROLLS OF THE PRIORY OF FINCHALE, IN THE COUNTY OF DURHAM. 8vo. Price to Non-Members, £1 12s.

VI. SANCTUARIUM DUNELMENSE ET SANCTUARIUM BEVERLACENSE, or REGISTERS OF THE SANCTUARIES OF DURHAM AND BEVERLEY. 8vo. Price to Non-Members, £1.

VII. CATALOGI VETERES LIBRORUM. Catalogues of the Library of Durham Cathedral at various Periods from the Conquest to the Dissolution, including Catalogues of the Library of the Abbey of Hulme, and of the MSS. preserved in the Library of Bishop Cosin at Durham. Price to Non-Members, £1.

VIII. A MISCELLANEOUS VOLUME of BIOGRAPHY, containing a Life of Oswin, King of Northumbria, two Lives of St. Cuthbert, and a Life of Eata, Bishop of Hexham. Price to Non-Members, 12s.

IX. HISTORIÆ DUNELMENSIS SCRIPTORES TRES, GAUFRIDUS DE COLDINGHAM, ROBERTUS DE GRAYSTANES, et WILLIELMUS DE CHAMBRE, with the omissions and mistakes in Wharton's Edition supplied and corrected, and an Appendix of 655 original Documents in Illustration of the Text. A Volume of nearly 700 pages. Price to Non-Members, £2 2s.

X. RITUALE ECCLESIÆ DUNELMENSIS. A Latin Ritual of the ninth Century, with an interlinear Northumbro-Saxon Translation. Price to Non-Members, £1 1s.

XI. JORDAN FANTOSME. An Anglo-Norman Poem, of an Historical Nature, by Jordan Fantosme; giving a minute Account of the War in the North of England in 1170 and 1171, between Henry II. and William King of Scotland. Price to Non-Members, £1 1s.

XII. LIBER VITÆ ECCLESIÆ DUNELMENSIS, NEC NON OBITUARIA DUO EJUSDEM ECCLESIÆ. Price to Non-Members, 16s.

XIII. THE CORRESPONDENCE, INVENTORIES, ACCOUNT ROLLS, and LAW PROCEEDINGS of the PRIORY OF COLDINGHAM. Price to Non-Members, £1 6s.

New Members may obtain the Publications of the Society at a lower rate.

BOOKS IN THE PRESS.

XIV. THE EPISTOLARY CORRESPONDENCE and OTHER PAPERS of DR. MATTHEW HUTTON, Archbishop of York, in the Time of Elizabeth and James, with an UNPUBLISHED MEMOIR of that PRELATE and his immediate Descendants, by Dr. ANDREW C. DUCAREL. For the year 1842.

XV. A PORTION of the CORRESPONDENCE & STATE PAPERS of SIR ROBERT BOWES, Ambassador to Scotland in the Time of Queen Elizabeth. For the year 1842.

The Books, of which a few only are set apart for sale, may be had of the Publishers, J. B. Nichols and Son, Parliament Street, William Pickering, Piccadilly, London; and of Charnley, Newcastle; Andrews, Durham; and Laing and Forbes, Edinburgh.

OFFICERS

of

THE SURTEES SOCIETY,

TILL THE ANNIVERSARY IN 1842.

President.
THE RIGHT HON. THE LORD BRAYBROOKE.

Vice-Presidents.
JOHN ADAMSON, Esq., F.S.A., &c., *Secretary to the Society of Antiquaries of Newcastle upon Tyne.*
THE RIGHT REVEREND JOHN BRIGGS, D.D.
John Trotter Brockett, Esq., F.S.A., Newcastle.
THE REV. TEMPLE CHEVALLIER, B.D., *Professor of Mathematics in the University of Durham.*
CHARLES PURTON COOPER, Esq., F.S.A., LL.D., &c., *Lincoln's Inn.*
THE REV. SAMUEL GAMLEN, M.A., *Vicar of Bossal.*
THE REV. W. S. GILLY, D.D., *Canon of Durham and Vicar of Norham.*
JAMES HAMILTON, Esq., M.A., *Reader in Languages in the University of Durham.*
THE REV. JOSEPH HUNTER, F.S.A.
SIR WILLIAM LAWSON, Bart., F.S.A., *Brough Hall, Yorkshire.*
THE REV. JOHN LINGARD, D.D., *Hornby, Lancashire.*
REV. GEORGE ORNSBY.
Henry Petrie, Esq., F.S.A., Keeper of the Records in the Tower of London.
SIR THOMAS PHILLIPPS, Bart., *Middle Hill, Broadway.*
REV. JOSEPH STEVENSON.
GEORGE TAYLOR, Esq., *Witton Hall.*
THE REV. GEORGE TOWNSEND, M.A., *Canon of Durham.*
WALTER CALVERLEY TREVELYAN, Esq., *Wallington.*
JOHN WARD, Esq., *Durham.*
THE REV. CHARLES WHITLEY, M.A., *Reader in Natural Philosophy in the University of Durham.*
SIR C. G. YOUNG, Knt., F.S.A., *Garter King of Arms.*

Treasurers.
ROBERT HENRY ALLAN, Esq., F.S.A., *Durham.*
JOHN GOUGH NICHOLS, Esq., F.S.A., *London.*

Secretary.
THE REV. JAMES RAINE, M.A., *Durham.*

MEMBERS OF THE SOCIETY—1842.

John Adamson, Esq., F.S.A., *Secretary to the Society of Antiquaries of Newcastle upon Tyne.* [Vice-President.]
E. N. Alexander, Esq., F.S.A., *Halifax.*
Robert Henry Allan, Esq., F.S.A., *Durham.* [Treasurer.]
Mr. George Andrews, *Durham.*
John Harrison Aylmer, Esq., *Walworth Castle.*
John Church Backhouse, Esq., *Darlington.*
The Rev. James Baker, M.A., *Spiritual Chancellor of the Diocese of Durham.*
Mr. Lewis Baker, *London.*
Samuel Bentley, Esq., *London.*
The Rev. John Besley, D.C.L., *Vicar of Long Benton.*
Christopher Blackett, Esq., *Wylam Oak Wood.*
Henry Collingwood Blackett, Esq., *Sockburne Hall.*
J. Blackwell, Esq., *Newcastle.*
G. T. Leaton Blenkinsopp, Esq., *Hoppiland.*
Edward Blore, Esq., LL.D., F.S.A., *London.*
Beriah Botfield, Esq., M.P., F.R.S., F.S.A., *Norton Hall, Daventry.*
John Bowes, Esq., M.P., *Streatlam Castle.*
Richard Bowser, Esq., *Bishop Auckland.*
The Right Hon. Lord Braybrooke, F.S.A. [President.]
The Rev. John Brewster, M.A., Rector of Egglescliffe.
The Right Rev. John Briggs, D.D. [Vice-President.]
John Trotter Brockett, Esq., F.S.A., Newcastle, Vice President.
William Brougham, Esq.
The Rev. J. H. Brown, M.A., *Rector of Middleton-in-Teesdale.*
The Right Hon. Sir J. L. Knight Bruce, F.S.A., *Vice Chancellor.*
His Grace the Duke of Buccleuch and Queensberry.
John Burrell, Esq., *Durham.*
Robert Burrell, Esq., *Durham.*
The Right Hon. the Earl of Carlisle, F.R.S.
Emerson Charnley, Esq., *Newcastle.*
Rev. Temple Chevallier, M.A., *Professor of Mathematics in the University of Durham.* [Vice President.]
The Rev. E. Churton, M.A., *Rector of Craike.*
John Clayton, Esq., *Newcastle.*
His Grace the Duke of Cleveland.
Thomas Clennell, Esq., *Harbottle Castle.*
Charles Purton Cooper, Esq., Q.C., D.C.L., F.R.S., F.S.A. [Vice-President.]
The Rev. George Elwes Corrie, M.A., *Fellow of Catharine Hall and Norrisian Professor of Divinity in the University of Cambridge.*
The Rev. Thomas Corser, M.A., *Stand, Manchester.*
The Rev. Anthony Cumby, M.A., *Master of Scorton School.*
Miss Currer, *Eshton Hall.*
The Rev. Francis Daniel, *Stonyhurst.*
Matthew Dawes, Esq., F.G.S., *Bolton-le-Moors.*
Pudsey Dawson, Esq., *Hornby Castle.*
The Rev. T. F. Dibdin, D.D.
William Dickson, Esq., *Alnwick.*

Henry Donkin, Esq., *Durham.*
The Rev. H. Douglas, M.A., *Canon of Durham.*
The Right Hon. Lord Viscount Dungannon, M.P.
The Hon. Lord Dunglas.
The Right Rev. the Lord Bishop of Durham, D.D., F.S.A. &c.
John F. Elliot, Esq., *Elvet Hill, Durham.*
The Rev. F. A. Faber, M.A., *Fellow of Magdalen College, Oxford.*
John Ralph Fenwick, Esq., *Durham.*
The Right Hon. the Earl Fitzwilliam.
Thomas William Fletcher, Esq., F.R.S., F.S.A., *Dudley.*
Matthew Forster, Esq., M.P.
Percival Forster, Esq., *Durham.*
Joseph Frank, Esq., Stockton.
The Rev. Samuel Gamlen, M.A., *Vicar of Bossal.* [Vice-President.]
Rev. W. S. Gilly, D.D., *Canon of Durham and Vicar of Norham.* [Vice-President.]
Rev. Thomas Gisborne, M.A., *Canon of Durham.*
T. C. Granger, Esq. M.P., *of the Inner Temple, London.*
The Rev. Robert Green, M.A., *Newcastle.*
William Thomas Greenwell, Esq., *Greenwell Ford.*
Sir Charles Edward Grey, Knight, M.P.
Stacey Grimaldi, Esq., F.S.A., *London.*
Edwin Guest, Esq., M.A., F.R.S., *Fellow of Caius College, Cambridge.*
The Venerable W. H. Hale, *Archdeacon of St. Alban's.*
James Hamilton, Esq., M.A., *Reader in Languages in the University of Durham.* [Vice-President.]
William Charles Harland, Esq., *Sutton Hall.*
Henry M. Hawkins, Esq., *Tredunnoch, co. Monmouth; Montague Place, London.*
Gilbert Henderson, Esq., M.A., *of Brazen Nose College, Oxford, and the Temple, London.*
John Fowden Hindle, Esq., *Woodford Park, Lancashire.*
John Hodgson Hinde, Esq., M.P.
The Rev. John Hodgson, M.A., F.S.A., M.R.S.L., *Vicar of Hartburn.*
John Holmes, Esq., F.S.A., *British Museum.*
Thomas Hopper, Esq., *Sharrow, Ripon.*
Rev. A. McDonald Hopper, *Fellow of St. John's College, Cambridge.*
Henry Howard, Esq., Corby Castle.
The Rev. Joseph Hunter, F.S.A. [Vice-President.]
R. C. Hussey, Esq., F.S.A., *Birmingham.*
Alan William Hutchinson, Esq., *Durham.*
William Hutton, Esq., F.R.S., *Newcastle.*
Robert Ingham, Esq., *Westoe.*
William Ward Jackson, Esq., Normanby.
George Edwin Ward Jackson, Esq., M.A., *Normanby.*
Rev. Henry Jenkyns, D.D., *Canon of Durham, and Professor of Greek in the University of Durham.*
Michael Jones, Esq., F.S.A., *London.*
John M. Kemble, Esq., M.A.
Richard John King, Esq., *Exeter College, Oxford.*
A. Kirkaldy, Esq., *Bishopwearmouth.*
David Laing, Esq., F.S.A., *Secretary to the Bannatyne Club, Edinburgh.*
Robert Laurie, Esq., *Windsor Herald.*
Sir William Lawson, Bart., F.S.A., *Brough Hall.* [Vice-President.]
George Lawton, Esq., *York.*
The Rev. H. G. Liddell, M.A., *Rector of Easington.*

Ralph Lindsay, Esq., *London.*
H. A. Littledale, Esq., *Bolton Hall.*
The Right Rev. the Lord Bishop of London, D.D., &c.
The Marquess of Lothian.
The Rev. John Lingard, D.D., *Hornby.* [Vice-President.]
W. J. Lysley, Esq., *Fitzroy Square, London.*
John Whitefoord Mackenzie, Esq. W.S., *Edinburgh.*
James Heywood Markland, Esq., F.R.S., F.S.A., *Treasurer of the Roxburghe Club, London.*
Thomas Mason, Esq., *Copt Hewick, Ripon.*
The Hon. Lord Milton.
Francis Mewburn, Esq., *Darlington.*
Sir Samuel Rush Meyrick, K.H., LL.D., F.S.A., *Goodrich Court, Hereford.*
The Right Hon. Lord Montague.
John Morice, Esq., F.S.A., *London.*
The Rev. James Morton, B.D., *Vicar of Holbeach, and Prebendary of Lincoln.*
The Rev. C. Newsham, D.D., *President of St. Cuthbert's College, Ushaw.*
John Bowyer Nichols, Esq., F.S.A., *London.*
John Gough Nichols, Esq., F.S.A., *London.* [Treasurer.]
Alexander Nicholson, Esq., F.S.A., *Ufford, Suffolk.*
George Ormerod, Esq. D.C.L., F.R.S., and F.S.A.
Rev. George Ornsby, *Durham.* [Vice-President,]
William Palmer, Esq., M.A., *Fellow of Oriel College, Oxford.*
J. H. Parker, Esq., *Oxford.*
The Very Rev. George Peacock, D.D., F.R.S., &c., *Dean of Ely, and Lowndian Professor in the University of Cambridge.*
The Rev. T. W. Peile, M.A., *Head Master of Repton School.*
John Pemberton, Esq., *Sherburn Hall.*

Henry Petrie, Esq., F.S.A., Keeper of the Records in the Tower of London. [Vice-President.]
Sir Thomas Phillipps, Bart., F.S.A., *Middle Hill, Broadway.* [Vice-President.]
William Pickering, Esq. *London.*
The Rev. F. C. Plumptre, D.D., *Master of University College, Oxford.*
The Rev. William Raine, M.A., *Swinbrook.*
The Rev. James Raine, M.A., *Durham.* [Secretary.]
The Rev. John Raine, M.A., *Vicar of Blyth, Co. Notts.*
Leonard Raisbeck, Esq., *Stockton.*
J. Reed, Esq., *Bishopwearmouth.*

The Rev. Wm. Richardson, B.D., Fellow of College, Oxford.
Edward Widdrington Riddell, Esq.
The Rev. Thomas Riddell, M.A., *Vicar of Masham.*

John Gage Rokewode, Esq., F.R.S., Director S.A., London.
The Rev. Christopher Robinson, M.A., *Vicar of Kirknewton.*
The Rev. Daniel Rock, D.D., *Buckland, Farringdon.*
Samuel Rowlandson, Esq., *Durham.*
William Russell, Esq., *Brancepeth Castle.*
Anthony Salvin, Esq., F.S.A., *London.*

William T. Salvin, Esq., Croxdale.
Robert Segar, Esq., *Preston.*
John Strangways Donaldson Selby, Esq., *Cheswick.*
Sir Cuthbert Sharp, Knight, *Bishopwearmouth.*

Edward Sharpe, Esq., M.A., *Lancaster.*
George Shaw, Esq., *Durham.*
R. C. Sherwood, Esq., *Cheltenham.*
Edward Shipperdson, Esq., *Durham.*
The Right Hon. the Earl of Shrewsbury, F.S.A.
The Rev. Richard Skipsey, M.A., *Bishopwearmouth.*
John Smith, Esq., LL.D., *Secretary of the Maitland Club, Glasgow.*
Thomas Sopwith, Esq., F.R.S., *Newcastle.*
H. J. Spearman, Esq., *Newton Hall.*
Thomas Stapleton, Esq., F.S.A., *London.*
Rev. Joseph Stephenson, *Durham.* [Vice-President.]
Robert Surtees, Esq., *Redworth.*
Robert Lambton Surtees, Esq., *Redworth.*
George William Sutton, Esq., *Elton.*
Clement Tudway Swanston, Esq., Q.C., F.R.S., F.S.A.
Sir John E. Swinburne, Bart., F.R.S., F.S.A., *President of the Society of Antiquaries of Newcastle upon Tyne.*
The Rev. James Tate, M.A., *Canon Residentiary of St. Paul's Cathedral.*
The Rev. Ralph Tatham, D,D., *Master of St. John's College, Cambridge.*
George Taylor, Esq., *Witton Hall.* [Vice-President.]
Joseph Francis Tempest, Esq., F.S.A., *Hemsworth.*
The Venerable Archdeacon Thorp, D.D., *Warden of the University of Durham, and Canon of Durham.*
The Rev. Mark Aloysius Tierney, F.R.S., F.S.A., *Arundel Castle.*
The Ven. H. J. Todd, M.A., *Archdeacon of Cleveland and Rector of Settrington.*
The Rev. George Townsend, M.A., *Canon of Durham.* [Vice-President.]
W. Calverley Trevelyan, Esq., F.S.A. [Vice-President.]
John Trotter, Esq., M.D., *Durham.*
Mr. William Trueman, *Durham.*
Thomas Turner, Esq., *Fellow of Trinity College, Cambridge, Lincoln's Inn.*
Henry Turner, Esq., Secretary S.A.N., *Killingworth.*
The Hon. Lord Harry Vane, M.P.
The Very Rev. George Waddington, D.D., *Dean of Durham.*
John Walker, Esq., *Cornhill.*
The Right Hon. Lord Wallace.
John Ward, Esq., *Durham.* [Vice-President.]
Robert Weddell, Esq., *Berwick.*
The Hon. and Rev. G. V. Wellesley, D.D., *Canon of Durham.*
His Excellency M. Van de Weyer, *Belgian Minister.*
Thomas Wheldon, Esq., *Barnardcastle.*
Rev. William Whewell, B.D.,F.R.S., *Professor of Moral Philosophy and Master of Trinity College, Cambridge.*
Rev. Robert Meadows White, B.D., *late Professor of Anglo-Saxon, Oxford.*
The Rev. Charles Whitley, M.A., *Reader in Natural Philosophy in the University of Durham.* [Vice-President.]
The Rev. John William Whittaker, D.D. *Vicar of Blackburn.*
Thomas Willement, Esq., F.S.A., *London.*
The Rev. W. Wilson, M.A., *Rector of Wolsingham.*
Henry T. Maire Witham, Esq., *Lartington.*
Sir Wm. Woods, Knight, Garter King of Arms.
The Ven. Francis Wrangham, M.A., Archdeacon of the East Riding of Yorkshire.
Sir C. G. Young, Knight, F.S.A., *Garter King of Arms.* [Vice-President.]

MEMBERS ELECTED AT THE ANNIVERSARY IN 1842.

John Fawcett, Esq., *Durham.*
Leonard L. Hartley, Esq., *Middleton Lodge.*
John Hubback, Esq., *Lincoln's Inn.*
Hedworth Lambton, Esq., M.P.
W. W. E. Wynn, Esq., *Peniarth, Merionethshire.*

MEMBERS OF THE SOCIETY WHO HAVE DIED SINCE THE LAST REPORT.

The Rev. R. W. Bamford, B.D. *Vicar of Bishopton.*
Geo. Fred. Beltz, Esq., *Lancaster Herald.*
Sir Ralph Bigland, Knight, *Garter King of Arms.*
The Hon. Sir William Bolland, Knight, *one of the Barons of the Court of Exchequer.*
Lieut.-Col. Cookson, *Neasham Hall.*
Rev. N. J. Hollingsworth, M.A., *Rector of Boldon.*
William Mills, Esq., *Durham.*
Rev. Marmaduke Prickett, M.A. *Bridlington.*
Crosier Raine, Esq., *London.*
The Rev. R. Richardson, D.D., *Chancellor of St. Paul's, London.*
Thomas Rickman, Esq., F.S.A., *Birmingham.*
Joseph Willis, Esq., *Gateshead.*
W. D. Wilson, Esq., *of Glenarbach,* F.S.A.

ACCOUNT

OF THE

TREASURERS OF THE SURTEES SOCIETY,

From September, 1837, to 20th September, 1842.

DR.

	£	s.	D.
To received 2 Subscriptions in arrear, for the year ending July, 1835,	4	4	0
To received 6 Ditto, for the year ending July, 1836,	12	12	0
To received 26 Ditto, (24 by Mr. Allan and 2 by Mr. Nichols,) for the year ending September, 1837,	54	12	0
To received 159 Subscriptions, (107 by Mr. Allan and 52 by Mr. Nichols,) for the year ending September, 1838,	333	18	0
To received 156 Subscriptions, (106 by Mr. Allan and 50 by Mr. Nichols,) for the year ending September, 1839,	327	12	0
To received 160 Subscriptions, (109 by Mr. Allan and 51 by Mr. Nichols,) for the year ending September 1840,	336	0	0
To received 145 Subscriptions, (98 by Mr. Allan and 47 by Mr. Nichols,) for the year ending September, 1841,	304	10	0
To received 71 Subscriptions, (55 by Mr. Allan and 16 by Mr. Nichols,) for the year ending September, 1842,	149	2	0
To received of Mrs. Andrews, for the Sale of Books published by the Society, from September, 1837, to September, 1842,	20	9	6
To received of Messrs. Laing and Forbes, of Edinburgh, for Sale of Books, from September, 1837, to September, 1841,	14	8	6
To received of Messrs. Nichols, of London, for Sale of Books, from September, 1837, to September, 1840,	22	11	6
To received of Mr. Pickering, London, for Sale of Books, from September, 1837, to September, 1840,	25	1	3
To received of same, for Sale of Books, from September, 1840, to September, 1842,	15	6	6
To received of Messrs. Nichols, for sale of Books, from September, 1840, to September, 1842,	65	13	7
To received of Beriah Botfield, Esq., towards printing the Preface to the "Monastic Catalogues,"	17	0	0
	£1,703	0	10

	CR.	£	s.	D.
By Balance due to the Treasurers, as per Account ending Sept. 1837,		66	9	6
Paid Messrs. Blackwell and Co. for printing 500 Copies of the "Monastic Catalogues," of the "Biographies," and of the "Three Historians," including the Carriage of Proof Sheets, &c., the Printing of Rules, Circulars, &c., and the Binding of 300 Copies of each of the above Publications, and 300 copies of the "Durham Ritual" and "Fantosme,"		352	14	6
Paid M. Michel for editing "Fantosme,"		52	10	0
Paid Messrs. Maulde and Renou, of Paris, for printing "Fantosme,"		68	19	6
Paid Mr. Bentley for printing Title of "Fantosme,"		2	10	6
Paid Mr. Russell Smith's Expenses in landing "Fantosme,"		13	17	0
Paid Mr. Bentley for printing the "Durham Ritual,"		86	15	0
Paid Messrs. Blackwell and Co. for printing 500 Copies of the "Coldingham Records," including the Carriage of Proof Sheets, &c. the Printing of the Report of the Society, of Rules, Circulars, &c., the Binding of 300 Copies of the above Work and of the "Liber Vitæ," and two Years' Rent for Warehouse Room for the Publications of the Society,		145	4	6
Paid Mr. Bentley for printing the "Liber Vitæ,"		48	10	0
Paid the Rev. Joseph Stevenson and Mr. R. A. Thompson for transcribing the several MSS.,		87	7	2
Paid for Binding the MS. "Durham Ritual,"		0	15	0
Paid the Rev. James Raine for editing the "Biographies," 9 Sheets, at £2 2s. each,		18	18	0
The like for editing the "Three Historians," 43 Sheets,		90	6	0
The like for transcribing Portions of the Appendix of Ditto,		17	8	0
The like for editing the Coldingham Records, 25 Sheets,		54	12	0
The like for transcribing Portions of Ditto,		5	0	0
The like for Index to Ditto,		5	5	0
Paid his Postages and other Expenses from September, 1837, to September, 1842,		15	16	7
Paid the Rev. Joseph Stevenson for editing the "Durham Ritual," 13½ Sheets, and the "Liber Vitæ," 9½ Sheets, and other incidental Expenses,		71	5	0
Paid the Rev. George Ornsby for Index to the "Three Historians,"		8	8	0
Paid Mrs. Andrews and Mr. Loraine for Stationery, and Carriage of Parcels,		10	17	9
Paid by Mr. R. H. Allan (the Treasurer), for Postages and various petty Cash Expenses, from September, 1837, to September 1842,		4	0	0
Paid by Mr. J. G. Nichols (the Treasurer), for Printing, Postages, and various petty Cash Expenses, from September, 1837, to September, 1842,		4	11	9
Paid for Advertising Publications for Sale,		17	14	0
Paid Mr. Nicholson for Woodcuts for the "Coldingham Records,"		6	14	6
Paid Mr. Collard for a Fac-simile of a Coldingham Proclamation,		5	0	0
Paid Mr. Netherclift for Fac-similes of the Anglo-Saxon Ritual,		3	2	6
Paid for Copy of Du Cange,		4	4	0
Paid the Rev. James Raine for Editing the "Finchale Records," (not included in the Account for September, 1837,) 42 Sheets		88	4	0
Paid Mr. Lemon and Mr. Fisher for Plates of "Finchale Priory," (not included in the Account for September, 1837),		7	10	9
By received less on Account of Subscriptions for the Year ending Sept. 1837,		4	4	0
By Balance,		334	6	4
	£,1703		0	10

We, the Auditors, appointed to Audit the Accounts of the Surtees Society, report to the Society that the Treasurers have exhibited to us their accounts, from September, 1837, to the 28th Day of September, 1842, and that we have examined the said Accounts, and find the same to be correct :—

And we further Report that the above is an accurate Abstract of the Receipts and Expenditure of the Society, during the Period to which we have referred. As Witness our Hands, this 19th Day of December, 1842.

(Signed)   CHARLES WHITLEY.
             TEMPLE CHEVALLIER.
             JOHN WARD.

London: J. B. Nichols and Son, Printers, 25, Parliament Street.

THIS BOOK

DOTH CONTEINE A DISCRIPTION OR BRIEFE DECLARATION

OF ALL

THE ANCIENT MONUMENTS, RITES, AND CUSTOMES

BELONGINGE, OR BEINGE WITHIN,

THE MONASTICAL CHURCH OF DURHAM

BEFORE THE SUPPRESSION,

WRITTEN 1593.

I. THE NINE ALTARS.

FIRST in the front or highest part of the Church were the NINE ALTARS dedicated and directed in the honour of several Saints, and of them taking theire names, as the inscription hereof shall declare. The Altars beinge placed north and south one from another, alonge the FRONT OF THE CHURCH.

Yn the midst of the front of the Church, where theise nine Altars were placed, was the Altar of the holy fathers SAINT CUTHBERT and SAINT BEDE, havinge all the foresaid Altars equally devided of either hand, as on the south hand foure and on the north hand foure.

On the south were theise foure Altars followinge :

First the Altar of SAINT OSWALD and SAINT LAURENCE.

The second was the Altar of SAINT THOMAS OF CANTERBURYE and SAINT KATHERN.

The third was the Altar of SAINT JOHN BAPTIST and SAINT MARGARETT.

The fourth was the Altar of SAINT ANDREW and MARY MAGDALENE, beinge the uttermost Altar towards the south.

[On the south-angle of the said Nine Altars, next the Cemitery, commonly called the Centry Garth, and next the said Altar, there was an almery set, wherein singing-bread and wine were usually placed; at which the Sacristan of the Abbey caused his servant or scholar daily to give attendance, from six of the clock in the morning till high mass was ended, from out thereof to deliver singing-bread and wine to those who assisted the monks to celebrate and say mass. *Dav.*]

RICHARD DE BURY, Bishopp of Durham, lyeth buryed before this Altar under a faire marble stone, wheron his owne ymage was most curiously and artificially ingraven in brass, with the pictures of the twelve Apostles decided imbordered [devided and bordered. H. 45.] of either side of him, and other fine imagery worke about it, much adorninge the marble stone.

On the north side of Saint Cuthbert's Shrine and Saint Bede's Altar were theise four followinge :

The Altar of SAINT MARTIN.

The second was the Altar of SAINT PETER and SAINT PAUL.

The third was the Altar of SAINT AIDAN and SAINT HELLINE.

The fourth was the Altar of the holy Archangell SAINT MICHAELL, beinge the outermost towards the north.

Betwixt the last two Altars lyeth buryed ANTHONY BEAKE, Bishopp of Durham and Patriarch of Jerusalem, in a faire marble tombe under neath a faire marble stone, beinge the first bishopp that ever attempted to lye so neere the saccred Shrine of Saint Cuthbert, the wall beinge broken at the end of the allye for bringinge him in with his coffin, [which contynued untill the suppression of the abbey. H. 45.]

All the foresaid nine Altars had theire severall Shrines and covers of wainscote over head, in very decent and comely forme, having likewise betwixt everye Altar a verye faire and large partition of wainscott, all varnished over, with fine branches and flowers and other imagerye worke most finely and artificially pictured and guilted, conteyninge the severall lockers or ambers for the safe keepinge of the vestments and ornaments belonginge to everye Altar; with three or four amryes in the wall pertaininge to some of the said Altars, for the same use and purpose.

There is in the east end of the church a goodly faire round window, called SAINT KATHERN'S WINDOW, the bredth of the Quire, all of stone, verye finely and cunningly wrought and glazed; havinge in it twenty-four lights verye artificially made, as it is called geometricall, and the picture of Saint Kathern is sett in glass on the right side, underneath the said window, in a nother glazed window, as shee was sett uppon the wheele to bee tormented to death, which wheele did burst in pieces and caught the turners of the said wheele, and with the pikes therof all to rent them in pieces, Saint Katherine beinge safe hir selfe by the provision of Almightie God. And in the said window was there a frame of iron wherein did stand nine very fine cressetts of earthen mettall filled with tallow, which everye night was lighted, when the day was gone, to give light to the Nine Altars and Saint Cuthbert's Feriture in that part, and over all the church besides, did burne unto the next morninge that the day was broken.

In the south alley end of the Nine Altars there is a good glazed window called SAINT CUTHBERT'S WINDOW, the which hath in it all the storye, life, and miracles of that holy man Saint Cuthbert, from his birth, of his nativitie and infancie unto the end, and a discourse of his whole life, marvelously fine and curiously sett forth in pictures in fine coloured glass, accordinge as he went in his habitte to his dying day, beinge a most godly and fine storye to behould of that holy man Saint Cuthbert.

In the north alley of the said Nine Altars there is another goodly faire great glass window, called JOSEPH's WINDOW, the which hath in it all the whole storye of Joseph, most artificially wrought in pictures in fine coloured glass, according as it is sett forth in the Bible, verye good and godly to the beholders therof.

II. IN SAINT CUTHBERT'S FERITORYE.

Next to theise Nine Altars was the goodly [stately, H. 45] MONUMENT OF SAINT CUTHBERT, adjoyninge to the Quire and the High Altar on the west end, reachinge towards the Nine Altars on the east, and toward the north and south containinge the breadth of the Quire, in quadrant forme, in the midst wherof his sacred SHRINE was exalted with most curious workmanshipp of fine and costly [green, H. 45, and *Dav.*] marble, all limned and guilted with gold, hauinge foure seates or places conuenient under the shrine for the pilgrims or laymen [lame or sick men, H. 45] sittinge on theire knees to leane and rest on, in time of theire devout offeringes and fervent prayers to God and holy Saint Cuthbert for his miraculous releife and succour, which beinge never wantinge, made the Shrine to bee so richly invested, that it was estimated to bee one of the most sumptuous monuments in all England; so great were the offerings and jeweles that were bestowed uppon it, and no lesse the miracles that were done by it [wrought att it, H. 45] even in theise latter days, as is more patent [apparent, H. 45] in the History of the Church at large.

At the west end of this Shrine of Saint Cuthbert was a little Altar adjoyned to it for masse to be said on, onely uppon the great and holy feast of Saint Cuthbert's day in Lent, at which solemnitie the holy [whole, H. 45] Convent did keepe open household [howse, H. 45] in the Frater House, and did dine altogether on that day, and on no day else in the yeare. And at this feast and certaine other festivall dayes, in the time of devine service, they were accustomed to drawe [up, H. 45] the cover of Saint Cuthbert's Shrine [beinge of wainescott, where unto was fastned unto every corner of the said cover, to a loope of iron, a stronge cord, which cord was all fest together over the midst over the cover. And a strong rope was fest unto the loopes or bindinge of the said cordes, which runn upp and downe in a pully under the vault which was above over Saint Cuthbert's Feretorie, for the drawinge upp of the cover of the said Shrine, and the said rope was fastned to a loope of iron in the north piller of the Ferretory, haveinge six silver bells fastned to the said rope, soe as when the cover of the same was drawinge upp the belles did make such a good sound that itt did stirr all the people's harts that was within the church to repaire unto itt, and to make ther praiers to God and holy Saint Cuthbert, and that the behoulders might see the glourious ornaments thereof. Also the cover had att every corner two ringes made fast, which did runn upp and downe on fower staves of iron, when itt was in drawinge upp, which staves were fast to every corner of the marble that Saint Cuthbert's coffin did lye upon, which cover was all gilded over, and of eyther syde was painted fower lively images curious to the beholders; and on the east end was painted the picture of our Saviour sittinge on a rainbowe to geive judgment, very lively to the behoulders; and on the west end of itt was the picture of our Lady and our Saviour on her knee. And on the topp of the cover from end to end was most fyne [brattishing of, Ed. H.] carved worke, cutt owte with dragons and other beasts, most artificially wrought, and the inside was vernished with a fyne sanguine colour that itt might be more perspicuous to the behoulders; and att every corner of the cover was a locke to keepe itt close, but att such tymes as was fitt to shew itt, H. 45] that the beholders might see the glorye and ornaments therof.

Also within the said Feretorye, both of the north side and the south, there was ALMERYES of fine wenscote, beinge varnished and finelye painted and guilted finely over with little images, verye seemly and beautifull to behould, for the Reliques belonging to Saint Cuthbert to lye in. And within the said Almeryes did lye all the holy reliques [and guifts, H. 45] that was ofered to that holy man Saint Cuthbert. And when his

Shrine was drawne [upp, H. 45] then the said almeryes were opened, that every man that came thither at that time might see the holy reliques therein [all the holy reliques and guifts and jewells that were in the Almeries, H. 45] so that for the costly reliques and jewels that was in the same almeryes, and other reliques that hung about within the said Feretorye uppon the irons, was accounted to bee the most sumptuous and richest jeweles in all this land, with the beautifullness of the fine little images that did stand in the FRENCH-PEIR within the Feretorye, for great was the gifts and godly devotion of kinges and queenes and other estates at that time towards God and holy Saint Cuthbert in that Church.

Within this Feretorye of Saint Cuthbert there was many fine little PICTURS of severall sorts [saints, Ed. H.] of ymagery worke, all beinge of alabaster, set in the frontispice [Frenchpeire, H. 45] in theire severall places, the pictures beinge verye curiously engraven and gilt, and the NEVELLES CROSSE and bull head [for his creast beinge, H. 45] sett uppon the heighest [on height, H. 45] and of either side of the two dores in the said French Peire besides, and also in divers other places of the French Peire [which Feretory and French Pierre, *Dav.*] was made at the charges of John Nevill, as may appeare at large in the Historie of the Church.

At the east end of Saint Cuthbert's Feretorie there was wrought uppon the height of the irons, towards the Nine Altars, very fine CANDLESTICKS of iron, like unto socketts, which had light sett in them before day, that every monke might have the more light to see to read uppon theire bookes at the said nine altars when they said Masse, and also to give light to all others that came thither to heare and see the divine seruice.

[The King of Scots Ancient and his Banner, with the Lord Nevil's Banner, and divers other noble men's Ancients, were all brought to Saint Cuthbert's Feretory, and there the said Lord Nevill, [after the battel done, in most solemne and humble manner, H. 45] did make his petition to God and that holy man Saint Cuthbert, [to accepte his offeringe, H. 45] and did offer jewels and banners [and the holy rood crosse which was taken on the Kinge of Scotts, H. 45] to the Shrine of the holy and blessed man Saint Cuthbert within the Feretory. [and soe after his orisons performed to God and Saint Cuthbert, he departed. H. 45] And there the said Banners and Ancients stood and hung till the suppression of the house. The Lord Nevil's banner staff was done [wrought, H. 45] about with iron [wrythen about with iron, Ed. H.] from the midst upward, and did stand and was bound to the irons on the north end of the Feretory, and the King of Scots banner was bound to the midst of the said irons [to the midst of the Ferretorie, H. 45] and did hang on [over, H. 45] the midst of the Alley of the Nine Altars, and was fasten'd [with a cord, H. 45] to a loop of iron being in a pillar under Saint Catharine's window, in the east end of the church. And a little after the suppression of the house they were all taken downe, spoiled, and defaced, that the memory thereof should be clean taken away [obliterated, H. 45] though a great honour to the realm and decent ornament to the church. *Davies.*] [and an honnour to the realme, beinge the ensignes and trophies of ther great victories, H. 45.]

III. THE QUIRE.

In the east end of the Quire, joyninge uppon St. Cuthbert's Feritore, stood the HIGH ALTAR, beinge the goodliest [and moste statelye, H. 45] Altar in all the church, and a verye rich thinge, with many pretious and costly ornaments appertaininge to it, both for every principall day, as also for every [of our Ladies, H. 45, and *Dav.*] dayes.

Betwixt the said High Altar and St. Cuthbert's Feriture is all of [the, H. 45] FRENCH PEERE, verye curiously wrought, both of the inside and outside, with faire IMAGES of alabaster being most finely gilted, beinge called in the antient history the LAORDOSE, the said curious workmanshipp of French Peere or Laordose reachinge in hight almost to the middle vault, and containinge the breadth of the Quire in lengthe, in the midst wherof, right over the said Hie Altar, were artificially placed, in very fine alabaster, the picture of OUR LADY standinge in the midst, and the picture of ST. CUTHBERT on the one side and the picture of ST. OSWALD on the other, beinge all richly gilded, and at either end of the said Altar was a wande of iron fastened in the wall, wheron did hang curtaines or hanginges of white silke dayly.

The dayly ornaments that were hunge both before the Altar, and above, were of red velvett, wrought with great flowers of gold in imbroydered worke, with many goodly pictures besides, beinge verye finely gilted; but the ornaments for the Principall Feast, which was the Assumption of our Lady, were all of white damaske, all besett with pearle and pretious stones, which made the ornaments more rich and gorgeous to behould. [At either end was a place to keepe the which ornaments, which were of white damask and such like stuffe, H. 45.]

Within the said Quire, over the High Altar, did hang a rich

and most sumptuous CANAPIE for the BLESSED SACRAMENT
to hang within it, which had two irons fastened in the French
Peere, very finely gilt, which held the canapie over the midst of
the said High Altar, (that the PIX did hang in it, that it could
not move nor stir,) wheron did stand a PELICCAN, all of silver,
uppon the height of the said canopie, verye finely gilded,
givinge hir bloud to hir younge ones, in token that Christ did
give his bloud for the sinns of the world; and it was goodly to
behould, for the blessed Sacrament to hange in, and a marveilous faire PIX that the holy blessed Sacrament did hange in,
which was of most pure fine gold, most curiously wrought of
goldsmith worke. And the white cloth that hung over the Pix
was of verye fine lawne, all embroydered and wrought about
with gold and red silke, and four great and round knopes of
gold, marvelous and cunningly wrought, with great tassells of
gold and redd silke hanginge at them, and at the four corners
of the white lawne cloth, and the crooke that hung within the
cloth that the pix did hang on, was of gold, and the cords, that
did draw it upp and downe, was made of fine white strong
silke.

And when the Monkes went to say or singe the High Masse
they put on theire vestments [they were vested, H. 45] in the
VESTRYE [revestrye, *Dav.*] both the Epistoler and the Gospeller.
They were always revest in the same place, and when the office
of the masse began to be sung the Epistoler came out of the
revestrie and the other two monkes following him, all three
arow, at the south Quire dore, and there did stand to [untill,
H. 45] the *Gloria Patri* of the office of the masse began to bee
sunge, and then, with great reverence and devotion, they went
all [three, *Dav.*] upp to the High Altar (and on of the vergers
that kept the vestrie did goe before them, with a tipt staffe in
his hand, as it was his office so to doe), bowinge themselves
most reverently to the blessed Sacrament of the Altar, the one
on the on side of him that said the masse and the other of the
other side, also the Gospeller [Epistler, H. 45] did carrye a
marvelous FAIRE BOOKE, which had the Epistles and Gospells
in it, and did lay it on the Altar, the which booke had on the
outside of the coveringe the picture of our Saviour Christ, all
of silver, of goldsmiths worke, all parcell gilt, verye fine to behould: which booke did serve for the PAX in the masse. The
epistoler, when he had sung the epistle, did lay by the booke
againe on the Altar, and, after, when the gospell was sunge,
the Gospeller did lay it downe on the Altar untill the masse
was done; and, the masse beinge ended, they went all three
into the Revestrie, from whence they came, and caryed the

booke with them; and, one of the vergers meetinge them at the south Quire dore, after the same sort they came, and went before them into the vestrie.

Also there was perteininge to the High Altar two goodly CHALICES. One was of gold, the other of silver and double gilt, and all the foote of it [them, H. 45] sett full of precious stones. That of gold was for principall dayes, and the other was to serve everye day.

Likewise there was perteininge to the High Altar two goodly gilt BASONS of silver, one for principall dayes, double gilt, a great large one; and the other bason for everye day, not so large, beinge parcell gilt and graven all over; and two gilt CRUITTS, that did hold a quart a piece, parcell gilt and graven all over, and two lesser crewetts, for everye day, all of silver; one payer of silver CENSERS for everye double feast, double gilded, and two paire of silver CENSORS parcell gilt, and the cheines also, for everye day, with two SHIPPS OF SILVER, parcell gilt, for principall dayes, and other two of silver ungilt, for everye day, to carry frankincence in [one pair of silver censers for every day, and two pair of silver censers for every double feast, double gilt, and two pair of silver censers, parcel gilt, and the chains also, for every principal day, with two ships of silver, parcel gilt, for principal dayes, and other two of silver ungilt for every day to carry frankincence in, *Dav.*], and two silver double-gilded CANDLESTICKS for two tapers, very finely wrought, of three [two, H. 45] quarters high, to be taken in sunder with wrests, other two silver candlesticks for everye dayes service, parcell gilt, with rich and sumptuous furnitures for everye festivall day of changable suites; divers of the VESTEMENTS was sett all round about, both stooles and fannels. There was also other very rich and costly jewells and ornaments that was perteininge to the said High Altar.

Also there was two [faire, H. 45] CROSSES to be borne [to be carryed in procession, H. 45] on principall dayes, the one of gold, and the staffe, that it did stand on, to beare it with all, was all of silver and goldsmiths worke, verye curiosly and finely wrought and double gilt, and the other crosse was of silver and double gilt, and the staffe of it was wood, that it did stand on, after the same workmanshipp, and double gilt.

IV. THE QUIRE—THE PASCALL.

Also there was a goodly monument pertaininge to the Church called the PASCALL, which was wont to be sett upp in the Quire, and there to remain, from the Thursday called Maundye thursday, before Easter, untill Wednesday after the Assention day, that did stand uppon a foure-square thick planke of wood against the first grees or stepp, hard behind the three basons of silver that hung before the High Altar. In the midst of the said greese is a nick wherein one of the corners of the said planke was placed, and at every corner of the planke was an iron ringe, wherunto the feete of the Pascall were adjoyned, representinge the pictures of foure flyinge dragons [att each corner one, H. 45] as also the pictures of the four Evangelists [with six faire candlesticks for six tapers to stand in, H. 45] above the tops of the dragons, underneath the nethermost bosse, all supportinge the whole pascall; and [in] the four quarters have beene foure christall stones, and in the four small dragons' four heads four christall stones, as by the holes doth appeare. And on everye side of the four dragons there is curious antick worke, as beasts and men, uppon horsbacks, with bucklers, bowes and shafts, and knotts, with broad leaves spred uppon the knotts, very finely wrought, all beinge of most fine and curious candlestick mettall [or Latten mettal glistering as the gold it self, having six candlesticks or flowers of candlestick mettall, *added by Dr. Hunter, in the margin.*] comminge from it, three of everye side, wheron did stand in everye of the said flowers or candlestick a taper of wax. And on the height of the said candlestick or Pascall of lattine was a faire large flower, beinge the principall flower; which was the seventh candlestick. The Pascall in latitude did containe almost the bredth of the Quire, in longitude that did extend to the height of the [lower, H. 45] vault, wherein did stand a long peece of wood reachinge within a mans length [height, H. 45] to the uppermost vault roofe of the church, wheron stood a great long square taper of wax [a large square wax taper, H. 45] called the Pascall, a fine conveyance through the roofe of the church to light the taper with all. In conclusion the Pascall was estimated to bee one of the rarest monuments in England.

V. The Quire—The Passion.

Within the Abbye Church of Durham, uppon Good Friday [theire was, H. 45] marvelous solemne service, in the which service time, after the Passion was sung, two of the eldest [ancient, *Dav.*] Monkes did take a goodly large Crucifix, all of gold, of the picture of our Saviour Christ nailed uppon the crosse, lyinge uppon a velvett cushion, havinge St. Cuthbert's armes uppon it all imbroydered with gold, bringinge that betwixt them uppon the said cushion to the lowest greeces [stepps, H. 45] in the Quire; and there betwixt them did hold the said picture of our Saviour, sittinge of every side, [on ther knees, H. 45] of that, and then one of the said Monkes did rise and went a pretty way from it, sittinge downe uppon his knees, with his shooes put of, and verye reverently did creepe away uppon his knees unto the said Crosse, and most reverently did kisse it. And after him the other Monke did so likewise [all the other Monckes, H. 45], and then they did sitt them downe on every [eyther, H. 45] side of the Crosse, and, holdinge it betwixt them, and after that [them, H. 45] the Prior came forth of his stall, and did sitt him downe of his knees, with his shooes off, and in like sort did creepe also unto the said Crosse [and all the Monkes after him one after another, in the same order, and, *not in* H. 45], in the mean time all the whole quire singinge an himne. The seruice beinge ended, the two [two *not in* H. 45] Monkes did carrye it to the SEPULCHRE with great reverence, which Sepulchre was sett upp in the morninge, on the north side of the Quire, nigh to the High Altar, before the service time; and there lay it within the said Sepulchre, with great devotion, with another picture of our Saviour Christ, in whose breast they did enclose, with great reverence, the most holy and blessed Sacrament of the Altar, senceinge it [singinge, H. 45] and prayinge unto it upon theire knees, a great space, settinge two tapers lighted before it, which tapers did burne unto Easter day in the morninge, that it was taken forth.

VI. THE QUIRE—THE RESURRECTION.

There was in the Abbye Church of Duresme verye solemne service uppon Easter Day, betweene three and four of the clocke in the morninge, in honour of the RESURRECTION, where two of the oldest Monkes of the Quire came to the Sepulchre, beinge sett upp upon Good Friday, after the Passion, all covered with red velvett and embrodered with gold, and then did sence it, either Monke with a pair of silver sencers sittinge on theire knees before the Sepulchre. Then they both rising came to the Sepulchre, out of the which, with great devotion and reverence, they tooke a marvelous beautifull IMAGE OF OUR SAVIOUR, representing the resurrection, with a crosse in his hand, in the breast wherof was enclosed in bright [most pure, H. 45] christall the holy Sacrament of the Altar, throughe the which christall the Blessed Host was conspicuous to the behoulders. Then, after the elevation of the said picture, carried by the said two Monkes uppon a faire velvett cushion, all embrodered, singinge the anthem of *Christus resurgens*, they brought it to the High Altar, settinge that on the midst therof, whereon it stood, the two Monkes kneelinge on theire knees before the Altar, and senceing it all the time that the rest of the whole quire was in singinge the foresaid anthem of *Christus resurgens*. The which anthem beinge ended, the two Monkes tooke up the cushions and the picture from the Altar, supportinge it betwixt them, proceeding, in procession, from the High Altar to the south Quire dore, where there was four antient Gentlemen, belonginge to the Prior, appointed to attend theire cominge, holdinge upp a most rich CANNOPYE of purple velvett, tached round about with redd silke and [a goodly, *Dav.*] gold fringe; and at everye corner did stand one of theise ancient Gentlemen, to beare it over the said image, with the Holy Sacrament, carried by two Monkes round about the church, the whole quire waitinge uppon it with goodly torches and great store of other lights, all singinge, rejoyceinge, and praising God most devoutly, till they came to the High Altar againe, wheron they did place the said image there to remaine untill the Ascension day. There was another CROSSE of christall, that served for every day in the weeke.

There was borne before the Crosse everye principall day a HOLY WATER FONT [fatt, H. 45] of silver very finely graven and parcell gilt, which one of the Novices did carrye.

VII. THE QUIRE—ALMERIES—LETTERNS—BASINS.

In the north side of the Quire there is an ALMERYE, neere to the High Altar, fastened in the wall, for to lay any thinge in pertaininge to the High Altar. Likewise there is another ALMERYE in the south side of the Quire nigh the High Altar, enclosed in the wall, to sett the chalices, the basons, and the crewetts in, that they did minister withall at the high masse, with locks and keys for the said almeryes.

At the north end of the High Altar there was a goodly fine LETTERON [lettern, H. 45] of brasse, where they sunge the epistle and the gospell, with a gilt pellican on the height [topp, H. 45] of it, finely gilded, pullinge hir bloud out hir breast to hir young ones, and winges spread abroade, wheron did lye the book that they did singe the epistle and the gosple. It was thought to bee the goodlyest [fairest, H. 45] letteron of brasse that was in all this countrye. It was all to bee taken in sunder with wrests, every joynt from other. [It went all in hernes to take asonder att plesure. H. 45.]

Also ther was lowe downe in the Quere another LETTORN of brasse, not so curiously wroughte, standinge in the midst against the STALLS, a marveilous faire one, with an EAGLE on the height of it, and hir winges spread a broad, wheron the Monkes did lay theire bookes when they sung theire legends at mattens or at other times of service. [Where the Moncks did singe ther Legends at Mattins and other tymes. Which same stood theire untill the yeare 1650, when the Scotts were sent prisoners from Dunbarr fight, and put prisoners into the church, where they burned upp all the wood worke, in regard they had no coales allowed them. And there was a fellowe, one Brewen, appointed to looke to the Scotts, by Sir Arthure Haslerige baronett, then Governour of Newcastle, and the fower Northeran Counties, which conveyed this said brasse letterne and eagle away, and many other thinges appertayninge to the Church, and sould them for his owne gaine, a man of a badd conscience, and a cruell fellowe to the poore prisoners. H. 45.]

Before the High Altar, within the Quire above mentioned, were three marveilous faire silver BASINS [at the stepps as one goes up, H. 45] hung in chaines of silver; one of them did hange in the south side of the Quire, above the stepps that go upp to the High Altar, the second on the north side opposite to the first, the third, in the midst, betweene them both, and just before the High Altar. Theise three silver basons had lattin basons within them, havinge pricks for serges, or great wax candles, to stand on, the lattin basons beinge to receive the drops of the candles, which did burne continually, both day and night, in token that the House was alwayes watchinge to God.

There was also another silver bason, which did hang in silver chaines before the Sacrament of the foresaid High Altar, but nerer to the High Altar then the other three, as almost dependinge or hanginge over the priests back, which was only lighted in time of masse and ther after extinguished.

VIII. THE QUIRE—LUDOVICKE DE BELLOMONTE.

LUDOVICK DE BELLOMONTE, Bishopp of Durham, lyeth buried before the High Altar, in the Quire, beneath the stepps that goe upp to the said High Altar, under a most curious and sumptuous marble stonn, which hee prepared for himselfe before hee dyed, beinge adorned with most excellent workmanshipp of brasse, wherein he was most excellently and lively pictured, as hee was accustomed to singe or say masse, with his mitre on his head and his crosiers staffe in his hand, with two angells very finely pictured, one of the one side of his head and the other on the other side, with censors in theire hands sensinge him, conteining most exquisite pictures and images of the twelve Apostles devided and bordered of either side of him, and next them is bordered on either side of the twelve Apostles in another border the pictures of his ancestors in theire coat armour, beinge of the bloud royale of France, and his owne armes of France, beinge a white lyon placed uppon the breast of his vestment, beneath his verses of his breast, with flower de luces about the lyon, two lyons pictured one under the one foote of him and another under the other of him, supportinge and holdinge up his crosier's staffe, his feete adjoyninge and standinge uppon the said lyons, and other two lyons beneath them in the nethermost border of all, beinge most artificially wrought and sett forth all in brasse, marveilously beautifyinge the said through of marble: wherin was engraven in brasse such divine and celestiall sayinge of the Scripture which hee had peculiarly selected for his spirituall consolation, at such time as it should please God to call him out of his mortalitie, wherof some of them are legeable to this day as theise that follow:—

Epitaphium ejus.

In Gallia natus
De Bellomonte jacet hic Ludovicus humatus
Nobilis ex fonte regum comitumque creatus
Praesul in hac sede coeli laetetur in ede
Preteriens siste memorans quantus fuit iste
Coelo quam dignus justus pius atque benignus
Dapsilis ac hilaris inimicus semper avaris.

Super caput.

Credo quod Redemptor meus vivit qui in novissimo die me resuscitabit ad vitam eternam et in carne mea videbo Deum salvatorem meum.

In pectore.

Reposita est haec spes mea in sinu meo. Domine miserere.

Ad dextram.

Consors sit sanctis Ludovicus in arce Tonantis.

Ad sinistram.

Spiritus ad Christum qui sanguine liberat ipsum.*

IX. THE QUIRE—THE ORGANS.

There was three paire of ORGANS belonginge to the said Quire, for maintenance of God's service and the better selebratinge therof.

One of the fairest paire of the three did stand over the Quire dore, only opened and played uppon at principall Feasts, the pipes beinge all of most fine wood and workmanshipp, very faire, partly gilded uppon the inside and the outside of the leaves and covers up to the topp, with branches and flowers finely gilted, with the name of JESUS [I H S., H. 44] gilted with gold. There was but two paire more of them in all England of the same makinge, one paire in Yorke and another in Paules. [But ther was a paire att the cominge in of the Scotts, 1640, far exceeded all which they destroyed. H. 45.] Also there was a LETTERNE of wood like unto a pulpit standinge and adjoyninge to the wood organs, over the Quire dore, where they had wont to singe the nine lessons in the old time on principall dayes, standinge with theire faces towards the High Altar.

The second pair stood on the north side of the Quire, beinge never playd uppon but when the four Doctors of the church was read, viz. AUGUSTINE, AMBROSE, GREGORYE, and JEROME, beinge a faire paire of large organs, called the CRYERS.

The third paire was daily used at ordinary service.

X. THE QUIRE—BOOK OF BENEFACTORS, RELIQUES, &c.

There did lye on the High Altar an excellent fine [faire, H. 45.] BOOKE, verye richly covered with gold and silver, conteininge the names of all the benefactors towards Saint Cuthbert's church, from the first originall foundation thereof; the verye letters, for the most part, beinge all gilded, as is apparent in the said

---

* Part of this Epitaph was legible in 1672. Durham Notes, in the possession of the Rev. W. Greenwell.

booke till this day. The layinge that booke on the Altar did show how highly they esteemed theire founders and benefactors, and the dayly and quotidian remembrance they had of them, in the time of masse and divine service, did argue not onely theire gratitude but a most divine and charitable affection to the soules of theire benefactors, as well dead as livinge. Which booke is as yett extant, declaringe the said use in the inscription thereof.* There is also another famous BOOKE, as yett extant, conteininge the reliques, jewels, ornaments, and vestments, that were given to the Church by all those founders, for the further adorninge of Gods service, whose names were of record in the said book, that dyd lye uppon the High Altar, as also they are recorded in this booke of the afore said reliques and jewells, to the everlasting praise and memorye of the givers and benefactors thereof.

XI. THE NORTH ALLEY OF THE QUIRE.

At the east end of the North Alley of the Quire, betwixt two pillars opposite, was the goodlyest faire PORCH, which was called the ANCHORIDGE, havinge in it a marveillous faire roode, with the most exquisite pictures of MARYE and JOHN, with an altar for a Monke to say dayly masse; beinge in antient time inhabited with an Anchorite, whereunto the Priors were wont much to frequent, both for the excellency of the place, as also to heare the high masse, standinge so conveuiently unto the High Altar, and, with all, so neere a neighbour to the sacred Shrine of Saint Cuthbert; wherunto the Priors were most devoutly adicted. The entrance to this porch or anchoridge was upp a paire of faire staires adjoyninge to the north dore of St. Cuthbert's Feretorie, under the which staires the Pascall did lye. And in the time of Lent the children of the Aumerie were enjoyned to come thither daylye to dresse, trim, and make it bright against the Pascall feast.

In this North Allye of the Quire, betwixt two pillars on the south side, before Saint Blese Altar, (afterwards called Skirlawes Altar,) lieth buryed WALTER SKIRLAW, Bishopp of Durham, under a faire marble stone very sumptuously [curiously, H. 45] besett with many brasen images [brasse pictures, H. 45] havinge his owne image [picture, H. 45] most artificially portred in brasse, in the midst therof, with this sainge engraven uppon his brest,

---

* This book has been published by the SURTEES SOCIETY.

𝕮𝖗𝖊𝖉𝖔 𝖖𝖚𝖔𝖉 𝖗𝖊𝖉𝖊𝖒𝖕𝖙𝖔𝖗 𝖒𝖊𝖚𝖘 𝖛𝖎𝖛𝖎𝖙 𝖊𝖙 𝖎𝖓 𝖉𝖎𝖊 𝖓𝖔𝖛𝖎𝖘𝖘𝖎𝖒𝖔 𝖉𝖊 𝖙𝖊𝖗𝖗𝖆 𝖘𝖚𝖗𝖗𝖊𝖈𝖙𝖚𝖗𝖚𝖘 𝖘𝖚𝖒 𝖊𝖙 𝖎𝖓 𝖈𝖆𝖗𝖓𝖊 𝖒𝖊𝖆 𝖛𝖎𝖉𝖊𝖇𝖔 𝕯𝖊𝖚𝖒 𝖘𝖆𝖑𝖛𝖆𝖙𝖔𝖗𝖊𝖒 𝖒𝖊𝖚𝖒.

[The place of his sepulcher was in antyent tyme invyrond with irons, artificially wrought, but of late tyme *his body was taken upp and interr'd before the High Alter, and the same stone layde over hym,* and a stall or pewe placed theire for gentlewomen to sitt in. *His body was not removed, onely the stone,* H. 45 and *marg. note.*]

Right over the entrance of this North Allye, goinge to the Song Scoole, which scoole was heretofore the Segresters exchequer, ther was a PORCH adjoyninge to the Quire on the south and Saint Benedicks altar on the north, the porch having in it an altar and the roode or picture of our Saviour, which altar and roode was much frequented in devotion by Doctour Swallwell, sometime monke of Durham, the said rood havinge marveilous sumptuous furniture for festivall dayes belonginge to it.

XII. THE SOUTH ALLEY OF THE QUIRE.

At the east end of the South Allye of the Quire [adjoining to the pillar next St. Cuthbert's Feretory, next the quire door on the south side, *Dav.*], opposite to the foresaid porch in the North Alley, was a most faire ROODE or picture of our Saviour, in silver, called the BLACK ROODE OF SCOTLAND, brought out of Holy Rood House, by Kinge David Bruce, and was wonn at the battaile of Durham, with the picture of our Ladye on the one side [of our Saviour, *Dav.*] and Saint Johns on the other side, very richly wrought in silver, all three havinge crownes of gold [pure beaten gold of goldsmiths work, *Dav.*] with a device or wrest to take them of or on, beinge adorned with fine wainscote [and on the back side of the said Rood and picture there was a piece of work that they were fastened unto, all adorned with fine wainscot-work and curious painting, well befitting such costly pictures, from the midst of the pillar up to the height of the vault, which wainscot was all red varnished over very finely, and all set forth with stars of lead, every star finely gilt over with gold. And also the said Rood and Pictures had every one of them an iron stuck fast in the back part of the said images that had a hole in the said irons, that went through the wainscot to put a pin of iron, to make them fast to the wainscot. *Dav.*]

THOMAS HATTFEILD, Bishop of Durham, lyeth buried over against the Revestorye doore, in the South Allye of the Quire, betwixt two pillars under the Bishopps seate, which hee did make before hee died, his tombe beinge all of alabaster, whereunto was adjoyned a little Altar which hee prepared for a Monke to say masse for his soule after his death, the Altar beinge invironed with an iron grate. [This monument remaynes still undefaced. His scutcheon, *Azure,* a chevron *or,* betwixt three lyons rampant *argent.* H 45.]

Within this south alley of the Quire was the VESTRYE [Revestry, *Dav.*] wher the Bishopp or his Sufraigne had a peculiar Altar, where they did use to say masse onely at such times as they were to consecrate priests or to give any holy orders.

XIII. THE CROSSE ALLYE OF THE LANTHORNE BEFORE THE QUIRE DORE GOINGE NORTH AND SOUTH.

In the former part of the Quire, of either side the West Dore, or chiefe entraunce therof, without the Quire dore, in the LANTHORNE, were placed in theire severall roomes, one above another, the most excellent PICTURES all gilted, verye beautifull to behould, of all the KINGES and QUEENES, as well of Scotland as England, which weere devout and godly Founders and Benefactors of this famous Church, and sacred monument of Saint Cuthbert, to incite and provoke theire posteritie to the like religious endeavours, in theire severall successions; whose names hereafter followeth.

    Edgarus rex Scotorum
    Katherina regina Angliæ
    David Broys rex Scotorum
    Ricardus secundus rex Angliæ
    Alexander rex Scotorum
    Henricus quartus rex Angliæ
    Richardus primus rex Angliæ
    Alexander rex Scotorum
    Matilda regina Angliæ
    David rex Scotorum
    Edwardus tertius rex Angliæ
    Henricus secundus rex Angliæ
    Edwardus primus rex Angliæ
    Henricus quintus rex Angliæ
    Alexander rex Scotorum
    Sibilla regina Scotorum
    Gulielmus Rufus rex Angliæ
    Richardus tertius rex Angliæ
    Gulielmus Conquestor rex Angliæ
    Heraldus rex Angliæ

Johannes rex Angliæ
Edwardus secundus rex Angliæ
Ethelstanus rex Angliæ
Stephanus rex Angliæ
Matilda regina Angliæ
Kenute rex Angliæ
Melcomus rex Scotorum
Duncanus rex Scotorum
Henricus tertius rex Angliæ
Helinora regina Angliæ
Henricus primus Angliæ rex
Elinora regina Angliæ
Melcomus rex Scotorum
Gulielmus rex Scotorum.

[*Some memorandums owte of the records of the Church of Durham which my ould booke wolde not contayne.*

Att the entrance of the Quier doore the pictures or statues of the severall Benefactors and Founders of the Church of Durham dedicated to Saint Cuthbert were placed, whose names are thus:

Edgarus rex Scotorum
Catherina regina Angliæ
David Bruce rex Scotorum
Ricardus primus rex Angliæ
Alexander rex Scotorum
Henricus quartus rex Angliæ
Matilda regina Angliæ
Edwardus tertius rex Angliæ
Henricus secundus rex Angliæ
Edwardus primus rex Angliæ
Henricus quintus rex Angliæ
Sibilla regina Scotorum
Willielmus Rufus rex Angliæ
Ricardus tertius rex Angliæ
Willielmus Conquestor rex Angliæ
Harold rex Angliæ
Johannes rex Angliæ
Edwardus secundus rex Angliæ
Ethelstan rex Angliæ
Stephanus rex Angliæ
Matilda regina Angliæ
Canutus rex Angliæ
Malcolmus rex Scotorum
Duncanus rex Scotorum
Henricus tertius rex Angliæ

Elinora regina Angliæ
Henricus primus rex Angliæ
Willielmus rex Scotorum.   H. 45.]

In the Lanthorne, called the NEW WORKE, was hanginge three fine [goodly, H. 45.] BELLS, which bells was runge ever at midnight, at twelve of the clock, for the Monkes went evermore to theire mattens at that houre of the night. There was four men appointed to ringe the said bells at midnight, and at all such other times of the day as the Monkes went to serve God; two of the said men apperteininge to the vestrye, which allwayes kept the Copes with the Vestments, and five paire of silver Sensers, with all such goodly ornaments, perteignige to the High Altar, which two men did lye everye night in a chamber over the west end of the said vestrye, and the other two men did lye everye night within the said church, in a chamber in the North allye, over against the Sexton's checker. These two men did alwayes sweepe and keepe the church cleanly, and did fill the Holy Water stones everye Sunday in the morninge with cleane water, before it came to be hallowed, and did lock in the church dores everye night.

Also there is standinge in the south pillar of the Quire doore of the Lanthorne, in a corner of the said pillar, a foure-squared STONN, which hath beene finely wrought, in everye square a large fine Image, whereon did stand a foure-squared stone above that, which had twelve cressetts wrought in that stone, which was filled with tallow, and everye night one of them was lighted, when the day was gone, and did burne to give light to the Monkes at midnight, when they came to mattens.

XIV. THE NORTH ALLEY OF THE LANTREN.

JOHN WASHINGTON, Prior of Durham, lyeth buryed under a faire marble stone with his verses [Epitaphe, H. 45] engraven in brasse uppon it, before the porch, over the entrance of the North allye, as you goe to the Song Scoole, adjoyninge to Saint Benedict's altar.

ROBERT BERINGTON de Walworth, Prior of Durham, did first obtaine the use of the Mitre with the Staffe. Hee lyeth buryed under a faire marble stone, beinge pictured from the waste upp in brasse, on the north side of Prior Washington, in the north plage, over against Saint Benedict's Altar, beinge the first of the three Altars in the North.

Next to SAINT BENEDICT'S ALTAR, on the north, is SAINT GREGORYE'S ALTAR, being the second Altar.

[The Altar of SAINT NICHOLAS and SAINT GILES was the last of the three Altars in the north plage towards the north.]

JOHN FOSSOUR was the first Prior that ever attempted to be buried within the Abbey church out of the Centorie Garth. He was buried in the north plage [under the north window in the lanterne alley, H. 45] before the Alter of SAINT NICHOLAS and SAINT GILES, being the last of the iij Alters in the north plage towards the north [the furthest north of the former, H. 45], over whom was layd a curious and sumptuous marble stone, which he had prepared in his liffe-tyme, ingraven in brasse, with his owne image and immagerie wourke [in brasse, *Cos.*] upon yt, with the xij apostiles devided and bordered of either syde of him with there pictures in brasse. *Roll.*]

XV. AN AUNTIENT MEMORIALL COLLECTED FORTHE OF THE BEST ANTIQUARIES CONCERNING THE BATTELL AT DURHAM IN JOHN FOSSOUR TYME.

[A collection forth of the best Antiquities of Durham church of the Battle fought theire against Daved Bruce kinge of Scotts and his brother in the time that John Forcer was Lord Prior, which was thus. H. 45.]

In the night before the battell of Durham stricken and begun [was petched, H. 45] the xvij. [xviij., H. 45] daie of October, Anno Domini 1346, ther did appeare to Johne Fossour, then Prior of the Abbey at Durham, a vision, commanding him to taike the holie CORPORAX CLOTH, which was within the corporax, wherewith Saint Cuthbert did cover the chalice, when he used to say masse, and to put the same holie relique, like unto a BANNER, [banner cloth, *Cos.*] upon a speare point, and on the morrowe after to goe and repaire to a place on the west parte of the citie of Durham, called the Readhills, and there to remayne and abyde till the end of the said battell. To which vision the Prior obeyinge, and taiking the same for a revelacion of God's grace and mercy by the medyacion of holie Saint Cuthbert, did, accordingly, early in the next morninge, together with the Monnks of the said Abbay, repaire to the said place, called the Readhills, there most devoutlye humbling [themselves, *Cos.*] and prostrating them selves in praier for the victorie in the said battell; a great multitude and nomber of Scotts runing and pressinge by them, both one waie and other, with intention to have spoiled them: but yett they had no power or suffrance to commytt any violence and force unto such holie persons, so occupied in praiers, being protected and defended by the mightie providence of Almightie God and by the mediacion of holy Saint Cuthbert, and the presence of the saide holie relique. And after many conflicts and warlike exploits there had and donne betwixte the Englishe men and the Kinge of Scotts and his company, the said battell ended, and the victorie was obteyned, to the great overthrowe and confussion of the Scotts there enemyes. And then the said Prior and monnkes, accompanied with Raphe L. Neivell [alias Daw Raby, H. 45] and John Neivell his sonne and the Lord Percy and many other worthie nobles of England, returned home and went to the Abbay Church, ther joyninge in hartie praier and thankes-geving to God and holie Saint Cuthbert for the conquest and victorie atchieved that daie. In which said battell a HOLY CROSS which was taken out of Holie Rude house [in Edinbrough, H. 45] in Scotland by kinge David Bruce was wonne and taiken [upon, H. 45] the said king of Scotland, at the said battell, which crosse, by most auncyent and credible writers, is recorded to have come to the said king most myraculouslie, and to have hapned and chaunced into his hand, being a hunting at the wylde harte in a forrest nygh Eddenbrowghe, upon Holy rude daie, commonlie called the Exaltacion of the Crosse, the said king, severed and parted from his nobles and company, suddenly there appered unto him (as it seamed) a most faire harte, runninge towards him in a full and spedy course, which so affraid the kings horse that he violently coursed away, whome the harte so fercely and swiftlye followed that he baire forciblie both the king and his horse to ground; who, so being dismayd, dyd cast backe his hands betwixt the tynds of the said harte to stay himselfe, and then and there most strangly slypped into the kings hands the said crosse, most wonderously. At the veiwe wherof immediatelye the hart vanished away, and never after was seane, no man knowing certenly what mettell or wood the said crosse was mayd of. In the place wherin this miracle was so wroughte doth now spring a fountaine called the Rude well. And the next night, after the said crosse so bechanced unto hym, the said king was charged and warned in his sleape by a vision to buyld an Abbey in the same place, which he most diligentlie observing, as a true message from God Almightie, did send for workemen into France and Flanders; who, at there commyng, were reteyned, and dyd buyld and erect the said Abbey accordinglie, which the king caused to be furnished with Chanons reguler, and dedicated the same in the honour of the Cross, and placed the said cross most sumptuously and richly in the said Abbey, ther to remayne as a most renowmed monument; and so there remayned till the said King, cummynge towards the said battell, did bring yt upon him as a most myraculous and fortunate relique. Notwithstandinge that the said Kinge, the said nighte, before he addressed him forwarde to the said battell, was in a dreame admonished, that, in any wise, he should not attempt to spoile or violate the churche goods of Saint Cuthbert, or any thinge that apperteyned unto that holie Saint. Which, for that he moste contemptuously and presumptuously dyd disdayne and contemne, violating and distroyinge, so much as he could, the said goods and lands belonging to Saint Cuthbert, was not onely punished by God Almighty, by his owne captivitie, being taiken at the said battell in the field, and therin very sore wounded, having first valiantly fought, and with him were taken foure Earles, two Lords, [eleven Lords, H. 45] the Archbushoppe of Saint Andrewes, one other Bushoppe, one knight, with many others. In which battell were slaine [the kings brother, H. 45], seaven Earles of Scotland, besyds many Lords and Scotishmen, to the noumber of, one and other, fifteane thousand, and also lost the said crosse, which was taiken upon him, and many other most wourthie and excellent jewells and monuments, which wear brought from Scotland, as his owne banner and other noblemen's aunncients [his owne banner, being the Royall standerd, with many more colours, H. 45] which all weare offred up at the shryne of Saint Cuthbert for the bewtifiynge and adorninge therof, together with the BLACKE RUDE of Scotland (so tearmed) with MARY and JOHN, maid of silver, being, as yt weare, smoked all over, which was placed and sett up most exactlie in the piller next Saint Cuthbert Shrine in the south alley of the said Abbey.

Shortelie after the said Prior caused a goodly and sumptuous BANNER to be maid, and, with pippes of silver, to be put on a staffe, being fyve yerds longe, with a device to taike of and on the said pipes at pleasure, and to be keapt in a chyste in the Ferretorie, when they weare taken down. Which banner was shewed and carried in the said Abbey on festival and principall daies. On the highte of the overmost pipe was a faire pretie crosse of silver and a wand of silver, having a fyne wroughte knopp of silver at either end, that went overthwart the banner cloth, whereunto the banner cloth was fastened and tyed, which wand was of the bignes of a man's fynger, and at either end of the saide wande there was a fyne silver bell. The wand was fast by the myddle to the banner staffe, hard under the crosse. The banner clothe was a yerd brode, and five quarters deape, and the nether part of it was indented in five parts, and frenged, and maid fast withall about with read silke and gold. And also the said banner cloth was maid of read velvett, of both sydes most sumptuously imbrodered and wrought with flowers of grene silke and gold. And in the mydes of the said banner cloth was the sayde holie Relique and Corporax cloth inclosed and placed therein, which Corporax cloth was covered over with white velvett, half a yerd square every way, having a red crosse of read velvett on both sydes over the same holie Relique, most artificiallie and cunynglie compiled and framed, being fynely fringed about the edge and scirts with frenge of read silke and golde, and three litle fyne silver bells fast to the scirts of the said banner cloth, like unto sackring bells, and, so sumptuouslie finished and absolutelye perfitted, was dedicated to holie Saint Cuthbert, of intent and purpose that the same should be alwaies after presented and carried to any battell, as occasion should serve; and which was (never) caryed or shewed at any battell, but, by the especiall grace of God Almightie and the mediacione of holie Saint Cuthbert, it browghte home the victorie. Which banner cloth, after the Dissolution [suppression, H. 45] of the Abbey, fell into the possession of one deane Whittingham, whose wife called Katherine, being a Freanche woman, as is most credably reported by those which weare eye-wittnesses, did most injuriously burne and consume the same in hir fire, in the notable contempt and disgrace of all anncyent and goodly reliques.

Further, on the west syd of the citie of Durham there was a most notable, famous, and goodly larg CROSS OF STONE WORK, erected and sett uppe to the honor of God and for the victorie had thereof, shortly after the battell of Durham, in the same place where the battell was fowghte, called and knowen by the name of NEIVELL'S CROSSE, which was sett upp at the cost and charges of the Lord Ralph Nevell, being one of the most excellent and chieffe in the said battell and feild. Which crosse had iij. [seven, *Cos.* and *Dav.*] steps aboute yt every way, four-squared to the sockett that the stalke of the crosse did stand in, which sockett was mayd fast to a four-squared brod stone, being the sole or bottom stone, of a large thicknes, that the sockett dyd stand upon, which is a yeard and a half square about every way, which stone was one of the steppes and the viij[th] in number. Also the said sockett was maid fast with iron and lead to the sole stone, in every syde of the corner of the said sockett-stone, which was three quarters deppe, and a yerd and a quarter square about every way. And the stalke of the crosse goinge upward conteyned in length three yerds and a halfe up to the bosse, being viij° square about, all of one holl peece of stone, from the sockett that yt did stand in to the bosse above, into the which bosse the said stalke was deply sowdered with lead and sowder. And in the mydest of the stalke, in every second square, was the Nevell's crosse, in a scoutchion, being the Lord Nevell's armes fynely cut out and wrought in the said stalke of stone. Also the nether end [part, *Cos.*] of the stalke was sowdered depe in the hole of the sockett, that it did stand in, with lead and sowder, and at every of the four corners of the said sockett belowe was one of the pictures of the four evangelists, being MATHEWE, MARKE, LUKE, and JOHNE, verie fynly sett forth and carved in stonemason worke: and on the hight of the said stalke did stand a most large fyne bosse of stone, being eight square rownde about, fynly cut out and bordered and mervylous curiously wrought. And in every square of the neither syde of the bosse in the mason worke was the Neivell's Crosse, in a scutchion, in one square, and the Bull's head, having no scutcheon, in an other square, and so contynued [conteined, *Cos.*] in every square, after the same sorte, rownd about the bosse: and on the hight of the said bosse, having a stalke of stone, being a crosse standing a little higher than the rest, which was sowdered deply with lead and sowder into the holl of the said bosse above, wheron was fynely cut out and pictured, on both sydes of the stalke of the said crosse, the picture of our SAVIOUR CHRIST crucified, with his arms stretched abrod, his hands nayled to the crosse, and his feete being naled upon the stalke of the said crosse belowe, almost a quarter of a yerd from above the bosse, with the picture of our Lady the blessed Virgin MARY of the one syde of him and the picture of Saint JOHN the Evangeliste on the other syde, most pitifully lamenting and beholding his torments and cruell deathe, standinge both on the highte of the said bosse. All which pictures was very artificially and curiously wrought all together and fynly carved out of one hole entyre stone, some part therof thorowgh-carved worke, both on the east syde and the west syde of the said crosse, with a cover of stone likewise over there heads, being all most fynly and curiously wrought together out of the said holl stone; which cover of stone was covered all over very fynly with lead. And also in token and remembrance of the said battell of Durham, and to the perpetuall memory and honour of the Lord Nevell and his posteritie for ever, it was termed by the title and name of Neivell's Crosse; which so did there stande and remayne most notorious to all passingers till of laite, in the yeare of our Lord God 1589, in the nighte tyme, the same was broken downe and defaced, by some lewde and contemptuous wicked persons, thereunto encouraged (as it semed) [seemeth, *Cos.*] by some who loveth Christe the worse for the crosse sake, as utterly and spitefully dispising all auncyent ceremonies and monuments.

And further, in the said place called the Read-hills, lying on the north syde of the said Neivell's crosse, a litle distant from a pece of grownd called the Flashe, above a close lying hard by north Chilton poole, and on the north side of the hedge where the Maydes bower had wont to be, where the said Prior and Monks standinge and makinge ther praiers to God with the holy Relicke of Saint Cuthbert during the tyme of the said battell, and, after the said battell finished and victorie atchived, was erected and sett up by the said Prior and Monks a faire CROSSE of WOOD, in the same place where they standing with the holie Relike mayd ther praiers, in token and remembrance of the said holy relique of Saint Cuthbert, which they caryed to the battell; which being a faire crosse of wood, fynely wrought, and verie larg, of highte two yeards, which there long stoode and contynued, by the remembrance of many now lyving; wher the said Prior and Monkes ever after, in memory of the said holy Relique, after the said victorie atchived, dyd in there tymes of recreacion, as they went and came to and from Beareparke to the monasterie and abbey of Durham, maike there humble and sollemne praiers to God and holie Saint Cuthbert, at the foote of the said crosse, in perpetuall prays and memory for the said victorie and recoverie of the said battell; tyll it was now of laite, within thes xxxv yeres, soddenly defaced and throwne downe by some lewde disposed persons, who dispised the antiquitie and worthynes of monuments after the suppression of Abbeys. And the collection of this memoriall antiquitie was in the yeare of our Lord God athowsand five hundreth nyntie and thre.

JOHN FOSSOUR was the first Prior that ever attempted to be buried within the Abbey church out of the Centorie Garth. He was buryed in the north plage [under the north window in the lanterne alley, H. 45] before the Alter of SAINT NICHOLAS and SAINT GILES, being the last of the iij Alters in the plage towards the north, [the furthest north of the former, H. 45] over whom was layd a curyous and sumptuous marble stone, which he had prepared in his liffe tyme, ingraven in brasse with his owne image and immagerie wourke [in brasse, *Cos.*] upon yt, with the xij Apostiles devided and bordered of either syde of him with there pictures in brasse.

XVI. THE SOUTH ALLEY OF THE LANTREN.

JOHNE HEMMYNGBROWGHE, Prior of Durham, lieth buried in the south plage, on the right hand, as yow goe to the Revestrie, under a faire marble stone, with his picture curiouslie ingraven upon it, having the xij Apostles pictured, of either syde of him vj, in brasse, with other immagerie woorke above his head, before the Alter of our LADYE, alias HOWGHELL'S ALTER, being the first of the iij Alters in the south plage [in the walke, H. 45].

WILLIAM EBCHESTER, Prior of Durham, lythe buryed in the south alley, under a faire marble stone, before the LADIE OF BOULTON'S ALTER, with his verses or epetaph ingraven upon the saide stone in brasse, which stone was taken up there, and removed, and lyeth nowe before the Quire door, the said Alter being the second of the iij Alters in that plage. Over the which Alter was a merveylous lyvelye and bewtifull Immage of the picture of our Ladie, so called the LADY OF BOULTONE, which picture was maide to open with gymmers [two leaves, H. 45] from her breaste [breasts, *Cos.*] downdward. And within the said immage was wrowghte and pictured the immage of our Saviour, merveylouse fynlie gilted, houldinge uppe his handes, and holding betwixt his handes a fair large CRUCIFIX OF CHRIST, all of gold, the which crucifix was to be taiken fourthe every Good Fridaie, and every man [moncke, H. 45] did crepe unto it that was in that church at that daye. And ther after yt was honng upe againe within the said immage. And every principall daie the said immage was opened, that every man might se pictured within her the Father, the Sone, and the Holy Ghost, most curiouslye and fynely gilted. And both the sides within her (? were) verie fynely vernyshed with grene vernishe and flowers of goulde, which was a goodly sighte for all the behoulders therof. And upon the stone that she did stand on, in-under, was drawen a faire crosse upon a scutchon, cauled the Neivell's cross, the which should signyfye that the Neivells hath borne the charges of ytt.

ROBERT EBCHESTER, Prior of Durham, lyeth buriede under a faire marble stone, with his picture and his versis, frome the waiste upe, in brass, before the said Lady Boulton Alter.

Next to the Lady of Bowlton's Alter, on the southe, was SANCTE FIDES ALTER and SANCTE THOMAS the Apostle, beinge the thirde Alter in the south plage.

There ys [was, H. 45] a LYBRARIE in the south angle of the Lantren, whiche is nowe above the Clocke, standinge betwixt the Chapter house and the Te Deum wyndowe, being well replenished with ould written Docters and other histories and ecclesiasticall writers.

In the north end of the allei of the Lantrene ther is a goodlie faire larg and lightsum glass wyndowe, haveinge in it xij faire, long, pleasant, and most bewtifull lights, being maid and buylte with fyne stone and glas, which in the ould tyme was gone to decaie, and the Prior at that tyme, called Prior Castell, dide renewe it, and did buylt yt all up enowgh againe, called the WYNDOWE OF THE FOUR DOCTERS of the church, which hath vj long fair lights of glas in the upper parte of the saide wyndowe. [of the upper parts in the same window. *Cos.*] And therin is pictured our blessed Ladie, with the picture of our Saviour Christ in her armes, and the picture of holie Sancte Cuthbert of the weste syde of her, both which pictures standing in the myds of the said wyndowe in most fyne coulored glasse, and of the east syde of our Ladie is ij of the Docters of the church pictured, and other ij of the Docters pictured on the west syde of Sancte Cuthbert, all being large pictures, and verie fynely and curiouslie sett furth in fyne coulored glas. And the picture of Prior Castell, who did make the hole coste of the buylding of the said windowe, both of stone and glasse, as is aforesaid, sytting on his kneis, in fyne blewe glas, in his habitt, and holding up his handes to our Ladie, under the feete of the said blessed virgin Marie, whose immage standing above his heade, sayinge,

"𝔙irgo 𝔐ater 𝔇ei miserere mei."

And other vj faire leights in the foresaid wyndowe, under our Ladie, Sancte Cuthbert, and the foresaid Docters beneath theme, being verie fynly glaised, with all the instruments of Christ's deathe sett in rownde [red coulered, H. 45] glasse, and wrowghte in fyne coulours in the said glasse wyndowe, being all but one wyndowe.

Also, in the southe end of the allei of the Lantren, above the CLOCKE, there is a faire large glasse wyndowe caulede the TE DEUM WYNDOWE, veri fair glased, accordinge as every verse of *Te Deum* is song or saide, so is it pictured in the wyndowe, verie fynly and curiouslie wrowghte in fyne colored glass with all the nyne order of Angells, viz. *Thrones, Dominations, Cherubins*, etc. [*Seraphines, Angells, Archangels*, &c. H. 45] with the pictur of Christ, as he was upon the cross crucified, and the blessed Virgin Marie with Crist in her armes, as he was borne.

XVII. THES MONNUMENTES FOLLOWINGE WEERE PLACEDE FROM THE LANTRENE IN THE MYDEST OF THE CHURCHE IN THERE SEVERALL PLACES TILL YOWE COMME TO THE WEST ENDE OF THE CHURCHE JOYNINGE UPON THE GALLELEIE.

In the body of the Churche, betwixt two of the hiest pillors supportinge and holding up the west syde of the Lanterne, over against the Quere dore, ther was an Alter called JESUS ALTER, where Jhesus mess was song every fridaie thorowe out the whole yere. And of the backsyde of the saide Alter there was a faire high stone wall: at either end of the wall there was a dore, which was lockt every night, called the TWO ROODE DORES, for the Prosession to goe furth and comme in at. And betwixt those ij dores was Jhesus Alter placed, as is afforesaide. And at either ende of the Alter was closed up with fyne wainscott, like unto a porch, adjoyninge to eyther roode dore, verie fynely vernished with fyne read vernishe; and in the wainscott, at the south end of the Alter, ther was iiij faire ALMERIES, for to locke the chalices and sylver crewetts, with two or thre sewts of VESTMENTS and other ornaments, belonginge to the said Alter for the holie daies and principall daies. And in the north end of the Alter, in the wainscott, there was a dore to come in to the said porch and a locke on yt, to be lockt both daie and nighte. Also ther was standing on the Alter, against the wall aforesaid, a moste curiouse and fine TABLE, with ij leves to open and clos againe, all of the hole Passion of our Lord Jesus Christ, most richlye and curiously sett furth in most lyvelie coulors, all like the burninge gold, as he was tormented, and as he honge on the cross, which was a most lamentable sighte to beholde. The which Table was alwaies lockt up but onely on principall daies. Also the fore parte of the said porch, from the utmoste corner of the porch to the other, ther was a dore with two brode leves to open from syde to syde, all of fyne joined and through-carved worke. The height of yt was sumthinge above a mans brest; and in the highte of the said dore yt was all stricken full of iron piks, that no man shold clymme over, which dore did hing all in gymmers, and clasps in the insyde to claspe theme. And on the principall daies, when any of the Monnks said mess at that Alter, then the Table was opened, which did stand on the Alter, and the dore with two leves, which stoode in the fore parte of the said closett or porch was sett open also, that every man might comme in and se the said Table in manner and forme as is aforesaid. Also there was, in the hight of the said wall from piller to piller, the whole storie and Passion of our Lord wrowghte in stone, most curiously and most fynely gilte, and, also, above the said storie and passion, was all the whole storie and pictures of the xij Apostles, verye artificiallye sett furth and verie fynelie gilte, contening frome the one piller to the other wrowght verie curiouslie and artificially in the said stone. And on the hight above all thes foresaide storyes, from piller to piller, was sett up a border very artificially wrowght in stone, with mervelous fyne coulers, very curiouslie and excellent fynly gilt, with branches and flowers, the more that a man did looke on it the more [desires he had and the greater, *Dav.*] was his affection to behold yt, the worke was so fynely and curiously wroughte in the said stone that it cold not be fynelyer wrowght in any kynde of other mettell. And also above the hight of all, upon the waule, did stande the most goodly and famous ROODE that was in all this land, with the picture of Marie on the one syde and the picture of John on the other, with two splendent and glisteringe Archangels, one on the one syde of Mary and the other of the other syde of Johne. So, what for the fairness of the wall, the staitlynes of the pictures, and the lyvelyhoode of the paynting, it was thowght to be one of the goodliest monuments in that church.

Also on the backsyde of the said Rood before the Queir dore there was a LOFT, and in the south end of the said loft the CLOCKE dyd stand, and in under the said loft, by the wall, there was a long forme, which dyd reche from the one Roode dore to the other, where men dyd sytt to rest themselves on and say there praiers and here devyne service.

Also, every frydaie at nyghte, after that the evinsong was done in the Queir, there was an anthem song in the bodye of the Church, before the foresaid Jhesus Alter, called JESUS ANTHEM, which was song every frydaie at nyght thorowgheout the whole yere by the M^r of the quiresters and deacons of the said church. And, when it was done, then the quiresters did singe an other anthem by themselves, sytting on there kneis all the tyme that ther anthem was in singinge, before the said Jesus Alter, which was verie devoutly song every fridaie at nyghte by the toulling of one of the Gallelei belles.

1. THOMAS CASTELL, Prior of Durham, lyeth buryed under a faire marble stone in the body of the church, being pictured from the waiste up in brass, in the mydest of the stone, with his versis or epetaph upon yt, before Jesus Alter, wher ther was on the north syde, betwixt two pillers, a looft for the M^r and quiresters to sing Jesus mess every fridaie, conteyninge a

paire of orgaines to play on, and a fair desk to lie there bookes on in tyme of dyvin service.

2. JOHANE AWCKLAND, Prior, lyethe buryed within the Abbey church of Durham.

3. JOHAN BURRNBIE, Prior of Durham, lieth buryed under a fair marble stone, pictured in brass from the waiste up, beneth the north dour, in the mydest of the church, not much distant from the Marble Cross, with his verses or epitaph adjoyninge therto.

Ther is betwixt the piller of the north syde, which the Holie Water stone did stand in, and the piller that standeth over against yt of the south syde, from the one of them to the other, a ROWE OF BLEWE MARBLE, and in the mydest of the said row ther is a CROSS of blewe marble, in token that all women that came to here devine service should not be suffered to come above the said cross. And if it chaunced that any woman to come above it, within the body of the church, thene, straighte wayes, she was taiken awaie and punishede for certaine daies, because ther was never women came where the holie man Sancte Cuthbert was, for the reverence thei had to his sacred bodie.

Also, yf any woman chaunced to come within the Abei Gaits, or within any presynckt of the house, yf she had bene sene but her lenth within any place of the saide house, she was taken and sett fast and punished, to gyve example to all others for doyng the like.

XVIII. THE CAUSES WHERFORE WOMEN MAY NOT CUMME TO THE FERRETORE OF SAINT CUTHBERT, NOR TO ENTER WITHIN THE PRECINCT ANNEXED IN THE MONASTERYE.

There are dyvers bookes written of the lyffe and miracles of that holy Confessour Cuthbert, partlie written by the Irishe, partly by Englishmen, and partlie by Scottishemen, being not able to comprehend the same in one worke. For, as Venerable Beede reporteth in the prologge of his Booke which he wrote of the liffe and miracles of Saint Cuthbert, that there weare many other things, nothing inferior to those which he wrote of the Liffe and vertews of that blessed man, which weare related unto him, and weare commaunded to be had in perpetuall memory, which woorkes, thowghe they weare not perfectly and delyberatlie finished, yt was thought unfitt and inconvenient to insert or adde any newe matter, of which books there is one intituled, *Of the cummyng of Saint Cuthbert into Scotland*, taiken furth of the Scottishe histories, whereupon, emongh other things, is sett downe the solitarie conversation of the said holie Saint Cuthbert, in this manner as followeth :

Blessed Saint Cuthbert for a long tyme led a [most, *Cos.*] solitarie liffe in the borders of the Picts, to which place great concourse of people daly used to visitt him, and from whome, by the providence and grace of God, never any returned without great cumforth and consolation. This caused both yong and old to resorte unto him, taking great pleasure both to se him and to heare him speake. In the meane tyme yt chanced that the daughter of the Kinge of that province was gott with child by some yong man in her father's house, whose belly swelling with her birth, which when the King perceyved, dyligently examined her who was the author of that fact. Upon dewe examynation wherof she maid this answere: " That solitarie young man, who dwelleth hereby, is he who hath overcum me, and with whose bewty I am thus disceived." Whereupon the King, furiouslye enradged, presentlie repayred with his deflowered dawghter, accumpaned with dyvers knyghtes, unto the solitary place, where he presentlie spake unto the servant of God in this manner : " What, are thowe he, who under the cullour of relligion, prophanest the temple and sanctuarie of God? Art thowe he, who, under the title and profession of a solytarie liffe, exerciseste all filthines of the world in incest? Behould, here is my dawghter, whom thowe with thy deceits hast corrupted, not fearing to make her dishonest, therefore now, at the last, openly confesse this thy falt, and plainly declaire heare before this cummpany in what sorte thow seduced her." The kinges dawghter, markinge the ferce speaches of her father, more impodentlye stepped furth, and bouldly affirmed that it was he which had done that wicked deade. At which thing the young man, greatly amased, perceiving that this forgery proceeded by the instigacion of the devell, wherwith he being browght into great perplexitie, applying his whole hart unto Almightie God, said as followeth : " My Lord, my God, who onely knowest and art the sercher of all secretts, make manifest also [all, H. 45] this worke of iniquetie, and by some example approve the same, which, thowgh yt cannott be done by humane pollecye, make it manifest by some dyvine oracle." Whenas the younge man, with grevous [greate, *Cos.*] lamentations and teares incredible to be reported, hadde spoken thes words, evin soddenlie, in the selfe same place wher she stod, the earth ther, making a hissing noyse, presentlie opened and swallowed her upe, in the presence of all the beholders. This place is cauled Corwen, where she for her corruption was conveyed and caried into hell. So sone as the king perceived this miraculous chaunce to happen, in the presence of all his cumpany, began to be greatlie tormented in his mynd, fearing, least throwghe his threates he should him selfe encur the like punyshment. Whereupon he, with all his cumpany, humbly craving pardon of Almightie God, with further desire and peticion to that good man Saint Cuthbert, that by his prayers he would crave at God's hands to have his dawghter again, to which peticion the said holie father graunted, upon condicion that no woman after that should have resorte unto him. Whereupon it came that the king did not suffer any woman to enter into any church dedecated to that Saint, which to this daie is dewly observed in all the churches of the Picts which weare dedicated to the honour of that holie man.

XIX. The northe alley of the bodie of the Churche.

In the NORTH ALLEI from the north church dor to the crose allei in the myds of the church, called the Lantren alley, where the Lantren standeth, in the entrance of the end of the said north allie into the said lanterne allie, from piller to piller, ther was a TRELLESDOURE, which did open and close with two leves, like unto a falden dor, and above the said dor it was likewaies trellessed, almoste to the hight of the valt above; and on the highte of the said trellesse was stricken full of iron piks, of a quarter of a yerd long, to th' entent that none should clyme over it; and was ever more lockt, and never opened, but of the Holie Daies, or of such daies as there was any Prosession. And likewise the north Rude dor, which was of th' other syde of the piller, at the north end of Jesus Alter, was never oppened but when there was any Prossession.

There was two faire HALLEWATER STONES belonging to the Abey church of Durresme, all of verie faire blewe marble. The fairest of them stoode within the north churche dour, over against the said dour, being wrowghte in the corner of the piller next adjoyning to the Lady of Pitties Alter, of the leaft hand, as yea turn into the Gallelei, having a verie faire skreene of waynscott over heade, fynely painted with blewe and litle gilted starres, being kept verie clene, and alwaies fresh water was provided against every sonnday morning by two of the bell ringers, or servitors of the church, wherin one of the Monncks did hallow the said water, veri early in the morninge befor devine service.

The other stood within the south church dour [right against

itt near the south doore, H. 45], not altogether so curyouse, yet all of fyne blewe marble, beinge verie decentlie keapt in the same manner with freshe water every sonndaie morninge by the said bell-ringers or servitoures of the church; when, in like sorte, one of the Monnks did hallow the said water very early in the morninge before dyvine service. The one of them, viz. that at the south dour, servinge the Prior and all the Covent with the whole house. The other, at the north dor, being joyned unto the piller, servinge all those that came that waie to here divyne service.

Ther was betwixt two pillers, on the leaft hand in the North Allie as yow tourne into the Galleley from the northe churche dour, our LADY OF PITTIES ALTER, being inclosed of either syde with fyne waynscott, with the picture of our Lady carying our Saviour on her knee, as he was taiken from the crosse, verey lamentable to behoulde.

Then on the right hand in the said north allie, as yow goe into the Galleley, under the belfraie called the GALLELY STEPLE, was SANCTE SAVIOUR'S ALTER, the north end of the sayd Alter stone being wrought and inclosed into the piller of the waul from the first foundacion of the church, for mess to be said at, as appered at the defacinge therof, and remayneth there to be knowne till this day by a corner of the sayd Altar stone not to be pulled furthe but by breaking of the wall.

In the weste end of the church, in the North Allie, and over the Galleley dour ther, in a belfray called the GALLELEY STEPLE, did hing iiij goodly great BELLS, and which was never rownge but at every principall feast, or at such other tymes as the Bushop dyd come to the towne. Every sonnday in the yere there was a sermon preched in the Galleley at afternonne, from one of the clocke till iij, and at xij of the clock the great bell of the Galleley was toulled, every sonndaie, iij quarters of an howre, and ronng the forth quarter, till one of the clock, that all the people of the towne myght have warnyng to come and here the worde of God preached. There was certaine officers perteyning to the said howse, which was allwayes charged, when so ever the said bells was knowlede, to be redy for the rynging of theme, viz. ij men of the kitching was charged with the ringing of on bell; and the iiij men of the church, that dyd lye allways in the church, was charged with the ringing of the third bell; and vj others was alwaies charged with the rynging of the great bell, viz. ij of the backhowse, ij of the brew house, and ij of the killne. And in the latter dayes of kyng Henrie the eighte the House was suppress, and after that tyme the said bell was never ronnge. Then Deane Whittingham, perceyving theme not to be occupied nor ronnge a great while before his tyme, was purposed to have taiken them downe and broken them for other uses [and make his profitt of them, H. 45]. Then Tho. Sparke, the Bushopes suffrigaine, lying at Durham, and kepinge howse there at the same tyme, havinge intelligence what the Deanes purpose was, dyd sende into Yorkshire with all speade for a workman, and caused iij of the said bells to be taiken downe,—the iiijth bell remaynes ther still, and was never ronnge synce yt was suspent* [the other did remayne a longe season, but yet after removed into the Lanterne, H. 45],—and caused them iij to be hoong up in the newe worke called the Lantren, and maide a goodly chyme to be sett on the said bells, the which dyd coste hime in charges thirty or fortie pownds; which chyme endureth to this daie; or els the saide bells had bene spoyled and defaced. [But, in the yeare 1650, this Abbey church was made a prison for the Scotts and quite defaced within, for ther was to the number 4,500, which most of them perished and dyed ther in a very short space, and were thrown into holes by great numbers together, in a most lamentable manner. But, in the yeare 1655, the clocke and chyme were repayred againe, which was taken downe and preserved from the said ruyne. H. 45.]

XX. THE SOUTH ANGLE OF THE BODIE OF THE CHURCHE.

ROBERT NEIVELL, Bushop of Durham, lyeth buryed in his anncestors Porch in the SOUTH ALLIE, nere unto the Cloyster dour on the southe, and Jesus Alter on the northe of the porche, conteyning iij pillers and so muche of the angle; having in yt an Alter withe a faire allablaster table above it, where messe was daly celebrated for their soules, and therein a seate or pew, where the Prior was accustomed to set to here Jesus messe. The est end of the Porche where the Alter stood was closed up with a litle stone wall, summwhat hier then the Alter, and wainscotted above the wall; the west end, with a litle stone wall, and an iron grait on the topp of the wall; and all the northe syd towardes the body of the churche invyroned with irone.

And also, in the backsyde, behynde the Neivells Alter, from the Neivells Alter to the mydst of the piller behinde the Churche doure, in compasse from piller to piller, ther was a chambre,

---

* Opposite to this word in *Cosin* Dr. Hunter has placed the word *indicted* in the margin.

where one that keapt the Churche, and rownge the bells, at mydnight did ly in; and also all over the Churche dour, the compasse of iiij pillers, two of either syd, when one entered within the Church doure, was all covered above with waynscott, verie fynely paynted and varnished blewe [azure, *interlined*] of the culler of the element, sett out with starres of goulde. And in the fore part of the wainscott, from piller to piller, within the Church, over the Holie Water stone, ther was a brattishing on the fore parte of the wainscott or rowffe, very fynely and curiouslie wrought, and all gilte [with gold, *interlined*] as fyne as the angell, and in the mydes of the saide brattyshing ther was a great starre of a great compasse, like unto the sonne, very artificially and most curiouslie gilt and ennamyled, very goodly to all the beholders therof, so that there coulde no duste nor fylthe falle into the Holy Water stone, it was so close above head, and so close within the Church doure.

In the west end of this south alley [angle, H. 45] betwixt the tow neithermost [lowest, H. 45] pillers, oppositt to the Ladie of Pitties Alter, ther was an Alter with a Roode representing the Passion [of our Saviour, H. 45] having his handes bounde, with a crowne of thorne on his head, being commonly called the BOUND ROODE, inclosed on etch syde with wainscott, as was the foresaid Alter of our Ladie of Pittie. [Neare to this Alter [on the south side adjoyning to the Galiley door, Ed. H.] was a grate whither the Sanctuary men did fly to when they came for refuge to Saint Cuthbert, H. 45] [where the sanctuary country men were wont to lye when they fled thither for refuge. *Davis.*]

XXI. THE SOUTH ALLEY OF THE BODIE OF THE CHURCH.
THE SANCTUARIE.

In the old tyme [the florishinge tyme, H. 45] longe before the house of Durham was supprest, the Abey Church, and all the Church yard, and all the circuyte therof, was a SAUNCTUARIE, for all manner of men that had done or commytted any gret offence, as killing of a man in his own defence, or any prisoners had broken out of prison and fled to the said church dore, and knocking and rapping at yt to have yt opened, there was certen men that dyd lie alwaies in two chambers [in a roome, H. 45] over the said north church dour, for the same purpose that when any such offenders dyd come, and knocke, streight waie they were letten in, at any houre of the nyght, and dyd rynne streight waie to the Galleley Bell and tould it, to th'intent any man that hard it might knowe that there was som man that had taken Saunctuarie. And when the Prior had intelligence therof, then he dyd send word, and commanding them that they should keape themselves within the Saunctuarij, that is to saie within the Church and churchyard; and every one of them to have a gowne of blacke cloth maid with a cross of yeallowe cloth, called Sancte Cuthbert's cross, sett on his lefte shoulder of his arme, to th'intent that every one might se that there was such a frelige graunted by God and Sancte Cuthbert,* for every such offender to flie unto for succour and safegard of there lyves, unto such tyme as they might obteyne their Prince's pardone, and that thei should lie within the Church or Saunctuarij in a GRATE, which grate ys remayninge and standing still to this daie, being maid onlie for the same purpose, standing and adjoining unto the Gallelei dore on the south syde, and likewise they had meite, drinke, and bedding, and other necessaries of the House cost and charg, for 37 † daies, as was meite for such offenders, unto such tyme as the Prior and the Covent could gett theme conveyed out of the dioces. This freedom was confirmed not onely by king Guthrid but also by king Alured.

In the weste end of the said Church, over the Gallelei, ther is a moste fyne large wyndowe of glass, being the holl storie of the RUTE OF JESSEI in moste fyne coloured glas, verie fynely and artifficially pictured and wrowght in coulers, veri goodly and pleasantlie to behoulde, with Mary and Christ in her armes in the top of the said wyndowe, in most fine coulored glass also.

XXII. THE GALLELY.

Wherefore the chappell dedicated in honor of Saint Mary was named and cauled the Galleley.

And for the cumforth of all women, and solace of theire soules, there was an ancyent Church in the Ferne ‡ iland, where the church of that towne nowe standeth, which was appoynted for women to repair unto, both for the hearing of masse for making there prayers, and receyving the sacraments; for which cause there was a chappell maide and dedicated to the blessed Virgin Marie, now cauled the Galleley. Upon the

* A coæval pen has altered *and Sancte Cuthbert*, into *unto Sancte Cuthbert's shrine.*
† The word *certaine* struck out and 37 placed in the margin.
‡ So in all the MSS. but a mistake, no doubt, for Lindisfarne, or Holy Island, where there is a church so situated.—ED.

namyng wherof is to be noted, as yow may reade in the booke entituled *The Acts of the B. ca. 26.*

HUGO, Bushop of Durham, who was consecrated in the yeare of our Lord God MCLIIII at Rome, by Pope Athanasius, upon the feaste day of Saint Thomas the Apostle, considering the deligence of his predecessors in buylding the Cathedrall Church, which was finished but a fewe yeres before his tyme, no Chappell being then erected to the blessed Virgin Marie, whereunto it should be lawfull for women to have accesse, began to erect a newe peice of woorke at the east end of the said Cathedrall Church, for which worke there weare sundry pillers of marble stone brought from beyonde the seas; but this worke, being browght to a small height, began throwghe great rifts apperinge in the same to fall downe, whereupon it manyfestlye appeared that that worke was not acceptable to God, and holy Saint Cuthbert, especially by reason of the accesse which women weare to have so neare his Ferreter. In consideration wherof the worke was left of, and a newe begun and finished at the west angle of the said Church, wherunto yt was lawfull for women to enter, having no holie place before where they mighte have lawfull accesse unto for there cumforthe and consolation.

In that it is called the GALLELY by reason (accordinge as some thinke) of the translatinge of the same, once begun and afterward removed, where upon it toke the name of Galleley, to which place such as maid repaire unto it had graunted unto them sundry pardons, as more plainly appereth in a table there sett up, conteyning the said pardons.

Within the said Gallelei in the Cantarie, being all of most excellent blewe marble, stood OUR LADIES ALTER, a verie sumptuous monument fynely adorned with curious wainscott woorke, both above the head, at the back, and at either end of the said Alter; the wainscott being devised and furnished with most heavenly pictures, so lyvely in cullers and gilting, as that they did gretly adorne the said Alter, where our Ladies masse was sung dalie, by the master of the Song Schole [cauled Mr. John Brimley, *interlined*], with certaine decons, and quiristers, the master playing upon a paire of faire orgaines the tyme of our Ladies masse, wherin the first founder of the said chantarie Bushop Langlei his soule was most devoutly praied for both in the begyning and ending therof. [This Bushop Langley did reedefye and buyld anew agayne the sayd Galliley. *Interlined.*] There was also belonging to the said Alter verey sumptious and gorgyous furneture, not onely for the principall feastes but for ordenary service, and for the preserving and saife keeping of these goodly suts of vestments and ornaments apperteyninge to the said Alter, ther was at either end therof behynd the portall two very fyne and close aumeries, all of wainscott, wherin after the celebrating of our Ladies mass they weare safely inclosed.

THOMAS LANGLEY, Bushop of Durham, lyeth buryed under a faire marble towme within the said cantaree, before our Ladies Alter. He founded upon the Place Grene a Grammer Scoole and a Songe Schole, with yerly stipends, wherof two prests weare maisters, which dyde dayly say masse, and also daily prayed for his soule. [His armes be pallie, argent and vert, a mullet of the first. H. 45.]

On the north syde of the saide Galleley was an Alter called the LADY OF PITTIES ALTER, with her pictur carryinge our Saviour on hir knee, as he was taiken from the crosse, a very dolorouse aspecte. The said Alter was ordeyned for a Chantry Preiste to saie masse every holy daie, having above the Alter on the wall the one parte of our Saviour's passion in great pictures, the other parte being above Saynt Beedes Alter on the south syde.

There was on the south syde, betwixt two pillers, a goodly monument, all of blew marble, the hight of a yeard from the ground, supported with v pillers, in every corner one; and under the mydest one, and above the said throwghe of marble pillers, did stand a second shrine to Saint Cuthbert, wherin the bones of the holie man Saint Beede was inshrined, being accustomed to be taiken downe every festival daie, when there was any solempe Procession, and caried with iiii Monnckes in tyme of Procession and devine service, which being ended they did convey it into the Gallely, and sett it upon the said tumbe againe [with great reverence, H. 45], havinge a faire [rich, H. 45] cover of wainscott verie curiously gilted and appointed to drawe up and downe over the shrine, as they list to showe the sumptuousness therof. And for the further veritie in this eneration of SAINT BEEDES SHRINE, I have sett downe the verces which are in the ancyent historie, declaring both the tyme of his Translation from Saint Cuthbert's toume, and withall the maker and founder of the shrine in the Galleley.

Hugo, Bushopp of Durham, after he had finished the chappell called the Gallely, did cause a Fereter of gold and silver to be mayd, wherin the bones of Venerable Bede, preiste and docter, translated and removed from Saint Cuthbert's shrine, weare laid. In the first woorke wherof, in the lower parte therof, these verses under-written were ingraven in Lattin, now translated into Englishe as followeth:

In cujus faretri prima fabricatura in parte inferiori isti versus sunt insculpti.

Continet hec theca Bede venerabilis ossa:
Sensum factori Christus dedit atque datori.
Petrus opus fecit, præsull dedit hoc Hugo donum;
Sic in utroque suum veneratus utrumque patronum.

In Englishe as followeth:

This coffin doth conteyne the bones of venerable Beede:
Christ to the maker sence did geve and to the giver gold.
One Peter framed the worke, the cost Bushopp Hugo maid;
So Peter and Hugo patrones both St. Bede inclosed in molde.

Anno milleno ccc ter cum septuageno
Postquam Salvator carnem de virgine sumpsit
Transtulit hoc feretrum Cuthberti de prope tumba
Istius ecclesiæ Prior huc (poscente Richardo
De Castro dicto Bernardi) cujus et ossa
Non procul hinc lapide sub marmoreo requiescunt.

In English as followeth:

In the yeare of our Lord a thousand thre hundreth and seventy
Richard of Barnardcastle did most earnestly procure
That the bones of Saint Beede lying nigh Saint Cuthbert shryne
Should be translated into the Galleley, there to remayne,
Which Richard disceased, for the love he did beare to Bede,
Caused his owne bones to be laid nere him under a marble stone indead.

It appeareth in the discription of the state of the Church of Durham that the bones of Saint Bede were first layde in the monastery of Jarrowe, and afterwards were browght to Durham and placed in the coffin [in a golden coffin, H. 45] on the right syde with the body [of the holy body, H. 45] of Saint Cuthberte.

Elfridus, a preaste, in that tyme, viz. Anno Gratiæ Mxx°, did affirme and certenly record that one coffyn dyd cover and conteyne both the body of Saint Cuthberte and the bones of venerable docter Bede.

On the south syde of the said Galleley was the ALTER OF SAINT BEEDE, before the which Alter lieth his bones and reliques interred under the same place where his shrine was before exalted.

Adjoyninge unto the lower parte of the great wyndow, in the weste end of the said Gallelee, was a faire IRON PULPITT, with barsse of iron for one to hould them by, going up the stepes unto the pulpett, where one of the Monncks did cume every holy day and sunday to preach, at one of the clock in the after noone.

In the west end of the south angle was a FONNTE for baptising of children, when the realme was interdicted by the Pope, which Thomas Langley, bushop of Durham, did onely procure as a priviledge, upon speciall favour, at the Popes handes.

[There are in this place (the Galilee), and all the church aboute, divers faire windows richly wrought with pictures and ymagery of Saints, which are now altogether broken, which I doe forbeare to meneion, for wante of roome and tyme, onely I have here inserted some thinges which were written, soe near as they could be read. H. 45.] (*The writer proceeds to give a few notices of the pictures and their inscriptions, of which the Roll contains a copious account as follows :*)

Also, in the west end of the said Galleley, there be foure faire coulered and sumptuous glasened WYNDOWES. In the first towards the south, there are three faire lights, the mydle lighte having in yt the picture of Christe, as he was crucified on the crosse, most curiously paynted and wrowghte in glasse, with the sonne and the moone above the head therof.

In the highest parte of which lighte ther is the picture of the starre which appered unto the thre Wise Men, or Kings of Colleine, underneth depictured, directing them into the East to search out the new-borne child Jesu, the holy one, borne betwixt an ox and an asse, to offer unto him oblacions and sacrifices of gold, myrr, and frankensence, together with the picture of our Ladye the Virgin Marie, with Christe naked sitting upon her knee, in most fyne coulored glasse.

In the light towards the north is dipictured God Almightie, having in his hand a ball or globe, conteyning and signyfying the heaven, earth, and sea. And, in under that, the salutacion of the angell Gabriell maid to the blessed Virgin Marie, and the picture of the Holie Ghost appearing to hir in the likenes of a dove, in fyne coulored glasse.

Also, in the light towards the southe, is the picture of our blessed Lady as she, assumpted into heaven, ascended glorified and crowned, and, underneth that, the picture of our blessed Lady with Christ new-borne naked, sitting of hir knee and sucking of hir brest, very lively sett furth, all in fine coloured glasse.

In the second, conteyning vj faire lights of glasse severed by stone, thre above and thre beneath, the mydle light above hath the picture of Saint Cuthbert, most lyvely coulered in glasse, in his ordinarie episcopall apparell to say masse, with his myter on his head, and a crosier or pastorall staffe in his lefte hand, having the immage of Saint Oswald's head painted upon his brest, upholden with his right hand, all in fyne coulored glasse. Under whose feate at the lowest parte of his picture is drawen or written in glasse:

𝖘𝖆𝖓𝖈𝖙𝖚𝖘 𝕮𝖚𝖙𝖍𝖇𝖊𝖗𝖙𝖚𝖘 𝖖𝖚𝖔𝖓𝖉𝖆𝖒 𝕷𝖎𝖓𝖉𝖎𝖘𝖋𝖆𝖗𝖓𝖊𝖓𝖘𝖎𝖘 𝕰𝖕𝖎𝖘𝖈𝖔𝖕𝖚𝖘 𝖊𝖙 𝖍𝖚𝖏𝖚𝖘 𝖊𝖈𝖈𝖑𝖊𝖘𝖎𝖆𝖊 𝖊𝖙 𝖕𝖆𝖙𝖗𝖎𝖆𝖊 𝖒𝖆𝖝𝖎𝖒𝖚𝖘 𝖕𝖆=𝖙𝖗𝖔𝖓𝖚𝖘.

The light on the north syde of Saint Cuthbert hath the picture of Saint Beede, in his blewe habitt apparell, in fyne coulered glasse, in under the foote of whose picture is in glasse writtin:

𝖘𝖆𝖓𝖈𝖙𝖚𝖘 𝕭𝖊𝖉𝖆, 𝖖𝖚𝖎 𝖛𝖎𝖙𝖆𝖒 𝖘𝖆𝖓𝖈𝖙𝖎 𝕮𝖚𝖙𝖍𝖇𝖊𝖗𝖙𝖎 𝖊𝖙 𝖒𝖚𝖑𝖙𝖆 𝖆𝖑𝖎𝖆 𝖆𝖇 𝖊𝖈𝖈𝖑𝖊𝖘𝖎𝖆 𝖆𝖕𝖕𝖗𝖔𝖇𝖆𝖙𝖆 𝖈𝖔𝖓𝖘𝖈𝖗𝖎𝖕𝖘𝖎𝖙, 𝖈𝖚𝖏𝖚𝖘 𝖔𝖘𝖘𝖆 𝖎𝖓 𝖍𝖆𝖈 𝖈𝖆𝖕𝖊𝖑𝖑𝖆 𝖎𝖓 𝖋𝖊𝖗𝖊𝖙𝖗𝖔 𝖈𝖔𝖓𝖙𝖊𝖓𝖙𝖆.

The light on the south syde of Saint Cuthbert hath the picture of Aydanus the bushop, most artificially sett furth, in fyne coulored glasse, as he was accustomed to say masse, with his myter on his head and a crosier staffe in his left hand, under whose feete this is written:

𝖘𝖆𝖓𝖈𝖙𝖚𝖘 𝕬𝖎𝖉𝖆𝖓𝖚𝖘 𝖊𝖕𝖎𝖘𝖈𝖔𝖕𝖚𝖘 𝕷𝖎𝖓𝖉𝖎𝖘𝖋𝖆𝖗𝖓𝖊𝖓𝖘𝖎𝖘 𝖊𝖈𝖈𝖑𝖊=𝖘𝖎𝖆𝖊 𝖕𝖗𝖎𝖒𝖚𝖘 𝖕𝖗𝖎𝖚𝖘 𝖎𝖓 𝖍𝖆𝖈 𝖘𝖆𝖓𝖈𝖙𝖎𝖘𝖘𝖎𝖒𝖆 𝕯𝖚𝖓𝖊𝖑𝖒𝖊𝖓𝖘𝖎 𝖊𝖈=𝖈𝖑𝖊𝖘𝖎𝖆 𝖋𝖚𝖎𝖙 𝖕𝖗𝖎𝖔𝖗𝖆𝖙𝖚𝖘.

Under whose iij lights by a particion are iij moe large pictures, in fyne coloured glasse, moste curiously depictured, conteyning the immages of Aldunus, Edmundus, and Eata, iij bushopps of Lindisfarne, in fyne coulored glasse, as they weare accustomed to say masse, with there myters on there heads and there crosier staves in there lefte hands. Under the feete of Eata his picture is written:

𝖘𝖆𝖓𝖈𝖙𝖚𝖘 𝕰𝖆𝖙𝖆 𝕷𝖎𝖓𝖉𝖎𝖘𝖋𝖆𝖗𝖓𝖊𝖓𝖘𝖎𝖘 𝕰𝖕𝖎𝖘𝖈𝖔𝖕𝖚𝖘.

And above, in the highest parte of this wyndow, ar six litle glasned lights, in tower manner, in fyne coulored glasse, conteyninge some parte of the historie of Christ's nativitie, the mariage in Gallelie and his miracles done upon the earth.

In the third wyndowe, being most faire and sumptuous, are also six lights, severed as before, in the highest parte therof are iij fyne portered [portred, *Cos.*] pictures in fyne colored glasse, the mydle being the immage of the glorious and blessed Virgin Mary, with Christe in her armes, most excellentlie wrowght in glasse, under whose feete is writtin:

Sancta Maria.

And on the north syde of her is the picture of Saint Oswold, the king, in fyne coulored glasse, very trymly sett furthe, with a faire crosse in his hand, under whose feete is written:

Sanctus Oswoldus fundator sedis Episcopalis Lindisfarnnensis quæ nunc est Dunelmensis cujus anima in feretro Sancti Cuthberti est humata.

And on the south syde of her is the picture of holie Kinge Henry, in fyne coulored glasse, with his princely scepter in his hand, under whose feete is written:

Rex Henricus.

Under them in other iij faire large lights oppositlie and firste to Saint Marie is placed the picture of Thomas Langley, Bushop, most curiouslie and worthelie in fyne coulored glasse, with his myter on his head and his crosier staffe in his lefte hand, as he was accustomed to say masse, having his armes verie excellentlie blasened in fine coulored glasse above his head, he being a most famous benefacter in reedifyinge and buylding againe this place, called the Galleley, as most truely and largly is recorded in the Historie of the Monasticall Church of Durham, under whome is written:

Thomas Langley Rector ecclesiae ad honorem Dei Episcopus Dunelmensis et duas cantarias in eadem fundavit et dotavit.

And under Saint Oswald is the picture of Wilfridus, Bushop, in fyne coulored glasse, as he was accustomed to say masse, with his myter on his head and his crosier staffe in his lefte hand, under whose feete is written:

Sanctus Wilfridus primo Lindisfarnensis monachus post Abbas Ripensis ultimo Archiepiscopus Eboracensis uno anno rexit episcopatum Lindisfarnensem.

And under king Henrie is the picture of Bushop Cedda, in fyne coulored glasse, as he was accustomed to say masse, with his myter on his head and his crosier staffe in his lefte hand, exquisitelie shewed, under whose fete is written :

Sanctus Cedda primo Lindisfarnensis monachus post Abbas in Lestingham tribus annis rexit Archiepiscopatum Eboracensem et etiam rexit Episcopatum Ligchfeilde.

And in this wyndowe, above all, are six litle glasened towre wyndowes, in fyne coulored glasse, conteyninge the Flight of Christe, Josephe, and Saint Marie into Egipt, being pursued by Herode, and the moste parte of the storie thereof.

In the fourth there be also six faire lights, severed as before, conteyning iij faire large pictures in iij lights, in the higher parte, most exactlie fashioned, being the images of iij holie Kings most goodly and bountifull to the church, and to Saint Cuthbert, viz. Alured, Gudred, and Elfride, most princely decked, and framed in ther royall apparrell, with there scepters in ther hands, in fyne coulored glasse, of whose liberalitye and marveilous munificence the historie of Saint Bede doth make mention. Under whome are pictured, in larg pictures, in fyne coulored glasse, iij Bushopes of Lindisfarne, as they weare accustomed to say masse, with there myters on there heads and there crosier staves in there left hands. Under there feete is to be seene,

Sanctus Godfridus [Egfridus] **Lindisfarnensis.**
Sanctus Ethelwoldus Lindisfarnensis.

The third no name to be discerned saving *Episcopus*. All which pictures aforesaid are most largly and sumptuously sett fourth in there formall apparell, as ys affore discribed.

In the highest parte of which wyndowe are six litle towre wyndowes, fynely colored and glasened, conteynninge the most parte of the storie of Christ's death, buryall, resurrection, and ascension, most excellentlye sett furth, pictured, and discribed, in fine colored glasse.

XXIII. The Ryte or Custome [Rytes and Ceremonies, H. 45] of the Church of Durham in Buryinge of Monnckes.

The Monncke, so soune as he sickneth, is conveyed, with all

his appurtinans or furniture, from his owne chamber in [owte of, H. 45] the Dorter to an other in the Fermery [another chamber in the place, called *Domus Infirmorum*, commonly called the Fermerey, H. 45], wher he might have both fyre and more convenyent kepinge, for that they were allowed no fyre in the Dorter. And, at such tyme as ytt appeared to them that accompeyned him in his sicknes that he was not lykly to lyve, they sent for the Prior's chaplaine, who staied with him till he yealded the ghoste. Then the barber was sent for, whose office is to put downe the clothes and baire him, and put on his feet socks and bowts [his foote sockes and his bootes, H. 45], and so to wynde hime in his cowle and habett. Then is he from thence immediatly caryed to a chamber called the Dead Mane's Chamber in the said Farmery, and there to remayne till nyght. [Then was he ymediately removed owte of the Fermery into a roome called the dead man's chamber, *over which was the Library of latter tymes,** and ther to remayne untill night. H. 45.] The Prior's chaplaine, so soune as that he ys wonne and conveyed into the DEAD MANE's CHAMBER, doth lock the chamber dour where he dyed and caryed the key to the Prior. At nyght ys he removed from the Dead Manes Chamber into ST. ANDREWES CHAPPELL, adjoyning to the said chamber and Fermery, there to remayne till eight of the clock in the mornynge, the said chappell being a place onely ordeyned for sollemne devocion. The nyght before there funeralles in this maner, two Monncks, either in kinred or kyndness the nerest unto him, were appoynted by the Prior to be speciall murners, syttinge all nyghte on ther kneys at the dead corsses feet. Then were the chyldren of th' Aumery sitting on there knees in stalls, of eyther syd the corpes, appoynted to read David's spalter all nyght over, incessantly, till the said hour of eight a clock in the morning, at which tyme the corse was conveyed to the Chapter house, where the [Lord, H. 45] Prior and the hole Covent did meat hime, and there did say there dergie [dirges, H. 45] and devotion, it not being permytted that any should cume neare the Chapter house duringe the tyme of ther devotion and praiers for his soule. And after there devocion the dead corpes was caryed by the Monnckes from the Chapter house thorowgh the PARLER, a place for marchannts to utter ther waires, standing betwixt the Chapter house and the Church dour, and so throwghe the said parler into the Sentuarie Garth, where he was buryed, and a chalice of wax laid upon his brest

---

* The words in italics are added in the margin.

with hime; havinge his blew bedd houlden over his grave by iiij Monncks during his funerall, which bedd is dew to the barber for his dewtie aforesaide and the making of his grave. And at the tyme of his buryall ther was but one peile ronnge for hime.

XXIV. The Rite or Custoume in Buryinge of Pryors.*

The Prior of the house of Durham was acustomed to be buryed in the oulde tyme in his bootes, and woune in his coole by the barber, accordingly as the Monncks was accustomed to be buryed, that is to say, he was caryed furth of his lodginge into a chamber in the Farmerye, called the Dead Manes Chamber, and there did remayne a certen spaice, and at nyght he was caried into a chapell over against the said chamber dore called Sancte Andrewes chappell, and was watched all that night with the children of the Almery, reading Davides splalter over him, and ij Monnckes, either in kindred or kyndnes, was appointed to sitte all night at his feet mourninge for him. And in the morninge he was caryed in to the Chapter house, and there did sollemne service for hime, as the Monnckes had at there buryall. From thence he was caryed thorowgh the Parlor into the Sentory Garthe, there to be buryed; wher every one of them did ly underneth a fair marble stone. And the Monnckes and barber did burye hime, with a litle challice of silver, other mettell or wax, which was laid upon his brest within his coffine, and his blewe bedde was holden over hime by iiij Monnckes till he was buryed, and the barber had it for his paynes for makinge of his grave and buryinge of hime, as he had for the Monnckes. And afterward the Priors came to be interred and buryed within the Abbey Church of Durisme, and not in Centori Garth in the latter daies, as followeth.

XXV. The names of the Priors buried out of the Centory Garth.

The names of all the Priors of Durham as weere buryed out of the Centory Garth within the Abbey Church of Durisme, in the same order and habitt, with [the mitre and, *Dav.*] all other there furnyture belonging therto, as there predicessors was

---

* MS. Hunter 45 enters into no detail on the burial of a Prior, but merely states that " it was in every respect performed accordinge to the buryinge of the monckes."

buryed before theme in the Centorie Garth, as is afforesaid, in every respects; all which Priors were great benefactors to the said Church, both during ther lives and at ther death, as the historie of the Church more at larg declareth.

JOHANNES FOSSER was the first Prior that ever attempted to be buryed within the Abbey church out of the Centore Garth.

ROBERT BERRINGTON de Walworth, Prior, dyd first opteyne the use of the myter with the crutch * or staffe.

JOHANNES HEMMYNGBROWGHE, PRIOR.

JOHANNES WESHINGTON, PRIOR.

WILLIELMUS EBCHESTER, PRIOR.

JOHANNES BURNBY, PRIOR.

ROBERTUS EBCHESTER, PRIOR.

JOHANNES AWKELAND, PRIOR.

THOMAS CASTELL, PRIOR.

HUGO WHITHEAD died at London, and lieth buried in the church of the Mineres nyghe the Towre of London. He was the laste Prior of the church of Durisme, and the first Deane.†

[ROBERT HORNE, Doctor of Devinity, Deane after hym. H. 45.]

The Bushopes of Durisme weare wonnte in anncyent tyme to be interred and buryed in the foresaid Chapter house, standing in the easte alley of the Cloysters,‡ in that they would not presume to ly any nearer to holie Sancte Cuthbert, whose naymes heare after enseweth.

---

* The words *the crutch or* are struck out, and *his crosier* placed above in the same hand, but in different ink.

† *And the first Deane*, is in a different, but apparently a coæval hand.

‡ Dr. Hunter has written opposite to this paragraph in *Cos.*, *This is better related in Mrs. Milner's manuscript.*

XXVI. A CATALOG OF THE BUSHOPS OF DURHAM, WHOSE BODIES AR FOUND BURYED IN THE CHAPTER HOUSE OF DURISME, AS APPERETH BY THER NAMES INGRAVEN UPON STONE WITH THE SIGNE OF THE CROSSE ✠ ANNEXED TO EVERY OF THERE SAID NAMES.

[AYDANUS* EPISCOPUS, H. 45] [qui obiit Anno Domini 651. *Cos.*]

✠ ALDUNUS EPISCOPUS [Aldwinus the first Bishop of Durham, and first founder of the Abbey Church, anno 990. *Cos.*]

✠ EADMUNDUS EPISCOPUS.† ⎫
✠ EADREDUS EPISCOPUS.   ⎬ These two were buried under one stone.

✠ WALCHERUS EPISCOPUS. [This Walter bishop was buried with Aldunus under one stone.] [" Short read, good read. Slay ye the Bishopp." H. 45.] ‡

✠ WILLIELMUS EPISCOPUS.

[Guilielmus primus episcopus de Karlipho, with Malcolme kinge of Scotts, and Turgott then Prior of this church, did pull downe the old church builded by Aldwinus, and did lay the foundation of this church, as it now is, theis three layinge the first three stones thereof in the foundation, July the 30th, or as others say Aug. 11, 1093. *Cos.*]

✠ RANULPHUS EPISCOPUS.

✠ GAUFRIDUS EPISCOPUS.

✠ WILLIELMUS SECUNDUS EPISCOPUS.

✠ HUGO DE PUTEACO EPISCOPUS. [King Stephen was his uncle. H. 45.]

* [There were many betwixt this Aydanus and theis mencioned who were Bishopps of Lindisfarne, now called Holy Island, before they came to Durham, but noe notable acts done by them. But I referr the reader to my other Booke where they are at large. H. 45.]

† [Forte fortuna a monachis dissidentibus electus, who dyed at Gloster, and was translated thence to bee buryed in the Chapter house, anno Domini 1048. *Cos.*]

‡ He was slaine in the church at Gateside in Newcastle, and was buryed privately in the Chapter house under the same stone with Aldwinus, without any inscription over him, anno 1081. *Cos.*

✠ Philippus episcopus.

✠ Richardus de Marisco episcopus.

✠ Nicholaus de Farnham episcopus.

✠ Walterus de Kirkham episcopus.

✠ Robertus Stichell episcopus.

✠ Robertus de Insula episcopus. ⎫ Both thes ly
✠ Richardus de Kellow episcopus. ⎭ buried before
the Bushop's seat under two marble stones, with ther immages in brasse curiouslie graven [but now defaced. *Cos.*]

Anno 1086. About which tyme king Malcolme caused the Church of Durrisme to be plucked downe, and buylded up a newe, begininge evin at the firste floore. In which season one Egelwyn, or William (as the Scottishe wryters have) was Bushop of that sea, and Prior of the Abbay was one Turgot, who afterward was maid Bushop of Saint Andrewes, and wrote lyves of Quene Margaret and Malcolme hir husband in the Scottishe tongue.

✠ This Turgotus prior of Durrisme [who laid one of the first three stones in the foundation of this church, *Cos.*] was afterward consecrated bushop [translated by Malcolme, Kinge of Scotts, to the Bishoprick, *Cos.*] of Saint Andreæ, in Scotland, Anno Domini mcix, upon whose request and petition, at his death he was carried to Durrisme, and lyeth buried in the Chapter house of Durrisme, there, emonges the rest of the Bushops.

In the which Chapter house in the upper end is a fair stall or Seat of Stone, [chaire of stone, *Cos.*] where the Bushopes have bene and are till this day installed, being also a place where the Bushope doth nowe keape his Visitation [where he keepeth his Visitation for the Cathedral church. And next to it there is a chair of wood fastened in the wall, where the Priors did and the Deanes doe now sit at the said Visitation. *Cos.*] Within [adjoyninge, H. 45; in the south side of, *Cos.*] the said Chapter house was a Prisonne for the Monnckes [whereunto the Monckes were committed for a certain space, *Cos.*] for all such light offences as was done emonges themselves.

In the same Chapter house, above the Chapter house door,

there is a faire glasse wyndowe, being the hole storie of the Rute of Jessei in most fyne coulored glas, verie fynelie and artificiallie pictured and wrowght in the said coulored glasse, verey goodlie and pleasantlie to behoulde, with Marie and Christ in her armes in the top of the said wyndowe, most fyne coulored glas also.

XXVII. THE RYTE OR CUSTUME IN BURYINGE OF BUSHOPPES IN THE CHAPTER HOUSE.

The Bushopes of Durrisme, when as they dyed, was browght to the Abbey Church of Durham, to be interred and buyried. The Prior and Monnckes of Durham dyd meite hime al at the Abbey Church garth gate, at the Place Grene, and receyved hime there, and brought hime thorowgh the said church into the Chapter house to be buryed. At which buriall there was usede greate solempnyte and devocion by the Prior and the Monnckes of that church of Durrisme, according to the customable burying of the Bushopes in the auncyente tyme. The accustomed burying of the Bushopes in that tyme was to be buried as he was accustomed to say masse, with his albe and stole and phannell and his vestment [other vestments, *Cos.*], with a myter on his heade and his crutch * with him, and so laied in his coffine, with a litle challice of sylver, other mettell, or wax; which wax challice was gilted verie fynly about the edge and knoppe in the myddes of the shanke of the challice, and aboute the edge of the patten or cover and the foote of it also was gilted; which one of the said challices [which challice, *Cos.*] was sett or laide upon his breast in the coffine with hime, and the cover therot nayled downe to yt, and verie solemne service don at there funeralls.

The Prior and the Monnckes had the horsses, charette, and all other thinges, which came with hime, [the deceased Bishopp, *Cos.*] being dewe unto themme by ther auncient custoume, as mor plainly doth appeare in the historie of the Church of Durrisme at large.

And afterwards the Bushopes came to be interred and buryed within the Abbay church of Durrisme, and not in the Chapter house in these latter daies, as followeth:

---

* Struck out and *crosier staffe* interlined in the same hand, but in different ink.

XXVIII. Bushops buried within the Abbaie Church.

The names of all the Bushops of Durisme as weare sumpteouslye buried out of the Chapter house, within the Abbaie church of Durrisme, in such forme and fashion as they weare accustomed to saie mass, with all there furniture belonging therto, as there predicessors had in the Chapter house, as is aforesaid, in every respectes, as by there severall monuments over them and inscriptions thereupon may appeare: all which Bushops were great benefactors to the said church, both duringe there lyves, and at there death, as the historie of the Church more at large declareth.

ANTHONY BEEKE, bushop of Durrisme and Patriarche of Hierusalem, was [buryed betwixt the two Alters of Saint Adyan and Saint Ellen in the utmoste east end of the Church, on the north side of Saint Cuthbert shrine, in a faire marble tombe under a large marble stone, beinge, H. 45] the first bushop that ever attempted to be buried in the Abbay church, out of the Chapter house, and to lye so neare the sacred shryne of Sancte Cuthbert, [the wall beinge broken downe att the end of the Abbey to bringe hym in with his coffin, which contynued untill the suppression of the Abbey, H. 45] [and the first layman that ever had any lycense to be buried within the said church was Raphe Lord Nevile, alias Daw-Raby, first Earle of Westmerland,* and John Lord Nevile, his sonne, with theire wives, who was admitted to be buried in the body of the said Church betwixt two pillers in the south angle of the same: whose tombes were standinge verie lately, untill the Scots were brought prisoners from Dunbarr and ymprisoned within the saide church, in the yeare 1651, which now are utterlye defaced. They had the honnour to be buried for the great battayle they wonne at Durham, where they tooke David Kinge of Scots prisoner and where his brother was slayne, with many more of the nobility of Scotland, soe itt may seeme that the Scotts defaced ther tombes in remembrance of that, but more of this shall follow of the manner of the battell. H. 45.]

---

* This is a mistake. The first Earl of Westmoreland was the grandson of the above.

LODOWICUS BELLOMONTE EPISCOPUS.

RICARDUS DE BERYE EPISCOPUS.

THOMAS HATFEILDE EPISCOPUS.

WALTERUS SKIRLEY EPISCOPUS.

ROBERT LANGLEY EPISCOPUS.

ROBERTUS NEIVELL EPISCOPUS.

CUTBERTUS TUNSTALL, episcopus, being at commandement with the Archbushoppe of Canterbery at Lambethe, there dyed a professed catholicke, and lyethe buryed in the church of Lambeth, where he was first maid Bushop.

[Cuthbert Tunstall Bishopp, beinge deprived of his Bishoppricke by Queene Elizabeth, was kept prisoner in the Archbishopps house at Lambeth, where he dyed and was buryed, under a faire marble in the parish church of Lambeth, where he was consecrated Bishopp, 40 yeares before. *Cos.*]

XXIX. THE CENTRIE GARTH.*

Att the easte end of the said Chapter howse [at the south side of the Quire, *Cos.*] there is a garth called the CENTRIE GARTH, where all the Priors and monnckes was buryed. In the said garthe there was a vaulte all sett within either syde with maison wourke of stone [free stone, *Cos.*], and likewise at eyther end, and over the myddes of the said vaut there dyd ly a faire throwgh stone, and at either syde of the stone was open [was a place open, *Cos.*], so that when any of the Monncks was buryed, looke what bones was in his grave they wer taiken when he was buryed and throwne in the saide vault, which vaut was maid for the same purpose [to be a charnell to cast dead mens bones in, *Cos.*]

Also ther was dyvers gentlemen, of good wourship, that was buryed in the said Centrie Garth, because they would be buryed [they desyred to lye, *Cos.*] neare unto that holy man Sancte Cuthbert. And amongs all other there was one gentleman of

* It will readily be perceived that *centrie* is a corruption of *cemetery*.

good wourth, cauled Mr. Rackett, which was buryed in the said Centry Garthe, nigh unto the Nine Alter dour, over against the holy man Saint Cuthbert, [Saint Cuthbert's shrine, *Cos.*] which had a faire toumbe over him, and a fair white marble stone above the said toumbe, wheron was pictured, very curyouslye, the picture of the said Mr. Rackett, all in brasse, in his cote armour, with his sword girdyd about him to his side, and at every corner of the said marble stone one of the four Evangelists, all in brass likewise.

There was an other gentleman, called Mr. Elmden, which was buryed in the said Garth, hard without the Nyne Alter dure, [besides him, *Cos.*] with a faire throwgh stone above hym, with dyverse other gentlemen whiche was buryed there, tyme out of memory, all which ar now defaced and gone [whose memoryes are now perished. *Cos.*]

Also in the said place, where all the Priors and Monnkes was buryed, in anncyent tyme, called the Centorie Garth; all which Priors, when thei diede, had every one a goodlie fair throwgh stone layd upon ther toumbes, [a tombstone either of marble or other stone, *Cos.*] which stones Deane Whittingham did cause to be pulled downe [and taken away, *Cos.*] and dyd breake and deface all such stones as had any pictures [of brass or other imagerie worke, *interlined.*] or challices wrought upon theme. And the residewe he caried them all awaie, and did occupie theme to his owne use, and dide make a washinge howse of many of them [at the end of the Centory Garth, *Cos.*] for women landerers to washe in, so that yt cannott be deemyd at this present that ever any hath bene buried in the Centorie Garth, yt is maid so plaine and streight [even. *Cos.*] For he could not abyde anye anncyent monuments, nor nothing that apperteyned to any godlie religiousnes or monasticall liffe. [By which act he shewed the hatred that he bare to the memories of his predecessors, in defacinge so rudely theire ancient and harmlesse monuments. *Cos.*]

XXX. HOLY-WATER STONES.

And also within the said Abbey Church of Durrisme ther was two HOLY-WATER STONES, of fyne marble, very artificially made and graven, and bost with hollow bosses upon the outer sydes of the stones, verie fynly and curiouslie wrowghte. The stone of the north dore [of the Church, *Cos.*] was a fair grete large one; the other, at the south dor, was not halfe so great, nor so large, but of the same worke that the other was of.

Which two holie-water stones was taken awaie by Deane Whittingham, and caryed into his kitching, and put unto profayne uses, and ther stoode during his liffe. In which stones thei dyd stepe ther beefe and salt fysh in, havinge a conveiance in the bottomes of them for letting furth the water, as thei had when they weare in the church. And [after his deathe, *Cos.*] the greater holie-water stone is removed into the lower end of the Deanes buttrie, where the water connditt is sett, and next unto the wyne seller, wher in now thei [the servants, *Cos.*] wash and make cleane ther potts and cuppes, before they serve theme at the table. The foote of the said greater holie-water stone was laid without the Church door, and now yt is [was afterwards, *Cos.*] placed in the earthe, in Lambe's shop, the black smyth, upon Framygaite brige end, and is there now to be sene.

Moreover Mrs. Whittingham, after the death of her husband, toke awaie the lessor holie-water stone out of the Deanes kitching, and browght yt into her howse in the Bailye [North Bailye, *Dav.*] and sett it there in her kitchinge, and also did carrye awaie dyverse grave-stones, of blew marble, and other throwgh stones, that did ly upon the Priors and Monnkes, out of the Centrie Garth, when she buylded her house in the Baley, which stones some of theme ar laid in the threshold of the dores, and two great ones lyeth without the doures, over against the walle before her dor [before her front stead, H. 44]. For the which facte she was complayned upon, and so laid those two without the dour that before was maid wall-fast within her house [which howse came after to Mr. Jo. Barnes, and after to Mr. Jo. Richardson, who lived theire a longe season: but, in his tyme, ther came an olde man with comly gray hayres to begg an almes, and lookeinge aboute hym upon the tombe stones, which lay in the court yard, saide to the party that came to hym, that whilest those stones were theire nothinge wolde prosper aboute the howse; and, after, divers of his children and others dyed. So he caused them to be removed into the Abbey yard, wher now they are: but before the almes came to serve the man he was gone, and never seen after. Which said howse is since sould by Mr. Jo. Richardson his grandchild to one Ambrose Myers, a . . . . . This is verified by divers nowe livinge. H. 45.] Thus may yow se how godlie things, which ar maid for the use of God's service in the church, are put to profayne uses, which were ordeyned affortyme for good and godly uses in the church. [Thus these sacred monuments, which were erected to continue the memories of good men here on earth, she rased and abused them, by imploying them to prophane uses. H. 44.]

XXXI. A Song Scoole in the Centory Garth.

There was in the Centorie Garth, in under the south end of the church, called the south end of the IX Alters [at the back syde of the IX Alters, H. 45] betwixt two pillers, adjoyning to the IX Alter dour, a Song Schoole, buylded for to teach vj children for to learne to singe, for the mayntenance of God's divine service in the Abbey Church; which children had there meat and there drinke of the house coste amonge the children of th' Almarie, which said schoole was buylded many yers since, without memorie of man, before the suppression of the House. And the said schoole [was builded together with the Church, and, *Cos.*] was verie fynely bourded within, rownd about, a mannes hight about the waules, and a long deske [did reache, *Cos.*] frome one end of the scoole to th'other, to laie there bookes upon; and all the floure bourded in under foote, for warmnes, and long formes sett fast in the ground for the children to sitt on. And the place where the master did sitt and teach was all close bordede, both behinde and of either syde, for warmnes. And the said master was bownd [his office was to teach those six children to singe and, *Cos.*] to plaie on the orgains every principall daie, when the Monnks did sing ther high messe, and likewise at evinsong. But the Monncks, when thei were at there mattens and service at mydnighte, thene one of the said Monnks did plaie on the orgains themselves and no other. So that the master was not bownd to plaie but on the principall daies, in the high messe tyme, and at evinsong, as is aforsaide. Also the master of the said children had his chamber nyghe unto the said schoole, a litle distant from it, where he did live, having his meite and drinke in the Priors Hall, emongs the Priors Gentlemen, and all his other necessaries found of the Prior and of the House coste besyds, untill such tyme as the House was supprest; and shortlie after, because ther was no techinge in that scoule any longer, but tawght in an other place or scoule appointed for that purpose, so that the foresaid scoole in the Centorie Garth is clene gone to decaie and pulled downe, that one cannot tell almost in what place yt did stand.

XXXII. The Cloysters.

The xiij. [day] of the callends of Aprill, DCLXXXVII° [684, H. 44] Sancte Cuthbert endyd his lyffe, and was buryed in Holy Eland, where he was buship iij yeres, in Sancte Peter's church,

by the Altar, of the east side, in a grave of stone that was for
him maid to be buried in. And also, xj yere after that he had
bene beryed and lyne there in Sancte Peter's church in Holy
Eland, he was taken out of the ground, the xiij of the callands
of Aprill, in the same callends that he died in, whole, lying like
to a man sleping, being found saife and uncorrupted and lyeth-
waike, and all his masse clothes saife and freshe as they weare at
the first houre that they weare put on him. And inshryned
him in a fereture light [a little, *Cos*.] above the pavement. And
there he stoode many a day. [He is said to be descended from
the blood-royal of the Kings of Ireland, being son of one
Muriardach and Sabina his wife, who was daughter to a King
there. He was brought up in the Abbey of Mailrose, first
under his predecessor Eata, and afterwards under Boisil, who
succeeded Eata. After the death of Boisil he was made Abbot
of that monastery, which he governed with great care and sin-
cerity. *Dav*.] He was anchore xiij yere, also he was monncke
xxxvij yere, and after xiiij yeares Abbot. [Also in the yeare
55 (? 875) Eardulf was bishop, at which time certain Danes
and Pagans, infidels, of sundry other nations, invaded and destroyed the realm of England in divers places. And after a
certain space Halden, King of the Danes, with a great
part of the navy and army of infidels, arrived at Tinmouth
haven, intending to sojourn there all the winter following;
and the next spring he meant with all his power to invade,
spoil, and destroy the County of Northumberland. Whereof,
when Eardulf the bishop had intelligence, with all his clergy
and people, after long consultation had amongst themselves
what course was to be taken in that extremity, to prevent the
barbarous cruelty of the savage and merciless infidels, they, in
the end, called to mind the words and monition delivered by
Saint Cuthbert to his brethren. The said holy man, before his
departure out of this life, amongst other wholesome counsels
and godly admonitions delivered, uttered these or the like
words, "If you, my brethren, shall be at any time hereafter
urged or constrained unto one of the two extremities following,
I do rather choose and wish that you would take my bones up
and fly from those places and take your place of abode and stay
wheresoever Almighty God shall provide for you, than that you
should by any means submit yourselves to the yoak and servi-
tude of wicked schismaticks." Which words he then spake by
the spirit of prophesie, foreseeing the perilousness of the time
to come. *Dav*.]* And also buship Eardulfe and abbott Edrede

* The above paragraphs from Davies are probably insertions of his own, upon
the authority of Bede.

did tacke, carry, and beare awaie the bodie of Sancte Cuthbert from Holy Eland southward and fledd vij yere from towne to towne for the great persecution and slawghter of the Panymes and Danes. And men of the shire, when they saw that Sancte Cuthbert body was gone, they left there lands and there goods and followed after. And so the bushop, the abbott, and the reste, being weirye of travellinge, thought to have stowlne awaye and caried Sancte Cuthbert body into Ireland, for his better saifftie. And being upon the sea in a shippe by myricle marveilous iij waves of water was turned into bloode. The shippe that they weere in was dreven back by tempest and by the mightie powre of God, as it should seame, upon the shore or land. And also the saide shippe that they weere in, by the grete storme and strong raging walls of the sea, as is aforesaid, was turned on the one syde, and the booke of the Holie Evangelists fell out of the ship into the bottom of the sea. The which booke, being all addorned with gould and presious stones of the out syde, and they being all troubled with great sorrowe for the losse of the said booke, one Hunredus, being admonished and commannded by the vision of Sancte Cuthbert [appearinge, *interlined*] to seeke the booke that was loste in the sea, iij myles and more from the land, and, as they weere admonishede, they found the booke much more bewtifull than it was before, both in lettres and leaves, excelling the utter bewtie of the cover, being nothing blemyshed by the water, as though it had been towched by some heavenly powere. And also by the foresaid viscion of Sancte Cuthbert [being upon the shore, *interlined*] they sawe a bridle hinging in a tree, and lookynge about him he dyd see a read horse, which cummyng towards him, by Gods provision dyd offer him selfe to be brydled, to ease their travell in carriage of the beare wherein Sancte Cuthbert's bodie laide.

And then they went with him to Crake Mynster, and rested there iiij monthes with his body, and afterward brought him to Chester [Cuneagester, now called Chester, *Dav.*] the yeare of the Incarnacion ccccccLxxxiii, from Sancte Cuthbert's daie at least cxxvi past since. Aldunus fledde awaie with the bodie of Sancte Cuthbert, when it had lyne at Chester cxiij yere, for great persecucion and robbing and spoiling of the Panemes or Danes, and fled to Rippon with his body, and within iiij monthes there warres dyd seas, and then, cumynge back againe, when all was in quietnes, thinkinge to have brought hime back to Chester againe and cummynge with him on the east syde of Durham, to a place called Ward Lawe, they could no further beare him. [They could not with all their force remove his body from thence, which seemed to be fastened to the ground, for that the chariot wherein the holy corpse was carried, miraculously stood unmoveable either by the strength of man or beast. *Dav.*] The Buship and the people fasted iij daies, and praied to God with great reverence and devocion to knowe from God what they shoulde doe with him, and revelacion had they to carry him to Dunhome. And, as they weare going, they had intelligence by a woman lacking her kowe, where that Dunhome was. And streight way they brought him to that place of Dunhome, myriculouslye, in the yere of our Lord DCCCCXCV, where there was nothing but a great rush of thornes and other thick woods growinge, and there for to reaste and remayne, for no further they could cary him. And there they buylded a litle CHAPPELL of WANDS, and ther in they him layd or sett, untill such tyme as a better kirke was buylded. The Buship came with the corse and with all his fource dyd wourship it. Also he fynes the place there defensable, with thick woods and great rushes, as is aforesaid, untill Uthred earle of Northumberland caused all the countrye to taike in hand to hew and cut downe all the woode that there was growing to make it habitable, and then the Buship beganne to worke and buylde, and to make a Mykle Kirke of stone. And, whels it was in makinge, from the wandyd kirke or chapell they brought the body of that holie man Sancte Cuthbert and translayted him into an other WHITE KIRKE, so called, and there his body remayned iiij years, while the more kyrke was buylded. Then the Buship Aldunus dyd hallowe the more kyrk or GRET KIRKE, so called, before the kallends of September, and translated Sancte Cuthbert's body out of the White Kirke into the Great Kyrke, as sone as the great kirke was hallowed, to more worship then before.

Also Aldunus dyd ordayne and make the BUSHIP SEA to be onely ther in Durham contynewally for ever. King Oswald and Aydane first beganne the Bushipes sea in Holy Eland, from the which tyme CCCLXI to the cummynge of Aldunus, who ordanyd the Bushipes sea of Durham, from the tyme that Sancte Cuthbert passed out of this world from theme, it was CCCIX yeares. And then Aldunus departed heme out of this world, iij yeres after that he had founded and stablished the Bushipes sea.

The buyldinge and first foundinge of the Abbei Church in Durham, that now is, was in the yere of our Lord MXXII yeres paste, by Bushippe William and Prior Turgott, with all the Monnkes, which caused the old Church, buylt by Aldunus, to be pulled downe, and buylding it anewe, beginning at the first floore. Thei weare the first that laid the first foundacion of the stones in the ground worke, where the Great Abbey Church is nowe founded. Bushippe William caused to make all the great kirke and caused the Monncks dalie for to worke at it out of service tyme. The Buship ordeyned before the people Prior Turgot to be Asdeacon, before he dyed, and also his Vicar-Generall. And the foresaid buship Wylliam did place the Monncks of Jarrowe and Wermouthe, being of St. Benedict's order, in the rowmes of the Cannons, for ther evill and nawghtie livinge. And when the Abbey Church was buylded and finished, then was he taiken up out of th' other church, called the White Church, and translaited and brought into the said Abbey Church, being inshryned above the ground, of iij yerds highte, in a most sumptuous and goodlie shrine above the High Alter, called the FERETURE. And the booke of the holie Evangelest, which was lost in the sea, as is aforesaide, was preserved and keapt in the said monasticall or Abbey Church of Durham, where the bodie of holie St. Cuthbert doth lie, as a place most worthie of so presyous a booke, browghte to light againe thorowgh his revelacion.

XXXIII. THE CLOYSTERS. SAINT CUTHBERTS TOUMBE.

And there was maide a faire TOUMBE OF STONE in the Cloyster garth, a yerde hight from the ground, where that holie man was first browght to and laide [when he was translated owte of the White Church to be laid in the Abbey Churche, H. 45] and a fair great broad playne throwghe stone layd above the said toumbe. Then afterward was there a goodlie and verie large and greate thicke IMADGE of stone, beinge the picture of that holie man Sancte Cuthbert, verie fynely and curiouslie pictured and wrowghte in the said stone with paintinge and giltinge, marveilous bewtifull and excellent to beholde, in forme and fashion as he was accustomed to saie masse, with his myter on his head and his croisier staff in his hand. And the said picture was caried and laid above the said toumbe of stone. It was rered up of either syde, and at both ends above the said stone wourke, verie close, with wood stanchels, that a man could not have gotten in his hand betwixt one stanchell and another, but have looked in and sene the picture of that holy man Saint Cuthbert lyinge therein, and covered over above, all verie fynelie and closlie with lead, like unto a little chappell or church. Which did stande contynewallie, unto the suppression of the House, as a memorie and special monument of the first cummynge of that holie man Saint Cuthbert, being onely maid and placed ther to that end. Which did stand in the Cloister Garth, over against the Parloure Dour, where thorough the Monncks was caried to be buried, which is nowe maid a Register house. And also it did contynue to the suppression of the House, as is aforesaid, and after, unto the tyme of Deane Horne, and then he caused the said monument to be pulled down, and converted the leads and all to his owne use; and the said image of St. Cuthbert was sett on the one syde, against the Cloister wall, over annenst the Parler Dor, as thei go thorough into the Senturie Garth. And, after, when Whittinghame came to be deane, he caused the said image to be defaced and broken all in pieces, to th' intent that there should be no memory nor token of that holie man Sancte Cuthbert, which was sent and brought thether by the powre and will of Almightie God, which was the occasion of the buylding of the said monasticall Church and House, where they have all there livings and commodities to lyve on at this daie. [Although he was sent by merveile from God, and by whose meanes there was soe great revenues geiven to the Church. And now all wholy taken away, and the Church and all therto ready to come down. And in the first yeare of King Edward the 6th, ther was certaine commissioners apoynted to deface all popishe ornaments in parishe churches, whose names were Doctor Harvy and Doctor Whitby, who did deface a goodly and rich shrine in Saint Nicholas Church, called CORPUS CHRISTI SHRINE, which Doctor Horne did treade and breake in peices with his feete, with many other ornaments. H. 45.]

[XXXIV. THE CLOYSTERS.*]

[The 13th day of the kalends of Aprill 684, [687, *note by Dr. Hunter.*] Saint Cuthbert ended this life, and was buryed in St. Peter's church in the Holy Island, where he was Bishopp three yeares, in a grave of stone that was made on purpose for him to bee buryed in. And eleven yeares after, hee was taken out of the ground, the 13th of the kalends of Aprill, in the same calends that hee dyed, and his bodye was found safe and uncorrupt, and lying like one asleepe, with all his masse cloathes safe and fresh as they were at the first when they were put on him, at which time they inshrined him in a Feretor, a little above the pavement of the church, where he lay a long space. And after-

---

* The two preceding Chapters or Sections as they stand in the *MS. Cosin* afford so many important additions and various readings that they are here subjoined at length.

ward Eardulphus bishopp and Abbot Eadred, about the yeare 890, did carrye away his bodye from Holy Island southward, and fled with it seven yeares from towne to towne, because of the great persecutions and slaughters which were made by the Painims and the Danes. And the men of that Iland, when they sawe that the body of theire holie Saint was gone, then left theire land and goods, and followed after him. And the Bishopp and the Abbott and the rest, beinge wearyed with theire dangerous travells, thought to have stollen away, and to have carryed the body of their holy Saint along with them into Ireland, hopinge there to bee safe and quiet. And beinge uppon the sea in a shipp, three waves miraculously were turned into blood, and the shipp was driven back by tempest unto the shore againe, and by boysterous windes and raginge waves it was turned on the one side, and the booke of the Holie Evangelists, curiously written and adorned with gold and pretious stones on the cover, did fall out of the shipp into the bottome of the sea, which disaster did sore perplex and afflict them. But Saint Cuthbert, beinge loath to see his honourers so sore troubled and so full of sorrow, did appear in a vision unto one Hundredus, and commanded him that they should seeke diligently for the booke uppon the coastes thereaboutes, where they found it three miles from the sea shore, (*sic*) cast, as it seemed, by the force of some wave and carried thither by the violence of some happye gale of winde, or by some divine power, for the comfort and confirmation of these faintinge monkes in theire religious worship of Saint Cuthbert. Which holy booke was far more beautifull and glorious to looke uppon, both within and without, then it was before, beinge nothinge blemished with the salt water, but polished rather by some heavenly hand; which did not a little increase theire joy. But beinge wearyed with the seekinge of that booke, and with bearinge about Saint Cuthbert's bodye, see againe the compassione of theire Saint, hee presented to theire eyes a bridle hanginge upp in a tree, and a redd horse runninge towards them, which did offer himselfe to bee bridled and to ease theire paines in carryinge of the chest wherein Saint Cuthbert's body was laid, uppon which horse they caryed him to Crake Minster, and rested them four months, and from thence brought him to Chester, Anno Domini 887 [883, *in marg. by Hunter*] where they remained 113 yeares, duringe the rest of the time of the Danes warrs, in the end whereof Aldwinus, then Bishopp, fledd with Saint Cuthbert's body to Rippon, to lye by the bodye of holy Saint Wilfride. But four monethes after theire arrivinge at Rippon the Danes warrs did cease, and then, intend-inge to bringe him backe againe to Chester, and comminge with him on the east side of Durham, to a place called Ward-lawe, they could not with all their force remove his body from thence, which seemed to bee fastened to the ground. Which strange and unexpected accident wrought great admiration in the heartes of the bishoppe's monkes and their associates, and *ergo* they fasted and prayed three dayes, with greate reverence and devotion, desiringe to know by revelation what they should doe with the holie bodie of Saint Cuthbert. Which thinge was granted unto them, and therin they were directed to carry him to Dunholme. But, being distressed because they were ignorant where Dunholme was, see their goode fortune, as they were goinge, a woman that lacked hir cowe did call aloude to hir companion to know if shee did not see hir, who answered with a loud voice that hir cowe was in Dunholme, a happye and heavenly eccho to the distressed monkes, who by that meanes were at the end of theire journey, where they should finde a restinge place for the body of theire honoured Saint. And, thereuppon, with great joy and gladnesse brought his body to Dunholme, Anno Domini 999 [*Hunter in marg.* 995], which was *inculta tellus*, a barbarous and rude place, replenished with nothinge but thornes and thick woods, save only in the midst where the Church now standeth, which was plaine and commodious for such a purpose. Where they first builded a LITTLE CHURCH of wands and branches, wherein they did lay his body (and thence the church was afterwards called Bough Church), till they did build a more sumptuous church, wherein they might inshrine him, which they assayed to doe with all theire power, Uthred earle of Northumberland aidinge them, and causinge all the country to cutt downe the wood and thorne bushes which did molest them, and so made all the place where the citye now standes habitable and fitt to erect buildinges on. Which gave great encouragement to Alwinus the bishopp to hasten the finishinge of his church. Which accordingly did, and then did translate St. Cuthbert's body from the wanded [or bough, *interlined*] church to the WHITE CHAPELL, for so it was called, which hee had newly built, which was a part of the great Church which was not yett finished, where it lay four yeares. But after the great Church was finished and consecrated, uppon the 20th of September, hee translated his bodye out of the White Chappell into the great Church, which hee made a CATHEDRALL, erectinge his Bishopp's sea at Duresme, where it still remaineth, about 377 [*Hunter in marg.* 361] yeares after it was first founded in the Holy Iland by Saint Aidaine and Saint Oswald, which was

Anno Domini 635, and 333 [*Hunter in marg.* 309] yeares after the death of Saint Cuthbert, which was Anno Domini 684. Which said Aldwinus bishopp dyed three years after hee had founded his bishopp's sea in Duresme, and finished his Cathedrall church in the yeare 1020. Which church was famous, with the succession of six bishopps in it. But William Carlipho, beinge not well content with the smallnesse and homelinesse of that buildinge, did pull it all downe 76 yeares after Aldwinus had finished it, and instead thereof did erèct the magnificent and famous buildinge which is now to bee seene, Malcolme kinge of Scotts, Turgott then Prior of the Church, and himselfe lyinge the first three stones in the new foundation, uppon the 30th day of July, as some say, or uppon the 11th of August, as others affirme, Anno Domini 1093, [for which famous work Anthony Beak one of his successors with a great sum of money got him to be canonized, *Dav.*] and caused the Monkes to labour in that holy worke all the daye longe, excepting onely meale times and times of prayer, [king Malcolm being the chief benefactor in the building thereof, *Dav.*] and appointed Turgott, ther Prior, to bee his Archdeacon and Vicar Generall within his diocese. And goinge to Rome, two yeares before his death, hee obtained license of Pope Gregory the 7th to remove the Monkes which were at Wermouth and at Jarrow, which were of the order of Saint Benett, to his church at Durham, where hee placed them in the roomes of the Cannons which hee expelled for theire lewd and lazy lives. But hee did not live to see his church finished, for he dyed Anno Domini 1095, two yeares after hee had laid the foundation. And Ranulph Flambard his successor, favoringe and with all his might furtheringe so good a worke, did, in the 29 yeares that he was Bishopp, build the said church from the foundation allmost to the coveringe. But it was not fully finished till the time that Nicholaus Farnam was Bishopp and Thomas Melscome [*Melsonby*] was Prior, which two good men did arch it over Anno Domini 1242, and lye buryed both under one stone in the Chapter House. But, longe before the church was finished, the body of Saint Cuthbert was translated againe out of the Cloyster garth where William Carlipho Bishopp had made him a verye sumptuous tombe to lye in, when he removed him out of the old church which Aldwinus built for him, which was then taken downe that this faire church now extant might bee erected in the same place where that old church was. In which new Church was builded a faire and sumptuous Shrine, about three yards from the ground, on the back side of the great Alter, which was at the east end of the Quire, where his body was solemnly placed in an iron chest

within the Shrine, where it lay quietly without molestation till
the suppression of the Church, as is above related, and the
Booke of the four Evangelists, which fell into the sea and was
so miraculously brought to land and found againe, was laid on
the great Alter, as a fitt monument to preserve the memory of
so great a Saint. And at the west end of the church Hugo
Pudsey bishop of Durham and earle of Northumberland [King
Stephen's nephew, *Dav.*] did build a very faire chappell which
hee dedicated to the Virgin Mary, [and was called the Galilee or
our Lady's chappel, but now simply called the Consistory, *Dav.*]
and there in a silver caskett gilt with gold hee laid the bones
of Venerable Bede and erected a costly and magnificent Shrine
over it as above is declared. [He also founded the Priory of
Finckley in honour of Saint Godrick the hermite. He founded
also the Hospitall of Allerton, and the famous Sherburn Hospitall neare Durham. He built also Elvett bridge over the
Wear with two chappels upon it. He also built both a Manor
and a Church at Darlington, and he bought of King Richard the
first the earldome of Sadberge for his successors. *Dav.*] And
because those holy Bishops and Monkes woold not bee un-
mindful of the least favour which was done for them and for
the honour of theire holy Saint, Aldwinus, on the outside of his
Church, and Ranulph Flambard, accordinge to the intention of
William Carlipho the founder, did erect a monument [made the
portraiture, *Dav.*] of a MILKE-MAIDE MILKINGE HIR KOUE, on
the outside of the north-west turrett of the Nine Altars, at the
buildinge of the new Church, in a thankful remembrance of that
maide which so fortunately in theire great perplexitye directed
them to Dunholme, where the body of theire great Saint was to
rest untill the resurrection, which monument, though defaced
by the weather, to this day is there to bee seen. *MS. Cos.*]

[XXXV. THE DISCRIPTION OF THE TOMBE WHICH WILLIAM
CARLIPHO ERECTED FOR SAINT CUTHBERT IN THE CLOYS-
TER GARTH TILL A FAIRE SHRINE MIGHT BEE MADE IN
HIS NEW CHURCH WHEREIN HE MIGHT BE INCLOSED.]

[William Carlipho, bishopp of Durham, before hee tooke
downe the old Church builded by bishop Aldwinus, did prepare
a faire and beautifull tombe of stone in the Cloyster garth, a
yeard high from the ground, where Saint Cuthbert was laid
untill his Shrine was prepared for him in the new Church that
now is. Over which tombe was layd a faire and comely marble.
But when his body was translated to the Feriture where it was

inshrined, in honour of him they made a goodly large and curious image of marble representinge Saint Cuthbert, in that forme in which he was wont to say masse, with his miter on his head and his crosier staff in his hand, and his other vestments very curiously engraven on the said marble, which, after his body was inshrined in the new church, was placed above the said tombe. And round about the said tombstone, both at the sides, and at either end, was sett upp neate stanchells of wood joyned so close that one could not put in his hand betwixt one and other, but might onely looke in and see that exquisite picture, which laid within them. And it was covered above with lead, like unto a chappell, which comely monument did stand in the Cloyster garth till the suppression of the Abbey, over against the Parlour Dore through which the Monkes were caryed unto the Centrye garth to bee buryed, which Parlour is now turned into a storehouse and a roome made above it for the Register's Office. But shortly after the Abby was supprest, deane Horne tooke downe that faire and ancient monument, and converted the leads and wood and stone thereof to his owne use, yet left the image of Saint Cuthbert perfect, and sett it on the side of the Cloyster wall, against the said Parlour Dore, through which the monks went into the Centrye garth. But when Deane Whittingham did beare authoritie in this church, he caused that image, as hee did manye other ancient monuments, to bee taken downe and broken in pieces, beinge religiously loath, as it should seeme, that any monument of Saint Cuthbert, or of any man who formerly had beene famous in this church and great benefactors thereunto, as the Priors his predecessors were, should bee left whole, and undefaced, in memorye or token of that holy man Saint Cuthbert, which was sent and brought thither by the power and will of Allmightie God, which was the occasion of the buildinge of the said monasticall Church and House, where they have all theire livinges and commodities to live on at this day. *MS. Cosin.*]

XXXVI. THE CLOYSTER. THE EAST ALLEY.

And also yt was long and many yeres after or [ever, *Cos.*] the CLOYSTER was buylded unto the tyme of Buship Skirley*

---

* He gave towards the building of the Cloisters two hundred pounds in his lifetime, and four hundred pounds in his will; and he bestowed also two hundred and twenty pounds in the building of the Dormitory. He sate Bishop of Durham eighteen years, and died in the beginning of the year 1406, and after him Thomas Langley, bishop, gave to the building of the said Cloisters £838 17s. 6d. *Dav.*

[Skirlawe, *Cos.*] and Bishop Langley, who were the first founders and buylders of the said Cloyster, and dyd bear all the charges of the buylding and workmanship of the said worke, and was the first that dyd cause from the Cloister dour to the Church dour to be sett in glasse in the wyndowes the hole storie and myricles of that holie man SAINTE CUTHBERT, from the daie of his nativitie and birth unto his dyinge daie. And ther yow should have sene and beholden his mother lying in her child bedd; [and how that, *Dav.*] after she was delyvered the brighte beames dyd shyne from heaven upon her and upon the child, where he did lye in the cradle, that to every mans thinking the Holie Ghoste had overshadowed hime. For every one that did se yt did thinke that the house had bene [set, *Cos.*] all on fyre, the beams dyd shine so bright over all the house, both within and without. And also the Bishop baptized the childe and did call him Mullocke [Hullocke, *Cos.*; Yllock, *Dav.*] in the Irish tonnge, the which is in Inglishe as much as to saie Cuthbert. The foresaid Bushops name, who [baptized and, *interlined*] had the keapinge of the vertuouse and Godly childe, is called Ugenius. The name of the citie that the childe Sainte Cuthbert was baptized in is called Hardbrecins [Hardbrecumb, *Cos.*], for he was blessed of God even from his mothers wombe, so that every myracle that he did after, frome his infancye, was sett there by it selfe, and in under every myracle there was sertain verses sett furthe in latten, that dyd declare the contents and meaning of every myracle and storie by ytselfe, in most excellent coulered glasse, most artificiallye sett furth and curiouslie [marvielouslye, *Cos.*] wrowght, being lyvelie to all the beholders thereof. And the storie which was in the Wyndowes there was onely sett up in that place by the charges of thes two godly and well disposed Bushopps, to be annexed and adjoined with the said toumbe [in the Cloister garth, *interlined*], and his picture thereupon most lyvely to beholde to be a memoriall of the said holie man Sainte Cuthbert, that every one that came throwghe the Cloyster mighte se all his liffe and myracles, from his birth and infancy unto his dying day; and he was commed of a princelie raice, for his father was Prynce and his mother a Princes dowghter, as may apeare by the history at large. And after, in kyng Edwards tyme vj., this story was pulled downe by Deane Horne and broken all to peces, for he might never abyde any anncient monuments, actes, or deades, that gave any light of godly religion.

Also ther is in the said Cloister, above hed, (in sellering in wainscot,*) certaine Bushops armes and Noble mens armes,

---

* Interlined in blacker ink, by a different but coæval hand.

both knights and men of worship, who had bestowed any thing of that church.

XXXVII. THE CLOISTER. MAUNDY THURSDAIE.

There was a goodlie ceremonye which the Prior and the Monnckes dyd use, every thursdaie before Easter, called MAUNDY THURSDAIE. The custoume was this. Ther were xiij [xviij, *Cos.* and *Dav.*] poore aged men appoynted to cume to the Cloyster, at that daie, havinge there feete clene washed, there to remayne till such tyme as the Prior and the whole Covent did cume thether, at ix a clock, or ther abouts, the aged men sytting betwixt the Parlor Dour and the Church Dour, upon a fair longe BROAD THICKE FOURME, which fourme laie on iij peces of wood, every pece pictured like unto a man, antick wourke, verie fynely wrought, being placed for the feite of the fourme, in under either end one, and one in the myddes, which forme dyd stand alwaies in the Church, beyond the Revester dour, betwixt two pillers, over against the Quere doure, on the south syd of the Quere. Which fourme was taiken and caried every maundie thursdaie before Easter to the Cloister, where the Prior, after certaine praiers said, one of his servants did bring a fair baison with clene water, and the Prior dyd washe the poore mens feete, all of theme, one after an other, with his owne hands, and dryed them with a towell, and kissed ther feite himeselfe, which being done he did verie liberally bestowe xxx^d in money of every one of theme, with vij reade herrings a pece, and did serve them him selfe with drinke and iij loves of bread with certaine wafers. And, when all was done, the forme, which was ordayned onely for that purpose, was caried againe into the Church and sett in the same place where yt was taken fro, that men might also sit on yt ther when they came to here devine servyce. [Which fourme is yet remayninge under the Te Deum wyndowe and the Clock. *]

[Also as you go out of the Cloister, through an entry to the Dean's lodging at the head of the stairs behind the door called the Usher Door, on the right hand behind the said door, there is another door, going into the Register, wherein certain old written Books of Records and Evidences of the monastical House of Durham did lye, as also a copy of the Foundation of the Hospital of Greatham, which was also registered in the said

---

* Added in a coæval hand.

Book of Records, and there to be found, if any misfortune should happen to the Foundation of the said Hospital of Greatham. The keeper of the said Register House was called George Baites, and he was also clerk of the Feretory at that time. And it was ever the Register House, till of late, that Mr. Tobias Matthew, Dean of Durham, altered the state of it unto another place called the Parlour, as is aforesaid. *Dav.*]

XXXVIII. The Cloister. The South Alley.

There was on the south syde of the Cloister, adjoyninge to the syde of the Cloister dour, a stoole or seat with iiij feete, and a back of wood joyned to the said stoole, which was maid fast in the wall for the porter to sytt on, which did keape the Cloister doure. And before the said stoole it was bourded in under foote, for warmeness. And he that was the last porter there was called Edward Pattinson. And from the said stoole west-ward on the south syde, there was a faire long Bench of Stone almost to the Frater house dour, whereon dyd syt certen childrin in a row, from the one end to the other, upon Maundy Thursday before Easter, being maide forth at purpose. Where all the whole Covent of Monnckes at that same present tyme had every one of them a boy appointed them, sytting upon the saide bench, wher the said Monks dyd wash the said childryns feete, and dryed them with a towell. Which being done, they dyd kisse the said childrins fete, every one of those he washed, giving to every childe xxx^d in money, and vij redde herrings and iij loves of bread and every one certaine wafercakes, [a wafercake, H. 44] the Moncks serving every childe with drinke themselves. The godly ceremony thus endyd, after certaine praiers said by the Prior and the whole Covent, they dyd all depart in great holynesse.

And at the end of the said bench, betwixt it and the Frater house dour, ther was a faire Almerie joyned in the wall, and an other of the other syd of the said dour, and all the forepart of the Almeries was thorowgh carved worke [for to geve ayre to the towels *], and iij dors in the forpart of either almerie, and a locke on every doure, and every Monncke had a key for the said almeryes, wherin did hinge in every almerie cleane towels for the Monncks to drie there hands on, when they washed and went to dynner. And the stoole and bench Tobie

---

* Interlined in a contemporary hand, but in different ink. Not in *Cos.*

Mathewe, dean of Durham, caused to be taiken downe, and maid as playne as is the rest of the floore of the Cloyster.

XXXIX. The Frater House.

In the said south allie of the Cloysters is a faire larg hall, called the FRATER HOUSE, wherein the greate feaste of Sancte Cuthbert's daie in Lent was holden.

[In the south alley of the Cloisters is a fair large Hall, called the FRATER HOUSE, finely wainscotted on the north and south sides, as also on the west. And on either part of the Frater House there is a fair long BENCH of stone-mason work, from the cellar-door to the pantry or covey-door. Above the bench is wainscot-work, two yards and a half in height, finely carved and set with embroidered work, and above the wainscot there was a fair large PICTURE of our Saviour Christ, the blessed Virgin Mary and Saint John, in fine gilt work, and excellent colours; which pictures, though washed over with lime, yet do appear through it. This wainscot-work hath engraven on the top of it,

Thomas Castell, Prior, Anno Domini 1518, mensis Julii.

So that Prior Castell wainscotted the Frater House round about. And within the said Frater House door, on the left hand as one goes in, there is a strong AMBRIE in the stone wall, where a great mazer, called the GRACE-CUP, did stand, which did service to the Monks every day, after grace was said, to drink in round the table. Which cup was largely and finely edged about with silver and double gilt with gold, and many more large and great mazers after the same sort. Amongst which was a goodly great mazer called JUDAS-CUP, edged about with silver and double gilt, with a foot underneath it to stand on, of silver and double gilt, which was never used but on Maundy Thursday at night in the Frater House, where the Prior and the whole Convent did meet and keep their Maundy. There lay also in the same ambrie the goodly cup called SAINT BEDE'S BOWL, the outside whereof was of black mazer, and the inside of silver double gilt, the edge finely wrought round about with silver and double gilt; and in the midst of it was the picture of the holy man Saint Bede, sitting as if he had been writing. The foot of the said bowl was of silver and double gilt, with four joynts of silver coming down, all double gilt from the edge to the foot, to be taken asunder. In that ambrie lay all the chief PLATE that served the whole Convent in the said Frater House on festival dayes, and a fine work of carved wainscot before it, and a strong lock, yet so as none could perceive that there was any ambrie at all; for the key hole was under the carved work of the wainscot. There is also another fair large AMBRIE within the said Frater House door on the right hand, as you go to the cellar, of wainscot, having divers ambries within it, finely wrought and varnished over with red varnish, wherein lay table-cloaths, salts, and mazers, a basin and ewer of latten, with other things pertaining to the Frater House and to the Loft, where all the Monks did dine and sup. And every Monk had his mazer severally by himself to drink in, and had all other things that served for the whole Convent and the Frater House in their daily service at their diet and at their table. And all the said mazers were largely and finely edged with silver, double gilt, and a fair basin and ewer of latten, the ewer pourtrayed like a man on horse-back, as he had been riding or hunting, which served the Sub-Prior to wash at the foresaid table, where he sate as chief. *Dav.*]

[And within the said Frater House the Prior and the whole Convent of Monks held their great feast of Saint Cuthbert in Lent, having their meat served out of the dresser-window of the great Kitchen into the Frater House, and their drink out of the great cellar. *Dav.*]

And in the east end, being the hiest part of the Frater house, and adjoyninge to the Deanes house, was taiken downe by Deane Whittingham the hie roufe of lead, and enclosed it to his house and use, and maid it a flatt roufe of lead, whereby the said Deane Whittingham gayned at the leaste xx^{li} by taikeing downe the said hie roufe of leade. Also in the said east end of the Frater House stoode a fair table with a decent skrene of wainscott over it, being keapt all the rest of the yeare for the master of the Novicies and the Novicies to dyn and sup in. [having their meat served in to them at a dresser window from the Great Kitchen and there drink out of the Great Cellar. *Dav.*] At which tyme the master observed this holsome and godlie order for the contynewallie instructing of ther youth in vertew and lerning, that is, one of the Novicies, at the election and appoyntment of the master, dyd reade summe parte of the Old and New Testament, in Latten, in dynner tyme, having a convenyent place at the southe end of the hie table with in a faire glasse wyndowe, invyroned with iron, and certaine steppes of stone with iron rayles of th'one syde to goe up to it, and to support an iron deske there placed, upon which laie the Holie Bible, where one of the Novicies elected by the master was appointed to read a chapter of the Old or New Testament in Latten as aforesaid in tyme of dynner, which being ended, the master dyd toule a gilden bell, hanging over his hed, therby givinge warnyng to one of the Novicies to cumme to the hie table and saie grace, and so, after grace said, they departed to their bookes.

XL. THE LAVER OR CONNDITT.

Within the Cloyster Garth, over against the Frater House dour, was a fair LAVER or CONNDITT, for the Monncks to washe ther hands and faces at, being maid in forme round, covered with lead, and all of marble, saving the verie * uttermost walls. Within the which walls you may walke round about the Laver of marble, having many litle cunditts or spouts of brasse, with xxiiij cockes of brasse, rownd about yt, havinge in yt vij faire wyndowes of stone woorke, and in the top of it a faire DOVE-COTTE, covered fynly over above with lead, the workmanship both fyne and costly, as is apparent till this daie. And, adjoyninge to the est syde of the Counditt dour, ther did hing a bell to geve warning, at a leaven of the clock, for the Monncks to cumme wash and dyne, having ther closetts or almeries on either syde of the Frater House dour keapt alwaies with swete and clene towels, as is aforesaid, to drie ther hands.

XLI. THE CLOISTER. THE NORTHE ALLEY.

In the north syde of the Cloister, from the corner over against the Church dour to the corner over againste the Dorter dour, was all fynely glased, from the hight to the sole within a litle of the grownd into the Cloister garth. And in every wyndowe iij PEWES or CARRELLS, where every one of the old Monks had his carrell, severall by himselfe, that, when they had dyned, they dyd resorte to that place of Cloister and there studyed upon there books, every one in his carrell, all the after nonne, unto evensong tyme. This was there exercise every daie. All there pewes or carrells was all fynely wainscotted and verie close, all but the forepart which had carved wourke that gave light in at ther carrell doures of wainscott. And in every carrell was a deske to lye there bookes on. And the

---

* This word interlined in a hand of the same date, but in different ink.

carrells was no greater then from one stanchell of the wyndowe to another. And over against the carrells against the church wall did stande sertaine great almeries [or cupbords, H. 45] of waynscott all full of BOOKES [with great store of ancient manuscripts to help them in their study, H. 45], wherein dyd lye as well the old auncyent written Doctors of the Church as other prophane authors, with dyverse other holie mens wourks, so that every one dyd studye what Doctor pleased them best, havinge the Librarie at all tymes to goe studie in besydes there carrells.

XLII. THE CLOISTER. THE WEASTE ALLEY.

In the weast alley of the Cloysters, towards the north ende, undernethe the Dorter, and adjoyning unto the staires that go up to the Dorter, is the THRESERHOUSE where there besst Evidennces and the Chapter seale ar keapt, of verie strong perfect workmanship, belonginge to the Prior and Covent.

[In that Angle on the south side of the Dormiter doore [a little distant from the said door, D.] there is a strong howse called the TREASURE HOWSE, where all ther tresure was kept. [having a strong door and two locks. D.] And in the midst of itt was a GRATE OF IRON, from the ground to the roofe of the howse, with a doore of iron into it. H. 45] [Within the said treasury was a strong iron grate, set fast in the groundwork, in the roof and in either wall, the breadth of the house, so fast as not to be broken, and in the midst of the grate a door of iron, according to the workmanship of the grate, with a strong lock upon it and two great shuts [slots, Ed. H.] of iron for the said door. And within the said grate was a four-square table, [a faire table, H. 45], covered with a green cloth, for the telling of their money. Within this treasury were likewise the Evidences of the house and the Chapter seale, as also the Evidences of several gentlemen's lands in the country, who thought them safer there than in their own custody. *Dav.*] [And many gentlemen sent ther Evidence to be kept ther for safety. H. 45].*

[Over against the said Treasury door was a fair stall of wainscott where the Novices were taught. And the master of the Novices had a pretty seat of wainscott, adjoyning to the south side of the Treasury door, over against the stall where the Novices sate. And there he taught the said Novices both fore-

---

* While now of late it is altered, the treasure and money being kept in a strong house over the east gates of the Abbey in the South Bailey now called the Exchequer, but in the old Treasury the common Chapter Seal is still kept. *Addition, Ed. H.*

noon and after noon. No strangers or other persons were suffered to molest or trouble the said Novices or Monks in their carrels [in their study, H. 45] while they were at their books within the Cloister. For to that purpose there was a Porter appointed to keep the Cloister door. *Dav.*]*

XLIII. THE DORTER.

Upon the west syde of the Cloyster there was a faire large house called the DORTER, where all the Monnks and the Novices did lye, every Monncke having a litle chamber of wainscott, verie close, severall, by themselves, and ther wyndowes towardes the Cloyster, every wyndowe servinge for one Chambre, by reasonne the particion betwixt every chamber was close wainscotted one from another, and in every of there wyndowes a deske to supporte there bookes for there studdie. In the weste syde of the said dorter was the like chambers, and in like sorte placed, with there wyndowes and desks towardes the Fermery and the water, the chambers beinge all well boarded under foute.

[The Novices had theire chambers severall by himselfe [in the south end of the said dorter, *Dav.*] adjoyning to the foresaid chambers, having eight chambers on each side, every Novice his chamber severall to himself, not so close nor so warme as the other chambers, nor having any light but what came in at the foreside of their chambers, beinge all close else both above and on either side. In either end of the said Dorter was a four [fair, *Dav.*] square stone, wherein was a dozen cressets wrought in either stone, being ever filled and supplied with the cooke as they needed, to give light to the Monks and Novices, when they rose to theire mattins at midnight, and for their other necessarye uses. *Cos.*]

Also there was a faire large house and a most decent place, adjoyninge to the west syde of the said Dorter, towardes the water, for the Monnkes and Novices to resort unto, called the PRIVIES, which was maide with two greate pillers of stone that did beare up the whole floore therof. And every seate and particion was of wainscott, close of either syde, verie decent, so

---

* A little south of the Treasury is a convenient room wherein is established the Song School for the instruction of boys for the use of the Quire. The Song School in the south isle of the Lanthorn being decently furnished with a reading desk, convenient seats, and all other laudable decencies, is appropriated to the service of God; where morning prayer is daily celebrated at six in the morning throughout the whole year, except on Sundays and Holydays. *Addition, Ed. H.*

that one of them could not see one another, when they weare in that place. There was as many seates of privies on either syde as there is litle wyndowes in the walls, which wyndowes was to gyve leighte to every one of the said seates. Which afterward was walled up, to make the howse more close, and in the height of the west end there was iij fair glass wyndowes and in the southe syde, in the hight over the said seates, is an other faire glass wyndowe, which greate wyndowes doth gyve lighte to all the whole house.

Also in the Dortre was every nyght [aboute 12 o'clock, H. 45] a privy serche, by the Supprior, who did caule at every Monnckes chambre [by ther names, H. 45], to se good order keapt, that none should be wanting [as also that ther were noe disorders amongest them, H. 45.] And the mydest of the said Dorter was all paved with fyne tyled stone, from th'one end to th' other. Also the said Supprior's chamber was the first chambre in the Dorter, for seinge of good order keapt. The Supprior dyd alwaies dyne and sup with the hole Covent, and did sytt at the over [high, H. 45] end of the table, and when every man had supped, which dyd end alwaies at fyve of the clock, upon the rynginge of a bell to gyve warninge to say grace, which being said, they departid all to the Chapter house, to meite the Prior, every night, ther to remayne in praier and devocion till six of the clocke. At which tyme, upon the ringing of a bell, they went to the *Salvi*. All the dures both of the Sell[er], the Fratre, the Dorter, and the Cloisters, weare locked evin at vj of the clocke, and the keys delyvered to the Supprior, untyl vij [six, *Cos.*] of the clock the next morninge.

XLIV. The Lofte.

The Monnckes dyd all dyne together at one table, in a place called the LOFTE, which was in the west end of the Fratree [Frater-house, *Cos.*] above the Seller. The Supprior dyd alwaies sitt att the upper end of the table as cheeffe, and theye had there meat served from the Great Kitching, the said Great Kitchinge servinge both the Prior and all the whole Covent.

[Ther was a paire of stayres within the Frater-howse, which did goe into a Loft over itt, where the ould Moncks did dyne and supp, where the Subprior was the cheife. They were served with meate from the Great Kitching, which hadd two dresser windowes into the Frater, a greater for principall feasts, the other for every day. H. 45.]

[Ther was also at the west end of the Frater-house, hard

within the Frater-house door, another door, at which the old Monks or Convent went in, and so up a greese, with an iron rail to hold them by, into a Loft which was at the west end of of the Frater-house, above the Cellar, where the said Convent and Monks dined and supp'd together. The Sub-Prior sate at the end of the table as chief; and at the greese-foot there was another door that went into the great Cellar or Buttery, where all the drink stood that did serve the Prior and the whole Convent of Monks, having their meat served them in at a dresser window from the Great Kitchen through the Frater-house, into the Loft, over the Cellar. *Dav.*]*

Also the Monnkes was accustomed every daie, aftere thei dyned, to goe thorowgh the Cloister, in at the Usher's dour, and so thorowghe the entrie, in under the Prior's lodginge, and streight into the Scentorie garth, wher all the Monnks was buried, and thei did stand all bair-heade, a certain longe space, praieng amongs the toumbes and throwghes for there brethren soules being buryed there, [departed, H. 45], and, when they hadd done there prayers, then they did returne to the Cloyster, and there did studie there bookes, untill iij of the clocke that they went to evensong. This was there dalie exercise and studie, every day after they had dyned.

The said Monnks weare the onlie writers of all the actes and deads of the Bushoppes and Priors of the Abbey church of Durham, and of all the cronacles and stories; and also did write and sett furth all things that was [thought, *Cos.*] wourthie to be noted, what acts and what miracles was done every yere and in what moneth. Which there doinges were most manifestly and undoubtedlie to be most just and trewe, and was alwaies most vertuouslie occupied, never idle, but either writing of good and goddly wourkes, or studying the Holie Scriptures, to the setting furthe of the honour and glorie of God, and for the edifieinge of the people, as well in example of good life and conversacion as by preaching the worde of God. Thus yow may se and perceave how the Monnks and religious men wer occupied in most godly writing and other exercissis in auncient tyme.

[The said Moncks were the onely writers of the lives and deedes of the Bishopps and Priors of Durham and of Cronicles and stories of memorable things and miracles of holy men, which were done every yeare, which writings were examined and found to be moste just and true. And sometymes studyinge

---

* This Loft since the Dissolution of the Monastery was made the dining-room of the Fifth Prebendaries house. *Addition, Ed. H.*

the Holy Scripture to the honour and glory of God and the edefying of the people by good example as well as by preachinge. H. 45.]

XLV. THE COMMON HOWSE.

On the right hand, as yow goe out of the Cloysters into the Fermery [or Infirmary, *Dav.*] was the COMMONE HOUSE, and a Maister therof. The house being to this end, to have a fyre keapt in yt all wynter, for the Monnckes to cume and warme them at, being allowed no fyre but that onely, except the Masters and Officers of the House, who had there severall fyres. Ther was belonging to the Common house a garding and a bowlinge allie, on the back side of the said house, towardes the water, for the Novyces sume tymes to recreat themselves, when they had remedy of there master, he standing by to se ther good order. [for the recreation of the Moncks, the master standinge by to see good order kept. H. 45.]

Also within this howse dyd the Master therof keepe his *O Sapientia*, ones in the yeare, viz. betwixt Martinmes and Christinmes, a sollemne banquett that the Prior and Covent dyd use at that tyme of the yere onely, when ther banquett was of figs and reysinges, aile and caikes, and therof no superflwitie or excesse, but a scholasticall and moderat congratulacion amonges themselves. [and that but a verye moderate one without superfluity, H. 45.]

XLVI. THE FERMERYE.

Within the FERMERY, under neth the master of the Fermeryes chamber, was a stronge prysonne call the LYNGHOUSE, [Lyingehouse, *Cos.*], the which was ordeyned for all such as weare greate offenders, as yf any of the Monnckes [and those which were in holy orders, H. 45], had bene taiken with any felony, or in any adulterie, he should have syttin ther in prisone for the space of one hole yere, in cheynes, without any company except the master of the Fermery [to see that he were strictlye looked to, accordinge to the orders of the house, H. 45] who did let downe there meate thorowgh a trap dour in a [great, *Cos.*] corde, being a great distance from them. [those who were in prison. *Dav.*] Other companye had they none. Yf any of the temporall men, [officers, H. 45] perteyninge to the said house had offended in any the premisses aforesaid, then weare they punyshed by the temporal lawe. [secular power, H. 45.]

XLVII. The Gest Hall.

There was a famouse house of hospitallitie, called the GESTE HAULE,* within the Abbey garth of Durham, on the weste syde, towardes the water, the Terrer of the house being master thereof, as one appoynted to geve intertaynment to all staits, both noble, gentle, and what degree so ever that came thether as strangers, ther interteynment not being inferior to any place in Ingland, both for the goodnes of ther diett, the sweete and daintie furneture of there lodgings, and generally all things necessarie for travellers. And, withall, this interteynment contynewing, not willing or commanding any man to departe, upon his honest and good behavyour. This haule is a goodly brave place, much like unto the body of a Church, with verey fair pillers supporting yt on ether syde, and in the mydest of the haule a most large rannge for the fyer. The chambers and lodginges belonging to yt weare swetly keept, and so richly furnyshed that they weare not unpleasant to ly in, especially one chamber called the KYNGS CHAMBER, deservinge that name, in that the King him selfe myght verie well have lyne in yt, for the princelynes therof. The victualls, that served the said geists, came from the great Kitching of the Prior, the bread and beare from his pantrie and seller. Yf they weare of honour they weare served as honorably as the Prior himselfe, otherwise according to ther severall callinges. The Terrer had certaine men appointed to wayte at his table, and to attend upon all his geists and stranngers, and, for ther better intertaynment, he had evermore a hogsheade or two of wynes lying in a seller appertayninge to the said halle, to serve his geists withall.

The Prior, whose hospitallie was soch as that there neaded no geist haule, but that they weare desyrouse to abound in all lyberall and fre almess geving, did keppe a moste honorable house and very noble intertaynement, being attended upon both with gentlemen and yeomen, of the best in the countrie, as the honorable service of his house deserved no lesse; the benevolence therof, with the releefe and almesse of the hole Covent was alwaies oppen and fre, not onely to the poore of the citie of Durham but to all the poore people of the countrie besides.

Also the lord Prior had two PORTERS, the one was the porter of his Hall dour, [called Robert Smyth, *interlined*,] and

---

* The houses belonging to the four following prebends, viz. the second, third, fourth, and tenth, were prepared out of the apartments and other offices belonging to the Guests' Hall, the hall itself being wholly demolished, nothing thereof remaining, except a part of the western wall. Nothing remains to let us know what was in the sixth and twelfth prebendaries' houses. *Addition, Ed. II.*

the other was the porter of the Usher dour, as ye goe frome the greate chamber to the Church, called Robert Clark, which two weare the last porters to the last Prior.

[The last Lord Prior was Doctor Whitehead, who after was the first Deane. H. 45.]

XLVIII. POOR CHILDREN. AGED WOMEN. THE FARMERY WITHOUT THE SOUTH GATES.

Ther weare certaine poor childrin onely maynteyned and releyved with the almesse and benevolence of the wholeHouse, which weare called the children of the Aumery, going daily to the Fermery schole, being alltogether mayntened by the whole Covent with meate drynke and lerninge.

[Ther was certayne poore children, called the children of the Almery, which was brought upp in learninge and mantayned with the almose of the Howse, havinge dyett in a Lofte on the north side of the Abbey Gates [before the suppression of the said house or abbey, *Dav.*] which had a longe porche over the gates [stairhead, slated over; and at either side of the said porch or entry there was a stairs to go up to it, *Dav.*] and a stable under itt [the said almery or loft having a door and an entry into it under the stairhead, *Dav.*] which after the suppression was turned into Mr. Stephen Marley's lodgings, and after converted to other uses. [Not long after the suppression he altered it and took down the porch and the two greeces that went to the said almery or loft, and made his kitchen where the stable was and his buttery where the said almery or loft was above. *Dav.*] The said children went to scoole to the Fermory chamber withowte the Abbey gates, which was founded by the Priors and mantayned att their cost. The last schoole-master's name was Sr Rob. Hartburne, which was injoyned to say masse two tymes in the weeke, att Magdelen's chappell near Kepyer, and once in the weeke at Kimblesworth chappell. They had ther meate from the Novices' table by the clarke of the Covent, owte att a windowe where the said clerke did looke to them, to see that they kept good order. [And the meat and drink of the foresaid children was what the Master of the Novices and the Monks had left and reserved, and it was carried in at a door adjoyning to the great kitchen window into a little vault at the west end of the Frater house like unto a pantry, called the COVEY, and had a window in it where one or two of the children did receive their meat and drink of the said clerk out of the said covey or pantry window, so called, and carried it to the almery or loft. *Dav.*]

Ther weare four aged women who lyved in the FARMERY WITHOUT THE SOUTH GAITS of the Abbey of Durham, every one having ther severall chamber to ly in, being founde and fedd onely with the releefe that came from the Priors own meyss, [table, *Cos.*] in which Farmerie there was a CHAPPELL, wher the schoolmaster of the Fermerye [and eyther the master of the fermerye, H. 45], having his chamber and schoule above yt, or soume other preest for hime, was ordeyned and appoynted to saye masse to the iiij^{or} ould womenne every holie daie and friday.

XLIX. THES BEYNGE MONNCKES AND OFFICERS WITHIN THE ABBEY CHURCHE OF DURHAM, AND NAMED AS FOLLOWITH.

Dane STEPHEN MARLEY the Supprior and Maister of the Fratere.

The Suppriors chamber was over the Dorter dour, to th' intent to heare that none should stir or go forth. And his office was to goe every nyghte, as a privy watch, befor mydnyght and after mydnyght, to every Monnckes chamber, and to caule at his chamber dour upon him by his name, to se that none of them shold be lacking or stolen furth, to goe about any kynde of vice or nowghtynes. Also the Supprior did sett alwaies in the Lofte amonges the Monncks, at meite, at the tables end, as cheefe amonges them, and to se that every mane did use him selfe according to the order that he had taiken him to. He did alwaies say grace at dynner and supper, and after v of the clocke at nyght to se all the dures, as the Seller dur, the Fratere dour, the Fawden getts, and the Cloister dures, every dur at nyghte to be locked. And he keapt the keyes of all thes foresaid dures all night, untill vij of the clocke in the morning, and at that tyme he caused the said doures to be opened, and delyvered the key of the Cloister to the Porter therof, and the keyes of the Fratere and the Seller to the Yeoman of the Celler.

Dane WILLIAM WATSONN, alias WILLIAM WYLOUME [Willome, *Cos.*] Maister and Kepper of the Fereture and deece Prior [the Deputy Prior, H. 45. Vice Prior, *Cos.*]

The Maister of the Feirture his chamber was in the Dorter.

He was the keper of the holy sacrede Shrine of Sancte Cuthbert. His office was, that when any man of honour or worshippe weere disposed to make there praiers to God and to Sancte Cuthbert, or to offer any thinge to his sacred Shrine, yf they requested to have yt drawen, and to se yt, then, streight waie, the Clarke of the Fereture, called George Baytes, did give intellegence to his Maister, maister deece [vice, *Cos.*] Prior, the Kepper of the Fereture. And then the said Maister dyde bring the keys of the Shrine with him, geving them to the clarke to open the locks of the Shrine. His office was to stand by, and to se it drawen, commanding the said clarke to drawe yt. Also it was ever drawen in the mattenes tyme, when *Te Deum* was in synginge, or in the hie mess tyme, or at evinsong tyme, when the *Magnificat* was song. And when they had maid there praiers, and dyd offer any thing to yt, yf yt weare either gould, sylver, or jewells, streighte-way it was honnge on the Shrine. And if yt weyre any other thing, as Unicorne horne, Eliphant tooth, or such like thinge, then yt was howng within the Fereture, at the end of the shrine. And when they had maid there praiers, the clarke did let downe the cover therof, and did locke yt at every corner, gyving the keies of the Shrine to the deice [vice, *Cos.*] Prior againe. Ther was many goodly Reliquies that belonged to the said shrine. The said George Baytes was Regester of the House, and did all that perteyned to the Register's office.

There was also a banner that perteyned to the said Shrine, in the keapinge of the said maister the deece [vice, *Cos.*] Prior, called SAINT CUTHBERTES BANNER [staffe, *interlined*], which was fyve yeards in length. All the pippes of it was of sylver, to be sleaven on a long speare staffe, [and on the overmost pype on the hight of yt was a fyne lytle silver crosse, *interlined*], [crosse staffe, *Cos.*] and a goodly banner cloth perteyned to yt. And in the mydes of the banner cloth was all of white velvett, halfe a yerd squayre every way, and a faire crose of read velvett over yt. And within the said white velvett was the holy relique, the CORPORAX [CLOTH, *interlined*] that the holy man Sancte Cuthbert did cover the chalyce with all, when he sayd masse. And the resydewe of the banner clothe was [all, *interlined*] of read [crimson, H. 45] velvett, imbrodered all with [grene sylke and, *interlined*] goulde, [most sumtuousle, as is aforesayd, *interlined*.]

The sayd banner was at the wynnyng of Bancks feilde [Brackinfeild,* *Cos.*] in King Henrie th'eights tyme, and dyd

---

* Brauxton, or Flodden-field.

bring home with it the Kinge of Scottes banner, and dyvers other noble mennes auncyentes of Scots, and that was loste that day. And did sett them up at Sancte Cuthbert's Fereture, where they dyd stande and hynge unto the suppression of the Howse. [And at the suppression of the House the aforesaid banner of Saint Cuthbert and all the auncients of the noblemen of Scotland were shortly after clearly defaced, to the intent there should be no memory of the said battel and of their aun‑ cients being spoiled, which were won at the said battle of Banfield, that there should be no remembrance of them in the monastical Church of Durham. *Dav.*] And the said Sancte Cuthbert's banner was at manye other places besydes. Yt was thought to be one of the goodlyest reliques that was in Eng‑ land, and yt was not borne but of principall daies when ther was a generall Prossession, as Easter daie, the Assention day, Whitsonday, Corpus Christi daie, and Sancte Cuthbert's day. And at other festivall daies it was sett up at the east end of the shrine, because yt was so chargeable. [weighty, *Dav.*]

Also, when so ever yt was borne, yt was the clarke [of the Fereture's, *interlined*] office to wayte upon yt [with his surplice on, *interlined*], with a faire reade paynted staffe, with a forke or clove on the upper end of the staffe, which clove was lyned with softe silke and softe downe, in under the silke, for hurt‑ inge or brusing of the pipes of the banner, being of sylver, to taike it downe and raise yt up againe, for the weightenes there‑ of. [There was also a strong girdle of white leather worn by him who carried Saint Cuthbert's banner, when it was carried abroad, and it was made fast to the said girdle by two pieces of white leather, and at either end of the two pieces of white leather, a socket of horn was made fast to them, that the end of the banner staff, might be put into it, for to ease him who car‑ ried the said banner of Saint Cuthbert, because it was so heavy. *Dav.*] There was iiij men alwaies appoyned to waite upon it besydes the clarke and he that dyd beare yt.

The deace [*so in Cos.*] Prior had the keyes and the keaping of Sancte Beeds Shrine, which dyd stand in the Galleley, and when so ever there was any generall Prossession, then he com‑ manded his clarke, geving him the keyes of Sancte Beedes Shrine, to drawe the cover of yt, and to taike yt downe and dyd carry yt into the Revestrie. Then it was caryed with iiij Monnckes about in Prossession, every principall day, and when the Procession was donne ytt was caryed into the Galleley and set upe there againe, with the cover letten downe over yt and lockte, the keyes browght by the clarke to the Maister of the Fereture againe.

Dane RICHARDE CROSBIE, Maister of the Novices.

Ther was alwayes vj Novices, which went daly to schoule within the House, for the space of vij yere [together, *Cos.*], and one of the oldest Monnckes, that was lernede, was appoynted to be there tuter. The sayd Novices had no wages, but meite, drinke, and clothe, for that space. The maister or tuteres office was to se that they lacked nothing, as cowles, frocks, stammyne, beddinge, bootes and socks, and whene they did lack any of thes necessaries the Maister had charge to calle of the Chamberlaynes for such thinges. For they never receyved wages, nor handled any money, in that space, but goynge daly to there bookes within the cloyster. And yf the maister dyd see that any of theme weare apte to lernyng, and dyd applie his booke, and had a pregnant wyt withall, then the maister dyd lett the Prior have intellygence. Then, streighte way after, he was sent to Oxforde to schoule, and there dyd lerne to study Devinity. And the resydewe of the Novices was keapt at there bookes tyll they coulde understand there service and the scriptures. Then, at the foresayde yeres' end, they dyd syng there first messe. The House was no longer charged with fyndinge them apparell, for then they entred to wages to finde them selves apparell, which wages was xxs. in the yere. [and noe more, H. 45.] The eldest Monncke in the House had no more, except he had an office [that did afford itt. H. 45.] His chamber where he dyd ly was in the Dorter.

Dane JOHANN PORTER, alias JOHAN SMYTHE, called Maister Sagersten [Saccraston, H. 45].

The Sexten's checker was within the Church, in the North Alley over against Bushop Skirley's Alter, of the lefte hand as yow goe up the Abbey to Saint Cuthbert's Fereture [which after was converted to a songe schoole, but sence itt is pulled downe by order of the Bishopp, att the cominge of King Charles in his progresse to Scotland, and the songe schoole made in the Cloisters, under the Moncks lodginge, where Maister Green now dwelleth, H. 45.] His office was to se that there should nothing be lackinge with in the Churche, as to provyde bread and wyne for the Church, and to provide for wax and lyght in wynter. He had alwaies one tonn of wyne lyinge in the said checker, for the use of the sayd Church. He had also Seggerstenhewgh in keping. It was his charge, and Saint Margarett's waird [wood, H. 45] in his office. Also his office was to se all the glass wyndowes repayred and mendid, and the plumbers wourke of the Churche, with mending of bells and belstrings [and leathering, *Dav.*], and all other workes that was necessary to be occupied, both with in the Church and with out the Church, and to se the Church to be clenely keapte. All thes things was alwaies to be called for at the Sagersten's hands, as neade requyred.

Also his office was to locke up, every day, all the keyes of every Alter in the Church (every Alter havinge there severall aumbree and some two), and to lye theme furthe every morninge, betwixt vij and viij of the clocke, upon the height [upon the topp, H. 45] of the aumbrie (being of waynscott), wherin they weare lockte, standing with in the north Quer dour, that every Monncke myght taike the key, and appoynt what Alter he was disposed to say mess at. Allso [And then, H. 45] thei went to the Chapter house, every day, where all the Bushops in the oulde tyme was buryed, betwixt viij and ix of the clocke, and there did pray for all [the soules of, H. 45] there benefactors and founders which had bestowed any thing of that Church. And, at ix of the clocke, ther ronng a bell to masse, called the Chapter masse, which was sonng alwaies [att the High Alter, H. 45] and he that sunge masse hadd alwaies in his MEMENTO all those that had geven any thinge to that Church [all the soules of theire benefactours, H. 45]. The one halfe of the Monnckes did say masse in the Chapter masse tyme, and the other halfe, that song the Chapter messe, seyd messe in the high messe tyme. Ther was at every Alter ij challices and ij sylver crewetts, apperteyninge to yt, both with albes and vestments, for the principall feastes, as also for all other daies besyde. Every Alter had ther duble furnitures, for adorninge all partes of the Aulter, servinge both for the holydayes and princypall feasts.

There founders and benefactoures was prayed for every daie and had in remembrance, in the tyme of masse. His chamber wher he dyd lye was in the Dorter. He had his meyt served from the Great Kitching to his checkre.

L. THESE BEINGE MONNCKES AND OFFECERES OF THE HOWSE OF DURHAM AND NAYMED AS FOLLOWETH:

Dane ROBERT BENNETT the Bowcer of the house.

The Bowcer's Checker is a litle stone house, joyninge of the

Cole garth, perteyning to the Great Kytchinge, a litle distant frome the Deanes haule greece [staires, H. 45].

His office was to receave all the rentes that was perteyning to the House, and all other Officers of the House mayde there accoumptes to him, and he discharged all the servants wages, and paide all the expences [and sommes of money as was laid furth about any work apperteining to the said Abey or, *interlined*] that the House was charged withall. His chamber, where he dyd lye, was in the Fermery. His meyt was served from the Great Kitching to his checker.

Dane ROGER WRYGHT the Cellerer of the House.

The Cellerer's Checker was afterward Docter Toddes chamber, joyninge of the west end of the Great Kitchinge, having a longe greece goynge up to yt over the Fawlden yeatts [folden gates, *Cos.*] His office was to see what expences was in the Kitchinge, what beffes [beives, H. 45] and muttones was spente in a weeke, and all the spyces and other necessaries that was spente in the Kitchinge, both for the Prior's table and for the hole Covent, and for all strangers that came [and to see that nothinge were wantinge, H. 45]. Yt was his office to se all things orderlye served, and in dewe tyme. The chambre where he dyd lye was in the Dorter.

Dane ROGER WATSON the Terrer of the House.

The Terrer's Checker was as yea goe into the Geste Haule, of your lefte hand, in the entrie, as yow goe in or (before) yea come into the Great Hall.

His office was to se that the Geste Chamber to be clenly keapt, and that all the table clothes, table napkings, and all the naprie with in the chambers, as sheetes and pillowes, to be sweate and cleane. And he provyded alwaies two hogsheds of wyne, to be redie against any strangers came, [for the entertaynement of strangers, H. 45.] and he provyded provender for there horses, that nothing should be lacking for any stranger, what degree so ever he was of, and iiij yeamen allowed to wayte upon the said strangers whensoever they came. His chamber where he dyd ly was in the Fermery.

Dane WILLIAM FOSTER the Kepper of the Garners.

The Maister of the Garner's Checker was over Maister Pilkington's haule doures. All his house and Maister Bonnies [Bunny's, H. 45] house was Garners,* where all there wheat and other corne did lye. His office was to receyve all the whet that came, and all the malte corne, and to make accompte what malt was spente in the weeke, and what malt corne was delyvered to the kylne, and what was receyved from the kylne, and howe moch was spente in the house. The kylne was where Maister Bennett's lodging [house, *Cos.*] was, hard beyond the Connditt, which lodging he ded buylde of his charges.† His chamber wher he dyd lie was in the Dorter.

Dan THOMAS SPARKE the Chamberlayne.

The Chamberlaynes Checker was where Maister Swifte hath his lodging, nyghe to the Abbey gaites.‡ His office was to provyde for stammyne, otherwaies called lyncye wonncye [and other lincy woncy, H. 45], for sheetes, and for sheirtes, for the Novices, and the Monnckes to weare, for they dyd never weare any lynynge, and he had a tailler wourkinge daily, makinge socks of white wollen clothe, both hole sockes and halfe sockes, and makinge shertes and sheetes of lyncye wonncey, in a shop underneth the sayde checker, which tailler was one of the servauntes of the House. His chamber where he dyd lye was in the Dorter.

Dane HENRYE BROWNE the Maister of the Common House. [Hall, H. 45.]

The Commoner's Checker was within the Common House. His office was to provide for all such spices against Lent as should be comfortable for the said Monnckes for there great austeritie both of fastinge and prayinge [because ther austerity of fastinge and praier was very great, H. 45], and to see a fyre [a good fyer, H. 45] contynewally in the Common House hall,

---

* These granaries are at present the houses of the eighth and ninth prebendaries.—*Addition Ed.* H.

† It is at this time the house of the eleventh prebendary.—*Id.*

‡ Now the mansion house of the first prebendary.—*Id.*

for the Monncks to warme theme, when they weyre disposed, and to have alwaies a hogshead of wyne for the Monnckes, and for the keaping of his O, called O Sapientia, and to provide for fyggs and walnutes against Lent. His chamber where he dyd lye was in the Dorter.

Dan William Watson the Prior's Chaplaine.

The Chaplaynes Checker was over the staires, as yow goe up to the Deanes haule.

His offis was to receave at the Bowcer's hands all such summes of money as was dewe for the Bowcer to paie unto the Lord Prior's use, for the mantenance of hime selfe and expencis of his whole howshold, and for all his other necessaries. The said Chaplen's office was to provide for the Lord Prior's apparell, and to se all things in good order in the Hall, and his furniture [lyninge, H. 45] for his table to be swete and cleane, and to se that every man applied his office diligentlie, as it owghte to be done, to se that no debaite nor strife to be within the house. He had in his charge and keapinge all the Lord Prior's plaite and treasure, as well in delyveringe therof as receiving yt in againe. And also he was to discharge and paie all gentlemen, yeomen, and all other servannts and officers of the Lord Prior's House [of what degree soever, H. 45] there wages, and to paie all other rackings of his house what so ever. His chamber where he did lye was next unto the Prior's chamber.

All thes Monnckes before rehersed was in thes Officies when the House was suppressed, and the Monnckes and Novices was alwaies named after this sorte, as thes Monncks ys named before the suppression of the House, and the Prior of the House was alwaise called the Lord Prior even to the suppression of the House also.

LI. Saynte Cuthbert's Shryne defacede.

The sacred Shryne of holy Sancte Cuthbert, before mentioned, was defaced in the Visitacion that Doctor Ley [Lee, H. 45], Doctor Henley, and Maister Blythman, held at Durham, for the subvertinge of such monuments, in the tyme of King Henrie 8, in his suppression of the Abbaies, where they found many woorthie and goodly jewells [goodly and rich ornaments and jewels of great value which the said Church and St. Cuthbert was adorned withall, but most especialle, H. 45], but especiallie one pretious stone [belonginge to the said shrine, H. 45], which by the estimate of those iij visitors and ther skilfull lapidaries [which they browght with them, H. 45] was of value sufficient to redeme a Prince [worth in value a King's ransome, H. 45]. After the spoile of his ornaments and jewells, cumming nerer to his [sacred, H. 45] bodie, thingking to have found nothing but duste and bones, and finding the chiste that he did lie in, very strongly bound with irone, then the goulde smyth did taike a great fore hammer of a smyth, and did breake the said chiste [open, H. 45], and, when they had openede the chiste, they found him lyinge hole, uncorrupt, with his faice baire, and his beard as yt had bene a forthnett's growthe, and all his vestments upon him, as he was accustomed to say masse withall, and his met wand of gould lieing besid him. Then, when the gouldsmyth did perceive that he had broken one of his leggs, when he did breake upe [open, *Cos.*] the chiste, he was verie sorie for it, and did crye "Alas, I have broken one of his leiggs." Then, Docter Henley, hereing him say so, did caule upon hime, and did bid him cast downe his bones. Then he made him annswer again that he could not gett it [them, H. 45] in sunder, for the synewes and the skine heild it, that it would not come in sunder [could not parte, H. 45]. Then Docter Ley did stepp up, to se if it weire so or not, and did turne hime selfe aboute, and did speke Latten to Docter Henley, that he was lieing holl. Yet Docter Henley would geve no creditt to his word, but still did crye "Cast downe his bones." Then Docter Ley maide annswere, "Yf ye will not beleve me, come up your selfe and se hime." Then dyd Docter Henlie step up [goe up, H. 45] to hime, and did handle him, and dyd se that he laid hole [was whole and uncorrupt, H. 45]. Then he did commaund them to taike hime downe, and so it hapned, contrarie ther expectation, that not onely his bodie was hole and incorrupted, but the vestments, wherin his bodie laie, and wherwith all he was accustomed to saie mass, was freshe, saife, and not consumed. Wherupon the Visitores commaunded that he should be karied into the Revestre [the Vestry, H. 45], where he was close and saiflie keapt, in the inner part of the revestrie, tyll such tyme as they did further knowe the King's pleasure, what to doe with hym, and upon notise of the King's pleasure therin, [and after, H. 45], the Prior and the Monnckes buried him, in the ground, under the same place where his Shrine was exalted [under a faire merble stone, which remaynes to this day, where his Shrine was exalted, H. 45].

LII. The Shrine of Holie Sancte Beede.

The Shrine of holie Sancte Beede [the Shrine of St. Beeda, H. 45], before mentioned, in the Gallelie, was defaced by the said Visitors, and at the same Suppression, his bones being interred under the same place where his Shrine was before erected [exalted, H. 45].

There ys two stones, that was of Sayncte Beede's Shrine in the Galiley, of blewe marble, which, after the defacinge thereof, was browght into the bodye of the Church, and lyeth nowe over against the estmost toumbe of the Neivells, joyned both together. The upper-most stone of the said Shrine hath iiij [three, H. 45] holes in every corner, for irons to stand and to to be fastned in, to guyde the coveryng, where yt was drawen up or letten downe, whereupon did stand Saincte Bede's Shrine. And the other ys a playne marble stone, whiche was loweste, and did lye above a litle marbel toumbe, where on the lower end of the v small pillers of marble did stande, which pillers did also support the uppermost stone. The said stones lyeth nowe bothe together (as is afforesaid) end-way, before [neare, H. 45] where Jesus' Alter did stande.

LIII. The Rite or Avncyent Custom of Prossessions within the Abbey Churche of Durham before the Suppression, as hereafter followeth.

Prossession by the Prior and the Monnckes on Sancte Mark's day.

Upon Sancte Mark's daie, after Easter, which was commonly fasted throwe all the countrie, and no flesh eten upon it, the Prior with the Monncks had a solemne Prossession at that daie, and went to the Bowe church with ther Prosession, and did verie solemne service ther, and one of the Monnckes did make a sermont to all the people of the parishe, and of the towne, that came thether.

LIV. Prosession of the iij Cross Daies by the Prior and the Monnckes.

Likewise, on Mondaie in Cross Weake, they had also an other solemne Prosession, and did goe to Sancte Oswald's Church, in Elvett, and there did verie solemne service, and had a sermont, that one of the Monnckes did make before the audyence of many people of the towne.

Likewise, the morowe after, being TEWSDAIE, they had an other solemne Prosession to Sancte Margaret's church in Framwelgate, and did solemne service there, and one of the Monnckes did make a sermount to the audience of much people of the said parishe.

Likewise on the morrowe after, being WEDINSDAY, they had an other solemne Prosession to Sancte Nicholas church, in the markett place, and there did devyne service very sollemly, and had a sermont made by one of the Monnckes, before the greatt audyence of many people.

LV. PROSSESSION OF HALLOWE THURSDAIE, WHITSONDAY, AND TRINITIE SOUNDAY, BY THE PRIOR, AND THE MONNCKES.

The next morninge, being HALLOW THURSDAIE, they had also a generall Prossession, with two CROSSES borne before theme, the one of the crosses, the stafe and all, of gould, the other of sylver and parcell gilt, both the cross and the staffe, with Sancte Cuthbert's Baner, that holy Reliquie, which was borne formest in the Prossession, with all the riche Copes that was in the Church, every Monnke had one, and the Prior had a marveilous riche cope on, of clothe of ffyne pure gould, the which he was not able to goe upright with it, for the weightines therof, but as men did staye it [but as some did goe by hym, H. 45], and holde it up of every side, when he had it on. [He went, H. 45] with his crutch in his hand, which was of sylver and duble gilt, with a rich myter on his head. Also Sancte Beede's Shrine, that holy Reliquie [and reliques, H. 45], was caryed in the said Prossession with iiij Monnckes, on there shoulders, and sertain other Monncks did cary about with theme in the saide Prossession dyvers other holy Relicks, as the picture of Sancte Oswald of sylver and gilt, and Sancte Margarett's crosse, of sylver and duble gilt. Which Prossession did goe furth of the north dore of the Abbey Church, and thorowe the church yeard, and down Lyegaite [Lidgate, *Cos.*] by the Bowe church end, and up the South Baley and in at the Abbey Gates [and soe to the Abbey Gates, H. 45], where a grete number of people did stand, both men, women, and childrine, with great reverence and devotion, which was a goodly and a godly sight to behold, and so went thorowe the Abbey Garth, and a number of men following it, but no women was suffered to goe further than the Abbey yeatts [in the Baylie, H. 45], and so thorow the Cloister into the Church.

Also upone WITSOUNDAIE was a generall Prossession, likewise, which was done with great solemnytie, after this foresaid prossession, as it was on Hallow Thursday, with Sancte Beede's Shrine and Sancte Cuthbert's Banner, and all the holie Reliques, as the image of Sancte Oswald, and the image of Sancte Aidan and the holie Relique of Sancte Margarett's cross, with dyvers holie Reliques besides.

Lykewise, on TRINITIE SOUNDAIE, there was another generall Prossession, after this sorte aforesaid, with all the aforesaid Reliques, and wente all the same sircuit that all the aforesaide Prossessions dyd goe before.

Many was the goodly riche Jewells and Reliques that did appurtaine to that same Churche: yt was accommpted to be the richest Churche in all this land, so greate was the rich jewells and ornaments that was geven and bestowed of that holie man Sancte Cuthbert. Besydes that, kyng Richard did geve his parlamente Robe of blewe vellet, wrowght with great lyons of pure gould, a marveilouse rich Cope, and another Cope of clothe of gould, geven to the same Church, in the worship of that holie man Sancte Cuthbert, by another Prince, so greate was the godly mynd of Kings, Quenes, and other great estaits, for the great devotion and love that they had to God and holy Sancte Cuthbert in that Church.

Looke what is further to be desyred in the nerration [generation, *Cos.*] of this auncyent Church, and godly ceremonyes therin frequented, you shall reade at large in the Historie of the Church, which coulde not be conveynyently sett downe in these particular notes, beinge but, as yt weare, a glass for the vewers and beholders therof.

LVI. THE AUNTIENT SOLEMNYTIE OF PROSSESSION UPON CORPUS CHRISTI DAY WITHIN THE CHURCH AND CITIE OF DURHAM. BEFORE THE SUPPRESSION OF THE SAID ABBEY CHURCHE.

There was a goodly Prossession upon the Place Grene, on the thursday after Trinitie soundaie, in the honor of CORPUS CHRISTI DAIE, the which was a pryncipall feast at that tyme. The Baley of the towne did stand in the Towle bowthe and did cawle the occupations that was inhabitens with-in the towne, every occupation in his degree, to bringe forthe ther Banners, with all the lightes apperteyninge to these severall Banners, and to repaire to the Abbey Church doure, every Banner to stand a rowe [in ranke, *Cos.*] in his degree, from the Abbey Church dour to Wyndshole yett : on the west syde of the waye did all the Banners stand, and on the easte syde of the way dyd all the Torges [torches, *Cos.*] stand, perteyninge to the sayd Banners.

Also there was a goodly Shrine in Sancte Nicholas church, ordeyned to be caryed the sayd daie in Prossession, cauled CORPUS CHRISTI SHRINE, all fynlye gilted, a goodly thing to behould, and on the hight of the sayd Shrine was a foure squared box, all of christall, wherin was enclosed the Holy Sacrament of th'Aulter, and was caryed the said daie with iiij prestes up to the Place Grene, and all the hole Prossession of all the Churches in the said towne goyng before yt, and, when it was a little space within Wyndshole yett, yt dyd stand still; then was Sancte Cuthbert's Banner browght fourth, with two goodly faire Crosses, to meet yt, and the Prior and Covent, with all the whole companye of the quere, all in there best Copes, dyd meet the said Shrine, sytting on there kneys and praying. The Prior did sence yt [fetch it, *Cos.*], and then, caryinge yt forward into the Abbey Church, the Prior and Covent, with all the Quere following yt, it was sett in the Quere, and solemne service don before ytt, and *Te Deum* solemnly songe and plaide of the Orgaynes, every man praysinge God. And all the Banners of the occupations dyd followe the said Shrine into the Church, goyng rownde about Sancte Cuthbert's fereture, lyghtinge there torches and burning all the service tyme. Then yt was caryed frome thence with the said Prossession of the towne, back againe, to the place from whence it came, all the Banners of the occupations following it, and setting yt againe in the Church, every man maiking his prayers to God did departe, and the said Shrine was caryed into the Revestrie, where yt remayned untill that tyme Twelvemonthe. Then afterward, in the first yere of Kyng Edwardes reigne, there was certaine Commyssioners appoynted to deface all suche ornaments as was lefte in the parishe Churches in Durham, undefaced in the former Visitation ; the names of the Commyssioners was docter Harvye and docter Whitby, the said docter Harvie did call for the said Shrine, and when it was browght before him he dyd tread upon it with his feete and did breake yt all in peces, with dyvers other ornaments perteyninge to the church.

APPENDIX.

I. A Description of the Glass Histories in the Windows.

IN THE NORTH ISLE OF THE BODY OF THE CHURCH,

1. Are six glass Windows. The lowest to the Lantherne hath three fair lights divided with stone work, having therein the picture of Christ crucified in the middle of the first light; and in the second light is the picture of our blessed Lady on the other side, the picture of St. John the Evangelist on the other side of the picture of Christ. A Monk in a blew habit, kneeling and holding up his hands, and six turret* windows in plaine glass.

2. The second Window hath two long lights, divided with stone work, and in white glass, with coloured glass about it.

3. In the third are two fair long lights, divided with stone work, having in the first light the picture of St. Catherine, and underneath her the picture of St. Oswald, and below St. Oswald's St. Cuthbert's picture. In the second light is pictured the blessed Virgin Mary with Christ in her armes [and underneath her the picture of St. Bede, and below him the picture of St. Osmond, bishop, and the arms of †], St. Cuthbert and St. Oswald set forth in colour'd glasse, and four turret windows without pictures, in colour'd glass.

4. The fourth Window was plain, and as the second with coloured glass about it.

5. In the fifth Window were two long lights, divided as aforesaid, in white glass without pictures, but having round about coloured glass; and five turret windows; first four, and one at the top.

---

* This word is generally written *turred* in the MS.

† The passages in brackets without reference stand in Hunter's Edition. The probability is that he corrected the MS. by actual inspection, the glass being most of it remaining in his time.

6. The sixth Window had two long lights, with stone work; in the first light the picture of St. Oswald, and under him St. Paul's picture; and in the second light is the picture of St. Peter, underneath him the picture of St. James, in fine coloured glass: and above four turret lights, with Bishop Skirlaw's arms.

In the end of the Church towards the west, over the north Galilee door, is a Window with two lights, divided with stone work, having in the south light the picture of our blessed Lady with Christ in her armes, and a sceptre in her hand [and the second or north light was in white glass: and above were four turret lights], with Bishop Skirlaw's arms on the top of all.

THE SOUTH ALLEY OF THE BODY OF THE CHURCH.

In this Alley are six Windowes in glass, finely colored, with pictures.

1. In the first, over the Church Doore going into the Cloysters, is a Window with three fair lights, divided with stone work, having in the first light the picture of St. Oswald, in the second the picture of the Virgin Mary, and underneath her is the picture of Bishop Langley, in his episcopal attire, praying on his knees, and holding up his hands, with his arms in a 'scutchon underneath, and these words, 𝕺rate pro anima Domini Thomae Langley quondam Episcopi hujus Ecclesiae. And in the third light was pictured St. Cuthbert, all set forth in fine colour'd glass, and three white turret windows.

2. In the second Window are five fair long lights, divided with stone worke, having in the first light the picture of St. George in armor, and a redd lyon under his feet; in the second light the picture of St. Oswald, king; in the third light the picture of our blessed Lady; in the fourth light the picture of St. Cuthbert, in his episcopal attire; and in the fifth light the picture of St. Christopher with Christ on his shoulder, having a staff flourishing in his hand, and the draught of the instruments wherewith Christ was crucified, and the manner thereof excellently set forth, and ten knots in coloured glasse, five above and five belowe; and six turret windows in white glasse.

3. In the third Window are two long lights, having in the first light the picture of God the Father, and Christ on his breast hanging on the cross; in the second light is pictured St. Cuthbert, with certaine Armes of the Nevills finely done; and four turret windows in the top, having in them all the Nevill's armes, as they were joined in matches.

4. In the fourth Window are two long lights, divided with

stone work, having in the first light the picture of our blessed Lady, and St. John Baptist, and St. Paul; and in the second light St. John the Evangelist, the chalice in his hand, St. Anne, and other pictures, with the Nevill's arms, and the arms of those that were joyned with them in marriage; and above four turret windowes, with the Nevill's armes in them all.

5. In the fifth Window are two fair long lights, having in the first light the picture of the Angel Gabriell saluting the blessed Lady; in the second light the picture of the Virgin Mary, and two other angells with 'scutchons of the Arms of the Nevils, and others with whom they have married, on their breasts, one angell under St. Gabriel, the other angel under our blessed Lady, all set out in fine coloured glass, and above four turret windowes in painted glass with knotts.

6. In the sixth Window [above the south great door of the Church] are two long lights, having in them no pictures; and above four tower lights, having in them the Arms of [four] several Noblemen.

7. Alsoe a Windowe over the south Galilee [door] and having noe pictures; four turret windows in white glass.

THE NORTH ALLEY OF THE LANTHORN.

[On the west side of this Alley, above the staircase door] there is a fair glass Window, having three long lights; in the first light is the picture of St. John Baptist, with the Lamb of God in his hands; in the second light is the picture of our blessed Lady, with the picture of a Monk in a blew habitt upon his knees, holding up his hands unto her underneath her; and above his heade written, **Mater Dei, miserere mei.** And in the third light the picture of St. John the Evangelist, with a reed in his hand, underneath him the Nevill's cross and bull's head, with two tower windowes above; and the picture of God Almighty in the highest, in fine coloured glass.

And further, in the said Alley are three Altars, and above every Altar one glass Window, having three long lights divided from each other by stone work.

1. The first Altar is called St. Giles's Altar; and in that Window, in the first light, is pictured St. Nicholas, having under his feete written, **Sanctus Nicholaus, Episcopus.** In the second light is pictured Nicodemus [some say it was Joseph of Arimathea, *in marg.*], with redd bloody hands and face, taking and bearing the weight of the cross in his armes;

and in the third light was pictured St. Giles in a blew habit, [with a hind at his feet shot with a shaft].

2. The second Altar is called St. Gregories Altar [and behind it a Window of three lights, divided with stone work]; in the first light is the picture of St. Gregory, and in the second light is the picture of our blessed Lady St. Mary, with Christ in her armes; and one [W.] Seaton, Sub-prior, pictured in his blew habit, kneeling and houlding up his hands, with these words underneath him, [𝔚.] 𝔖𝔢𝔞𝔱𝔬𝔫, 𝔖𝔲𝔟-𝔭𝔯𝔦𝔬𝔯; and in the third light a Bishopp with a cross on his shoulder, called St. Ambrose.

3. The third Altar is called St. Bennett's, and hath the like Windowe. In the first light is the picture of St. Bennett in a blew habit, with a crosier staff in his hand; underneath him is the picture of St. Hirome, with a Cardinal's hat on his head; and in the second light is the picture of Christ as hee arose from the dead*, and the picture of a Prior in a blew habit, kneeling and holding up his handes before the Altar, with a mitre sett upon it; in the third light was the picture of St. Catherine, with the wheele in her hand; underneath her the picture of Mary Magdalene, with an alabaster box in her hand, as she anointed Christ; and above are three tower windows with angels in fine coloured glasse.

And the Orders of St. Bennett were set forth in their pictures about the Altar in wainscott, with a partition, the Fryars within, and the Monks without.

THE SOUTH ALLEY OF THE LANTHORNE.

In this Alley are three Altars, called Houghwell's Altar; 2. the Lady of Bolton's Altar; 3. St. Fides's Altar towards the south [each having a window behind it].

1. The first Altar had a fair glasse Window with three long lights; in the first light is the picture of St. Catherine, with the wheele in her hand, and under her an axe, and in the second light the picture of our blessed Lady, with Christ in her armes; and under her a Monk in blew habit, kneeling and praying; and in the third light is the picture of St. Margarett, and under her the picture of St. Christopher, bearing Christ on his shoulders over the water, having a staff flourishing in his hand; and three turrett windows, with the picture of St. John the Baptist in prison, and a grate before him, and a book in his hand, with

* [As he did descend from death, MS.]

the Lamb of God upon it, pointing unto it with his other hand; when Christ sent divers messengers to John, then in prison, who pointing unto the Lamb with his finger, saying, 𝕰𝖈𝖈𝖊 𝕬𝖌𝖓𝖚𝖘 𝕯𝖊𝖎, &c., which was Christ, who was questioned of those sent to him to learn of him who he was. [who had sent them to learne of him who he was, MS.]

2. The second Altar hath a Window with three like lights, having in the first St. John the Evangelist, with a reed in his right hand, and an eagle upon his book in his left hand; and under him the picture of St. Nicholas; in the second light, the picture of our Lady of Bolton, with a golden mace in her hand, and a crowne of gold on her heade, and a Monk under her feet kneeling and praying; in the third light, the picture of St. Stephen, with stones in his hands [wherewith he was martyr'd]; and under him the picture of St. John Baptist, with the lamb in his hand; with three towers in coloured glass [with angels pictured in them].

3. The third Altar had the like Window; in the first light the picture of the blessed Virgin, with Christ in her armes; and under her the picture of St. Fides; in the second light, the picture of God the Father, with Christ in his armes, as proceeding from the Father; under him, the picture of St. Thomas; under St. Thomas is a Monk in a blew habit, houlding up his hands and praying; in the third light is the picture of St. Leonard; under him, St. Laurence; and in the high part of the windowe in a little turret is St. Bede in a blew habit, and the other two little turretts had two angells.

4. In the end of the said Altar, southward, is a fair glass Window with three long lights; in the [middle or] first light is the picture of Christ [crucified], and underneath the picture of a Monk in a blew habitt kneeling and holding up his hands, having written above his head, 𝕮𝖍𝖗𝖎𝖘𝖙𝖊 𝕵𝖊𝖘𝖚 𝕿𝖍𝖔𝖒𝖆𝖊—𝖉𝖊𝖘 𝕲𝖆𝖚𝖉𝖎𝖚𝖒.* And in the second light, the picture of the Virgin Mary on one side of Christ; and in the third light, the picture of St. John the Evangelist on the other side of Christ; and above all three lights, with the picture of God Almighty, with a globe in his hand, in the middle light; the picture of two angels on either side of God Almighty, in either of the other two lights.

5. There is a Window towards the Cloyster, west of the Clock, which had three lights; in the first, the picture of our Lady; under her, the picture of St. Cuthbert, with St. Oswald's head

---

* The inscription was an hexameter line 𝕮𝖍𝖗𝖎𝖘𝖙𝖊 𝕵𝖊𝖘𝖚 𝕿𝖍𝖔𝖒𝖆𝖊 𝕳𝖊𝖝𝖍𝖆𝖒 𝖉𝖊𝖘 gaudia coeli. Hexham occurs as a monk in 1436. See St. Cuthbert, p. 171. The glass has been lately removed.

in his hand; in the second light, our Saviour Christ on the cross, with **INRI** over his head, with Angells receiving blood and water from his side, and two Angells receiving blood from his feete, and the picture of the sonne and moone wanting light above his heade; under the picture of Christ is the picture of our Lady, and under her, the picture of a Monk in a blew habit, kneeling and holding up his hands, having above his head, **Mater Dei, miserere mei:** and in the third light is the picture of St. John the Baptist, and St. Oswald under him, as he was king, in his princely attire.

THE NORTH ALLEY OF THE QUIRE.

1. In the North Alley of the Quire are four fair coloured glass Windows; the first having four long lights [and a casement]; in the first light is pictured our blessed Lady, with Christ in her armes, with a triple crown of gold on her head; in the second light is pictured St. Anne; in the third light, St. Mary Magdalen; in the fourth, St. Mary, Cleophas, and Salome, being the three Maries [and one tower window].

2. In the second are four long lights; in the first is St. Michael the Archangel, with a sword in his hand, and a staff with a cross thereon in the other hand, killing the dragon; the second light hath St. Catherine with the wheele in her hand, [and a naked sword]; and written above her head **Sancta Catherina;** in the third light, our Lady, with Christ in her arms; above her head is written **Sancta Maria**—St. Mary; under her feet, the picture of a Monk in a blew habit praying, and written above his head, **Mater Dei, miserere mei;** and under his feet is written **Dominus Georgius Cornforth;** and in the fourth light, St. Cuthbert, with King Oswald's head in his hand, and above him written, **Sanctus Cuthbertus;** [and above all were seven tower lights of white glass, and below two knots of white glass].

3. [In the third were four lights; in the first] is the picture of St. Oswald, King, with a cross on his breast; in the second light, St. Cuthbert [with **Sanctus Cuthbertus** written under him]; in the third light, St. Gregory [with **Sanctus Gregorius** under him]; in the fourth light, a Monk travelling to the sea-side and washing his feet, found St. Cuthbert standing in the sea, above his shoulders, holding up his hands and saying his prayers; also another Monk lying on the topp of a rock, leaning his head on his hand, and beholding holy St. Cuthbert, where hee stood in the sea at his prayers.

[Above these were seven tower Windows, in fine coloured glass, having several pictures in them.]

4. In the fourth Window [were four lights containing in the first the picture of] Bishop Aidane; [in the second] St. Cuthbert; [in the third] St. Mary; and [in the fourth] St. Oswald the King, finely set out in coloured glass. And the three turret windows, having the pictures of two Angels offering incense to the picture of Christ in the highest, with twelve coloured knots.]

THE SOUTH ALLEY OF THE QUIRE.

1. In the South Alley of the Quire are four Windows; the first Window having four lights; the first hath St. Cuthbert, with King Oswald's head in his hand; the second St. Oswald, King, with his scepter in his hand; the third, Mary, with Christ in her arms; the fourth, St. George in blew armour, killing the dragon, and underneath four severall escutchions, viz. St. Cuthbert's, St. Oswald's, our Ladyes, and St. George's. [And above all three turret windows in white glass, with knots finely wrought in coloured glass upon them.]

2. The second Window hath four lights; having in them the picture of St. Peter, with keys in his hand and part of the creed; [under his feet,] **Ss Petrus,** above his head **Credo in Deum;** in the second light, St. Andrew, with **Scus Andreas** under his feet; above his head, **Et in Jesum Christum,** &c.; in the third light, St. James, with a staff and crosse on it in his hand; under his feet **Scus Jacobus,** and above him, **Qui conceptus,** &c.; in the fourth light, St. John, under him **Scus Johannes;** and above him, **Passus sub Pontio,** &c. [And 13 turrets and] the picture of God Almighty, in fine coloured glass, [above all.]

3. In the third Window [were four lights; in the first] is St. Thomas, with **Scus Thomas** under him, and above [his head **Descendit ad inferos & resurrexit a mortuis**—In the second light is St. James, under him **Scus Jacobus minor,** and above him, **Et sedit ad dextram,** &c.; in the third light, St. Philip, under him, **Ss Philippus,** and above, [**Inde venturus,** &c.—And in the fourth, the picture of St. Bartholomew, and under him, **Ss Bartholomeus;** and above,] **Credo in spiritum sanctum.** &c. [And four fine knots, in coloured glass, and sixteen tower windows, in white glass.]

4. In the fourth Window are four lights; in the first is St.

H

Barbara, with a castle in her hand; in the second, St. Andrew; in the third, [St. John the Evangelist; and in the fourth,] St. James, with a pilgrim staffe in his hand, and his scripp about him. And above three tower windows; [and in the highest,] the picture of Christ crucified, with Mary and John on each hand of him, [in finely coloured glass.]

IN THE VESTRY ARE FOUR WINDOWS.*

In the first towards the east is the finest Window, containing five long lights, divided with stone work; having in the middle the picture of Christ crucified, and above his head a pelican pictured, giving her blood to her young ones, as Christ gave his for the whole world; on one side, the picture of our blessed Lady wringing her hands, and lamenting most pitifully his death: and the picture of St. John the Evangelist, leaning his head upon the ball of his hand, with tears falling from his eyes, on the other side; and the picture of Venerable Bede in a fine blew habit, on the north side of our Lady; and St. Leonard on the south side of St. John; all finely set out in coloured glass.

In the second Window are three proportionable lights; in the first is the picture of St. Oswald, with a ball and a cross in one hand and a scepter in the other; in the second is the picture of our Lady with Christ in her arms; and in the third light is the picture of St. Cuthbert with St. Oswald's head in his hand, and the picture of a Monk, called Thomas Moresby, devoutly kneeling, with **Mater Dei miserere mei,** written above his head.

In the third Window are three lights; in the first is the picture of the salutation of the angel Gabriel to the blessed Virgin Mary. In the second is our blessed Lady with a little pot before her, and underneath her the picture of the Prior of Coldingham, named W. Draxe†, having a crosier staff in one hand, a book in the other, in a black habit, kneeling and holding up his hands with **Mater Dei miserere mei,** written above his head, and under him, **W. Draxe, Prior de Coldingham;** and in the third light, the picture of St. Ebba, a Prioress, at her prayers, with these words, **Ave Maria gratia plena Dominus tecum.**

In the fourth Window are three lights; in the first, the picture of Bishop Aidanus, in his episcopal attire, with his crosier

---

* The description of the windows in the vestry is not found in any MS. It first occurs in Hunter's Edition, the result no doubt of personal examination. The vestry was demolished in 1802.

† Prior of Coldingham in 1422, &c.

staff in his hand; in the second is the picture of William, Bishop, in his mass apparel and a staff in his hand, with a crosier thereupon; and under him a Monk in a blew habit, called Thomas Rome,* having written under **Tho. Rome, Sacrista,** and above him, **Sancte Willelme ora pro nobis**; and in the third light the picture of St. Bede in a blew habit; all set forth in fine coloured glass.

THE NINE ALTARS.

In the midst is the Altar of St. Cuthbert and St. Bede, above which there is a fair long Window, [with stone work partitions] with a cross division toward the midst; in the first light is St. Cuthbert, with King Oswald's head in one hand, and his crosier staff in the other, [in his habit] as he used to say mass, viz. his albe and red vestment; in the second light is St. Bede in a blew habit; these two are in a higher light, and under their feet is the pictures of two Bishops with crosier staves in their hands, kneeling and looking up to them, in their episcopal attire, and mitres on their heads, one under St. Cuthbert, and the other under St. Bede; in the lower light is the birth of St. Cuthbert, (vide Cloyster Windowes); and the picture of St. Oswald, blowing his horne, and St. Cuthbert appearing to St. Oswald; with the draught of Bishop Langley's armes in fine coloured glass; and four turret windows containing our Blessed Lady, and the lilly before her, and the Salutation.

On the south side of St. Cuthbert and St. Bede's Altar was the Altar of St. Oswald and St. Lawrence, [having above it a Window of the shape with the last, as all the windows of the Nine Altars were,] all the windows of the Nine Altars alike, [as the first, H. 44], having the picture of St. Oswald with a sceptre in his hand, a golden crowne on his head, and a cross and ball in his left hand, under him Bishop Langley in his pontificall habit, and above him was written **O Sancta Mater Dei ora pro me,** and under him, **Orate pro Thoma Langley, Episcopo Dunelm**; and the picture of St. Laurence with his gridiron, the armes and escutchions of Bishop Langley under him, viz. a crowne of gold above his helmett, and within the crowne the crest, being a bush of ostrich feathers, finely sett forth in redd and green painted glasse.

The lower lights containe the stories of St. Oswald's behead-

---

* Thomas Rome took his degree in Theology at Oxford in 1412.

ing, and being on his beare, accompanied by St. Cuthbert and others, and the sunn-beames shining on them, when they laid him on his beare, together with the story of St. Laurence his death. In the cross division are four little lights, bearing four starrs or mulletts, and four little turret windows, with our Saviour Christ, our Blessed Lady, and others, in most curious worke.

2. The second Altar was the Altar of St. Thomas of Canterbury and St. Catherine, above which the Window was made with the like lights; the martirdome of St. Thomas in one light; and the story of St. Catherine being brought before the King and tortured on the wheels, with two Angells severing the wheels from torturing; and after committing her to prison, looking forth of a grate, and her beheading afterwards in the King's presence; with certain escutchions, in four turret windows, [under the midst of the said window, divided, and the picture of four Bishops in four little turret windows, and the picture of our Blessed Lady above all, in a blew habit.]

3. The third was the Altar of St. John the Baptist and St. Margaret; having the Baptist on the one side, with the Lamb and Cross in his hand, with these words written above him, **Ecce Agnus Dei**; under him a Monk, called Thomas Battersby, in a blew habit, and these words written above him, **Adjuva me Divine Magister Sancte Cuthberte;** also his baptizing of Christ in Jordan, being brought before Herod, and soe after beheaded. Then follows St. Margaret having overcome the dragon, with these words above her, **Sancta Margareta;** and being brought before the King, by his command was hanged by the hair of her head, and drawn up by a windlass, [pulley, H. 45], and put into a tun of oyl, which would not kill her, because the fire would not consume it, and so she was beheaded. And above all are four turret windows, containing the picture of our blessed Lady, and others finely coloured.

4. [The fourth Altar was surmounted by its Window, or] the window of St. Andrew and Mary Magdalen. In the first light is St. Andrew, with a cross over his body, and above his heade, **Sanctus Andreas.** On the other side, St. Mary Magdalene, and under her, **Sancta Maria Magdalena;** and the story of her kneeling at her prayers, and being brought before the King and sentenced to die; with some part of the story of Christ's anointing and visiting the sick. In the four turret windows are the pictures of the four Doctors of the church, [St. Augustine, St. Hierome, St. Ambrose, and St. Gregory, in fine glass.]

On the north side of St. Cuthbert and St. Bede's Altar, was the altar of St. Martyn and St. Edmund.

1. [In the Window above, of the same architecture,] St. Martyn is in a black habit, and his mitre on his head, a staff in his hande, with a cross on the topp of it; above him these words, **Sanctus Martinus Archiepiscopus**; besides the picture of St. Martin, are certain [escutcheons charged with coats of] armes, and the picture of a wicked spirit, in the likeness of a woman who had gotten into the chamber and bedd of St. Edmund, intending to tempt that holy man to the abominable sin of leachery, who by the prayers and devotion of the said holy Saint, and his contempt of the sinne, was so abhorred and detested, that hee with a rodd did switch and beate her forth of his bed. And the picture of St. Edmund is in his redd episcopall attire, with a cross, having a staff under it, in his hand; the words over him are, **Sanctus Edmundus Episcopus**. Above in the turret windows are Bishopp Skirlaw's picture, [armes, H. 44.] and an Angell finely painted on each side. On the other side, under St. Edmond, were the arms of Doctors and Noblemen, perfectly drawn on the breasts of four Angels [in four turret windows.]

2. The second was the Altar of Peter and Paul [having the like Window and lights,] conteyning the picture of St. Peter, with cross keys in his hand, and underneath **Sanctus Petrus**. Here was the miracle of Peter's walking towards Christ upon the sea, and his danger of sinking, till Christ tooke him by the hand and helped him. Under the middle stone-work were the pictures of four escutcheons charged with arms. Then was represented St. Paul persecuting the church at Damascus; and his being strook blind, and of his becoming an apostle, having written on his breast, **Saule, Saule, quid tu me persequeris**; and after his bringing before Cæsar, and his beheading. And above four little turret windowes, with four fine pictures, viz. St. Cedda, St. Cuthbert, St. Aidane, and another Bishop unknown; and above all the picture of God Almighty.

3. The third was the Altar of St. Aidane and St. Helena, [with the like Window and lights,] conteyning the picture of St. Aidane in his episcopal attire, with a crosier in his hand; whose soul after his death is reported to be carried to heaven in a sheet by two Angels; and parcell of the history of Christ; and the picture of a King and two other Saints; and the picture of St. Helena in a blew habit, being a princess, conteyning the story, [soveraignty, H. 44.] of the religious of all orders of her sex, [of her order, H. 44.] resorting to their churches; and the picture of our Lady and the angel Gabriel [appearing to her, and the

Holy Ghost overshadowing her, with the lilly springing out of the lilly pot; and] underneath the middle stone-work are four Angels. Above are four turret windows, with four Apostles, and the picture of God Almighty above all, in another little window, with Christ in his arms.

4. The fourth was the Altar of the Archangel St. Michael; its Window contained the pictures of eight several orders of Angells in eight several pictures; viz. one Angel, and under him written, **Cherubins, Seraphins.** A second, and under him, **Archangeli.** A third, and under him, **Angeli.** A fourth, and under him, **Principatus.** A fifth, and under him, **Dominationes.** A sixth, and under him, **Potestates.** And above all, in four turret windows, the pictures of four Archangels winged, with wheels under their feet, and their names written on their wings, [armes under their winges, H. 44.] Above all, in a little tower window, the picture of God Almighty.

II. DE ADVENTU REGIS HENRICI SEXTI AD ECCLESIAM DUNELMENSEM.

Illustrissimus, benignissimus, graciosissimus, et omnibus eum intuentibus amabilis Rex noster Henricus sextus post Conquestum visitavit Tumbam Sancti Cuthberti Pontificis in Dunelmo, causa peregrinationis, Anno Domini 1448, anno papatus domini Nicholai quinti secundo, anno regni Regis ejusdem Henrici vicesimo sexto, anno etatis ejusdem vicesimo septimo, anno pontificatus domini Roberti Nevill Dunelmensis Episcopi undecimo, et anno prioratus domini Magistri Willielmi Ebchester sacræ paginæ professoris in Theologia secundo, litera dominicalis F., 6 kal. Octobris, et mansit in Castello Domini Episcopi in Dunelmo, usque in ultimum diem ejusdem mensis, hoc est pridie kal. Octobris in Festo Si. Hieronoymi Presbyteri; et in Dominica, in die Si. Michaelis Archangeli, in propria persona erat in primis Vesperis, in Processione, in Missa, in secundis Vesperis.

LITERA DOMINI REGIS HENRICI SEXTI, MAGISTRO JOHANNI SOMERSET MISSA, ANNO DOMINI 1448, DE PREMISSIS.

Right trusty and well beloved, Wee greet you hartly well, letting you witt, that, blessed be our Lord God, we have been right merry in our pilgramage, considering three causes; one is, how that that the church of the province of York and diocesse of Durham be as nobill in doing of divine service, in multitude of ministers, and in sumptuous and glorious buildinge as anie in our realme. And alsoe how our Lord has radicate in the people his faith, and his law, and that they be as Catholicke people as ever wee came amonge, and all good and holy, that wee dare say the first commandment may be verified right well in them, *Diligunt Dominum Deum ipsorum ex totis animis suis, et tota mente sua.* Alsoe they have done unto us als great herty reverence and worshipp as ever we had, with als great humanity and meekness, with als celestiall, blessed, and honourable speech and blessinge, as it can be thought and imagined: and als good and better then wee had ever in our life, eaven as they had beene *cœlitus inspirati.* Wherefore we dare well say, it may be verified in them the holy saying of the prince of the Apostles St. Peter, when he sayeth, *Deum timete, Regem honorificate—Qui timent Dominum et Regem honorificant cum debita Reverentia.* Wherefore the blessing that God gave to Abraham, Isack, and Jacob, descend upon them all, &c. Wryten in our citty of Lincolne, in crastino St. Lucæ Evangelistæ 1448.

III. INSCRIPTIONS BENEATH THE FIGURES OF SUCH MONKS OF THE BENEDICTINE ORDER AS WERE PAINTED UPON THE SCREEN WORK OF THE ALTAR OF SAINT JEROME AND SAINT BENEDICT, IN DURHAM CATHEDRAL.*

Quia de ortu sacrosanctæ religionis Monachorum plerisque vertitur in dubium, asserentibus quibusdam, minus sane sapientibus, prefatam religionem per Sanctum Benedictum habuisse exordium, et sic quasdam picturas et scripturas ymaginum ad altare Sanctorum Jeromini et Benedicti in ecclesia Dunelmensi non esse veras; asserunt etiam sic opinantes ordinem Canonichorum Regularium, quem allegant a beato Augustino habuisse exordium, ordinem præcessisse Monachorum, sicut dictus Sanctus Augustinus ante Sanctum Benedictum per spacium annorum   nec ante ejus tempora extitisse, ut hiis erroribus contraveniatur et veritas clarius elucescat, ex sententiis diversorum Sanctorum et Doctorum, prout inferius continetur, liquebit, quid de ejusdem inchoacione et felici successu est indubie sentiendum. . . . . Nunc superest, veritate duce, ostendere picturam ymaginum prefatarum veram esse, et plurimorum auctorum fideli testimonio confirmatam.

SCRIPTURÆ SUB IMAGINIBUS MONACHORUM AD ALTARE SANCTORUM JERONIMI ET BENEDICTI IN ECCLESIA DUNELMENSI.

Nomina sanctorum subscribuntur monachorum,
Sub normis quorum plures vixere virorum.
Sancti monstrantur, ac scriptis intitulantur,
Celo letantur, hiis plures sanctificantur.

NOMINA PAPARUM.

IN SUPREMO GRADU SUPERIORIS TABULÆ.

SANCTUS GREGORIUS. *Primus ex parte boriali.*

---

* Extracted from Prior Wessington's Treatise " De Origine Monachatus cum aliis de Statu Monachili." MS. Eccles. Cath. Dunelm. B. III. 30.

SANCTUS DIONISIUS, ex monacho in Papam consecratus. *Primus ex parte australi.*

SANCTUS DEODATUS, ex monacho Papa factus. *Secundus ex parte boriali.*

SANCTUS GREGORIUS VII. prius dictus Hildebrandus, Prior Cluniacensis. *Secundus ex parte australi.*

EUGENIUS TERCIUS, Abbas Sancti Anastasii, postea in Papam creatus. *Tertius ex parte boriali.*

ADRIANUS QUARTUS, natione Anglus, monachus Monasterii Sancti Ruphi. *Tertius ex parte australi.*

CELESTINUS QUINTUS, monachus et heremita. *Quartus ex parte boriali.*

URBANUS QUINTUS, Abbas Sancti Victoris Marsiliæ. *Quartus ex parte australi.*

NOMINA IMPERATORUM.

LOTARIUS IMPERATOR ROMANORUM, monachus. *Quintus ex parte boriali.*

MICHAEL IMPERATOR CONSTANTINOPOLITANUS, monachus. *Quintus ex parte australi.*

JOSAPHAT REX INDORUM, per Barlaam conversus et monachus factus. *Primus ex parte boriali.*

KAROLOMANNUS REX FRANCORUM, in monachum attonsus. *Primus ex parte australi.*

COENREDUS REX MERCIORUM, monachus. *Secundus ex parte boriali.*

ETHELREDUS REX MERCIORUM, in monasterio de Bardnay monachus factus. *Secundus ex parte australi.*

OFFA REX ORIENTALIUM SAXONUM, monachus. *Tertius ex parte boriali.*

SEBBA REX ORIENTALIUM SAXONUM, monachus. *Tertius ex parte australi.*

SIGBERTUS, REX ORIENTALIUM SAXONUM, monachus. *Quartus ex parte boriali.*

CEOWLPHUS REX NORTHANHIMBRORUM, monachus, ad quem Beda Historiam Anglorum scripsit. Plures res et villas Monasterio Lindisfarnensi contulit. Tandem, relicto regno, monachus ibidem effectus, post gloriosæ vitæ cursum in eodem est sepultus. Cujus caput, decursis multorum annorum curriculis, ad Dunelmum translatum, cum aliis Sanctorum reliquiis in ecclesia Sancti Cuthberti, quem semper amaverat, est locatum. Ex Li°. de Fundacione Ecclesiæ Dunelmensis, sub anno gratiæ 738. *Quartus ex parte australi.*

ERACLIUS REX BULGARORUM, monachus. *Quintus ex parte boriali.*

RACHIS REX LONGOBARDORUM, monachus. *Quintus ex parte australi.*

SANCTUS ATHANASIUS, Egiptiorum sacratissima lux, Alexandrinus patriarcha, et monachus.

SANCTUS JOHANNES CRISOSTOMUS, patriarcha Constantinopolitanus, et monachus. *Primus ex parte boriali.*

THEOPHANIUS, monachus, Patriarcha Antiochenus. *Primus ex parte australi.*

NOMINA ARCHIEPISCOPORUM.

SANCTUS MARTINUS, primo miles, monachus. *Secundus ex parte boriali.*

SANCTUS BASILIUS, Archiepiscopus Capadociæ, monachus. *Tertius ex parte boriali.*

SANCTUS BONIFACIUS monachus, natione Anglicus, in Archiepiscopum Maguntinensem ordinatus. *Secundus ex parte australi.*

SANCTUS AUGUSTINUS monachus et Archiepiscopus Cantuariensis. *Tertius ex parte boriali.*

RABANUS monachus et Abbas Fuldensis, postea Magunciæ Archiepiscopus. *Tertius ex parte australi.*

SANCTUS DUNSTANUS monachus. *Quartus ex parte australi.*

SANCTUS THEODORUS monachus, Archiepiscopus Cantuariensis, Sanctum Cuthbertum apud Eboracum in presencia Regis Egfridi et septem episcoporum in episcopum Lindisfarnensem consecravit. *Quintus ex parte boriali.*

SANCTUS LANFRANCUS, monachus, Archiepiscopus Cantuariensis. *Quintus ex parte australi.*

SANCTUS ANSELMUS, Abbas Beccensis, Archiepiscopus Cantuariensis. *Sextus ex parte boriali.*

SANCTUS LEANDER, Archiepiscopus Hispalensis et monachus. *Sextus ex parte australi.*

SANCTUS HONORATUS monachus, Archiepiscopus Arelatensis. *Septimus ex parte australi.*

SANCTUS HILLARIUS, monachus, Archiepiscopus Arelatensis. *Octavus ex parte australi.*

SANCTUS ODO, Archiepiscopus Cantuariensis, monachus. *Septimus ex parte boriali.*

SANCTUS ELPHEGUS, monachus, Archiepiscopus Cantuariensis. *Octavus ex parte boriali.*

SANCTUS PAULINUS, monachus, Eboracensis Archiepiscopus. *Primus ex parte australi.*

SANCTUS LAURENCIUS, monachus, Archiepiscopus Cantuariensis. *Primus ex parte boriali.*

SANCTUS JUSTUS, monachus, Archiepiscopus Eboracensis. *Tertius ex parte boriali.*

SANCTUS MELLITUS, monachus, Archiepiscopus Cantuariensis. *Secundus ex parte boriali.*

SANCTUS WILFRIDUS, monachus Lindisfarnensis, postea Abbas Rypensis, deinde Archiepiscopus Eboracensis. Sedem episcopalem Haugustaldensem et monasterium de Selesey fundavit. Vectam insulam et gentem Australium Saxonum ad fidem convertit. Cum Scotis in sinodo apud Qwytby, coram Oswyn Rege, de observatione termini Paschalis disputavit et vicit, et apud Rypun sepultus quiescit. Beda de Gestis Anglorum. L. 5. C. 19. sub anno Gratiæ, 629. *Secundus ex parte australi.*

SANCTUS OSWALDUS, monachus, Archiepiscopus Eboracensis. *Tertius ex parte australi.*

SANCTUS HONORIUS, monachus, collega Sancti Augustini, Cantuariensis Archiepiscopus. *Quartus ex parte boriali.*

SANCTUS HILDEFONSUS, Abbas Agaliensis, postea Archiepiscopus Tholetanus. *Quintus ex parte australi.*

SANCTUS AUSBERTUS, monachus, Rothomagensis Archiepiscopus. *Decimus ex parte boriali.*

SANCTUS AUSTREGESILUS, Archiepiscopus Bituricensis. *Undecimus ex parte boriali.*

SANCTUS SULPICIUS, monachus, Bituricensis Archiepiscopus. *Duodecimus ex parte boriali.*

THURSTINUS, sine subjectione canonica Cantuariensi Archiepiscopo facta, in Archiepiscopum Eboracensem ordinatus, Monasterii quod apud Fontes dicitur, aliorumque octo fundator fuit eximius. Cujus exhortacionibus et monicionibus David Rex Scotiæ per barones Eboracencis provinciæ, apud Moram de Alverton, commisso gravi prælio, cum suo exercitu est devictus, et tandem apud oppidum quod Pons Fractus dicitur, monachico habitu est indutus, ubi et quiescit sepultus. Ex Policronica, L. 7. C. 15 & 18. sub anno Gratiæ, 1141. *Quartus ex parte australi.*

SANCTUS CUTHBERTUS, monachus, undecimus Cantuariæ Archiepiscopus. *Quintus ex parte boriali.*

SANCTUS BREGWINUS, monachus, Archiepiscopus Cantuariensis. *Sextus ex parte boriali.*

BARTHOLOMEUS, Lugdunensis Archiepiscopus, monachus. *Nonus ex parte boriali.*

SANCTUS DAVID, vulgo Davy, Archiepiscopus Urbis Legionum, 147 ætatis suæ anno celestia regna petivit. *Nonus ex parte australi.*

SANCTUS MAGLORIUS, Archiepiscopus Dolensis, monachus. *Undecimus ex parte australi.*

SANCTUS MALACHIAS, monachus, Archiepiscopus Armachanus. *Duodecimus ex parte australi.*

SANCTUS SAMPSON, monachus, Archiepiscopus Dolensis. *Decimus ex parte australi.*

SANCTUS EUCHERIUS, monachus, et Archiepiscopus Lugdunensis. *Sextus ex parte australi.*

NOMINA EPISCOPORUM.

SANCTUS HERCULIANUS, in episcopum Perusinum electus.

SANCTUS EUTROPIUS, ecclesiæ Valentinæ episcopus.

SANCTUS HELENUS, monachus, episcopus Heliopoleos.

SANCTUS CEDD, monachus Lindisfarnensis Monasterii, unus ex discipulis Sancti Aydani, et germanus Sancti Ceddæ, Lichefeldensis episcopi, a Finano episcopo Lindisfarnensi in episcopum ordinatus, gentem Orientalium Saxonum et Swythelmum regem Orientalium Anglorum cum suo populo ad fidem convertit. Monasterium de Lestingaen ex donacione et concessione Ethelwaldi regis Northumbriæ filii Sancti Oswaldi fundavit, et religiosis moribus, juxta ritus ubi educatus fuerat, instruit. Regem Orientalium Saxonum Sigibertum, pro eo quod contra prohibicionem suam in domo cujusdam comitis per eundem episcopum excommunicati epulaturus intravit, in eadem domo per dictum comitem occidendum fore predixit. Beda de Gestis Anglorum, li°. 3. ca[is]. 22 & 28. Floruit anno Gratiæ 706.

SANCTUS GERMANUS, monachus, Antisiodorensis episcopus.

SANCTUS JOHANNES, Gerundensis Episcopus et monachus.

SANCTUS MARTINUS, monachus, Dumiensis sanctissimus pontifex.

SANCTUS THEODULPHUS, Abbas Floriacensis, deinde Episcopus Aurelianensis.

SANCTUS ETHELWOLDUS, primo monachus Glastoniæ, postea Abbas Abendoniæ, deinde episcopus Wintoniensis, a beato Dunstano consecratus, co-operantibus regibus Edredo et Edgaro. Sex monasteria monachorum fundavit et reparavit, videlicet Abendoniæ, Hely, Thorney, Burgh, et duo in civitate Wintoniæ. Hic semel ad Dunelmum est profectus, ubi, quod magnæ videbatur audaciæ, revulso sepulcri operculo, cum Sancto Cuthberto quasi cum amico loquebatur, munusque amoris deposuit et abiit, et Wintoniæ sepultus quiescit, ubi meritis ejus multa miracula usque in hodiernum diem operari dignatus et Deus. Ex Historia Aurea, C. 55, 56, 57, sub anno Gratiæ 960.

SANCTUS FRANCISCUS, Terraconensis episcopus et monachus.

SANCTUS LAMBERTUS, monachus, Trajectensis ecclesiæ episcopus.

SANCTUS FAUSTUS, Abbas Lirinensis, episcopus in Gallia.

SANCTUS ERCOMWALDUS, Londoniensis episcopus.

SANCTUS ANDOMARUS, monachus, Episcopus Tavernensis.

SANCTUS FRONCO, monachus, Petragoricensis episcopus.

SANCTUS WLSTANUS, monachus, episcopus Wigorniensis.

SANCTUS PETRONIUS, Bononiensis Ytaliæ episcopus.

SANCTUS ALDELMUS, monachus, episcopus Shyreburnensis.

SANCTUS SERAPION, monachus, Tymensis episcopus.

SANCTUS FULGENCIUS, monachus, Ruspensis ecclesiæ episcopus.

SANCTUS HERACLIDES, monachus, et episcopus Bithiniæ.

SANCTUS EATA, unus de xij pueris Sancti Aydani, quos ab initio de natione Anglorum suscepit et educavit, postea monachus et abbas Mailrosensis et Lindisfarnensis factus, Sanctum

Cuthbertum in monachum creavit, ac prepositum sive priorem, primo Mailrosensem, post Lindisfarnensem fecit. Monasterium monachorum in Ripon, dato loco ab Alfrido rege, fundavit, ubi Sanctus Cuthbertus Angelum Dei hospicio suscepit. Deinde per Theodorum Magnum Cantuariensem archiepiscopum ordinatus episcopus regimen Haugustaldensis et Lindisfarnensis ecclesiarum, duarum videlicet sedium, aliquamdiu accepit, et tandem apud Hexham obiit: quem intra ecclesiam, in scrinio honore condigno, Alfred filius Westou, presbiter Dunelmensis, collocavit. Beda de gestis Anglorum. Et ex vita ejusdem, sub anno Gratiæ 678.

SANCTUS CUTHBERTUS, patronus ecclesiæ, civitatis, et libertatis Dunelmensis, nacione Hibernicus, regiis parentibus ortus, nutu Dei Angliam perductus et apud Mailros monachus est effectus, deinde in ecclesiam Lindisfarnensem per Abbatem suum Eatam translatus, postea vitam anachoreticam in insula Farne ducebat solus. Demum per Egfridum regem et Theodorum archiepiscopum Cantuariensem, in plena sinodo, in episcopum Lindisfarnensem eligitur, et a septem episcopis Eboraci consecratur. Cujus corpus per Aldunum episcopum Dunelmiam translatum, ibidem post 418 deposicionis suæ annos incorruptum et flexibile, dormienti quam mortuo similius est inventum. Beda de Gestis Anglorum L. 4, C. 25, 26, 27, 28, 29, 30, 31. Et ex Libro de Exordio et Progressu ecclesiæ Lindisfarnensis simul et Dunelmensis. Floruit anno Gratiæ 680.

SANCTUS GERMANUS, monachus, episcopus Parisiensis.

SANCTUS EGWINUS, monachus, Wigorniæ episcopus.

SANCTUS MAURELIUS, monachus, Andegavensis episcopus.

SANCTUS MOISES, monachus, Saracenorum episcopus.

SANCTUS LUPUS, monachus, Trecasinæ urbis episcopus.

SANCTUS AMANDUS, monachus, Trajectensis episcopus.

SANCTUS JACOBUS, cognomine Sapiens, Nizibenæ, quæ et Antiochia, Persarum civitatis, episcopus.

SANCTUS BRITHWOLDUS, monachus, Wintoniensis episcopus.

SANCTUS EADBERTUS monachus, et septimus episcopus

Lindisfarnensis, vir sciencia scripturarum divinarum simul et preceptorum cælestium observantia, ac maxime elemosinarum operacione insignis, sæpius per intervalla temporum in aliqua insularum Domino solitarius militavit, in quibus predecessor ejus Cuthbertus aliquamdiu morari consuevit, corpusque Sancti Cuthberti post undecim sepulturæ suæ annos cum pannis et vestimentis, quibus fuerat involutum intemeratis incorruptum et flexibile inventum de terra levavit novaque in theca recondidit; corpusque ejusdem, juxta quod vivens petierat, in sepulcro Sancti Cuthberti positum fuit, sed modo ejus ossa in thecis extra Feretrum Sancti Cuthberti ut sanctæ reliquiæ sunt servata. Beda de Gestis Anglorum. L. iv. C. 29.

SANCTUS KENTEGERNUS, qui et Mungo, monachus, Episcopus Glascuensis.

SANCTUS EPIPHANIUS, monachus, Cypri Salaminæ episcopus,

SANCTUS AIDANUS, natione Scotus, monasterii de Hii, vir eximiæ sanctitatis, a sancto Oswaldo rege vocatus, primus Lindisfarnensis fuit episcopus, sedemque episcopalem simul et monachorum congregacionem, jubente rege prefato, anno gratiæ 635, ibidem instituit, ac gentem Berniciorum, suffragante et co-operante eodem rege, ad fidem convertit. Cujus doctrinam id maxime commendabat quod non aliter quam vivebat cum suis ipse docebat. Nihil enim ex omnibus, quæ ex propheticis evangeliis et apostolicis literis facienda cognovit, prætermisit. Ex hac eciam ecclesia omnes ecclesiæ et monasteria provinciæ Berniciorum sumpserunt originem. Demum, peractis in episcopatu 17 annis, obiit; cujus animam Sanctus Cuthbertus, conversacionis angelicæ juvenis egregius, ab angelis in cœlum deferri conspexit. Beda de Gestis Anglorum, sub anno Gratiæ supradicto.

SANCTUS GREGORIUS, Nazanzenus episcopus, monachus.

SANCTUS ALBINUS, monachus, episcopus Andegavensis.

SANCTUS CEDDA, monachus, episcopus Lichefeldensis.

SANCTUS VIGOR, monachus, Baiocensis episcopus.

SANCTUS FINANUS, nacione Scotus, et monachus de insula Hii, secundus episcopus Lindisfarnensis, ibidem ecclesiam sedi episcopali congruam edificavit, quam postea Theodorus magnus,

Archiepiscopus Cantuariensis, in honore beati Petri dedicavit. Mediterraneorum Anglorum regem Peadam in provincia Northanhimbrorum baptisavit, et quatuor monachos suos, videlicet Cedd, Adda, Becti et Dymna, qui erudicione et vita videbantur ydonei, ut ejus genti predicarent, de ecclesia sua cum eo direxit; postea Sigbertum regem Orientalium Saxonum lavacro baptismi perfudit, et predictum Cedd monachum suum eidem regno in episcopum ordinavit, ubi et duo monasteria construxit. Beda de Gestis Anglorum, L. III. C. 17. 21. 72. sub anno Gratiæ 152.

SANCTUS LEODEGARIUS, monachus, Episcopus Ednensis.

NOMINA ABBATUM.

SANCTUS LEONARDUS, monachus et abbas.

SANCTUS KARILEPHUS, monachus et abbas.

SANCTUS WANDRAGESILUS, monachus et abbas.

SANCTUS JOHANNES, monachus et abbas.

SANCTUS ARSENIUS, monachus et abbas.

SANCTUS JOSEPH, monachus et abbas.

SANCTUS PAFUNCIUS, monachus et abbas.

SANCTUS PAMBO, monachus et abbas.

SANCTUS YSIDORUS, monachus et abbas.

SANCTUS AMMONIUS, monachus et abbas.

SANCTUS MACHARIUS, monachus et abbas.

SANCTUS EGIDIUS, monachus et abbas.

SANCTUS PACHOMIUS, monachus et abbas.

SANCTUS JOHANNES CASSIANUS, monachus et abbas.

SANCTUS EUAGRIUS, monachus et abbas.

Sanctus Antonius, monachus et abbas.

Sanctus Maurus, monachus et abbas.

Sanctus Johannes, archicantor ecclesiæ Sancti Petri Romæ, Abbas.

Sanctus Alquinus, qui et Albinus, abbas.

Sanctus Theonas, monachus et abbas.

Sanctus Benedictus Biscopp, abbas, et nutricius Bedæ presbiteri ministerque Regis Oswini, patriam relinquens in insula Lyrinensi in monachum attonsus est. Inde, Romam veniens, Theodorum Cantuariensem archiepiscopum et Adrianum ejusdem collegam Britannias adduxit, ac monasterium Sancti Petri Cantuariæ regendum suscepit. Postea duo monasteria, quorum unum, 70 familiarum, in honore Sancti Petri, ad ostium Wiri fluminis, quod nunc Wermouth-monachorum dicitur, et aliud, 40 familiarum, in ripa Tyny fluminis, quod modo Jarowe nuncupatur, construxit, quibus utrisque abbatis jure præfuit. Usque quinquies Romam visitavit, libros et reliquias sanctorum ad monasteria sua revexit, et artem vitriariam primus ad partes suas attulit. Beda, ex vita ejusdem sub anno Gratiæ 676.

Sanctus Dionisius, monachus et abbas.

Sanctus Johannes, monachus et abbas.

Sanctus Adrianus, abbas.

Sanctus Columbanus, monachus et abbas.

Sanctus Stephanus, abbas.

Sanctus Brendanus, abbas.

Sanctus Columba, monachus et abbas.

Sanctus Eugippus, monachus et abbas.

Sanctus Adampnanus, monachus et abbas.

Sanctus Danyell, monachus et abbas.

Sanctus Theodorus, monachus et abbas.

Nomina Doctorum.

Sanctus Didimus Alexandrinus, monachus et doctor.

Marianus Scotus, doctor.

Oresiesis, monachus et doctor.

Johannes Scotus, monachus et doctor.

Gracianus de Tuscia, monachus et doctor.

Ursinus, monachus et doctor.

Sanctus Severus, qui et Sulpicius, monachus et doctor.

Vincentius Lirinesis, monachus et doctor.

Sophronius, monachus et doctor.

Cassiodorus, doctor.

Paulus diaconus Cassinensis, monachus et doctor.

Effrem, monachus et doctor.

Venerabilis Beda, doctor, presbiter, et monachus, septimo ætatis suæ anno traditus est Benedicto Biscopp, abbati monasterii Giruensis, quod nunc Jarowe dicitur, educandus, qui, 19 ætatis suæ anno, in diaconum, et 30 in presbiterum, a Sancto Johanne Archiepiscopo Eboracensi est ordinatus, sicque cunctum vitæ tempus in eodem monasterio peragens vitam Sancti Cuthberti conscripsit et omnem meditandis et exponendis scripturas (*sic*) operam dedit. Libros edidit quos in fine Historiæ suæ Anglicanæ enumerat, post quorum editionem ibidem obiit ibique sepultus fuit. Sed postea apud Dunelmum, primo cum corpore Sancti Cuthberti, deinde in Galilea Dunelmensi in feretro per Hugonem episcopum constructo, ejus ossa sunt translata. Ex libro de Exordio et Progressu Ecclesiæ Dunelmensis. Et ex libro ejusdem de Gestis Anglorum, L. V. C. 25. Sub anno Gratiæ 729.

Helinandus, monachus et doctor.

Sanctus Boisilus, monachus et prepositus ecclesiæ Mailrosensis, magnarum virtutum et prophetici spiritus sacerdos fuit. Sancto Cuthberto, jubente Abbati Eata, habitum monachalem tradidit; cujus monitis et exemplis instructus quod episcopus foret futurus cognovit. Mortem propriam et alia plurima predixit. Beda de Gestis Anglorum, L. IV. C. 25. Floruit anno Gratiæ 651.

SANCTUS PAULUS, primus heremita et monachus.

SANCTUS NEOTUS, regis West Saxonum Eldulphi filius, monachus.

SANCTUS GUTHLACUS, monachus.

IV. Scripturæ sub imaginibus regum, ad ostium chori ecclesiæ Dunelmensis ex parte australi.

Octo Reges totius Angliæ, qui antiquas possessiones et libertates ecclesiæ S. Cuthberti confirmaverunt, et plures de novo addiderunt.

Aluredus Rex.—1. Rex West Saxonum Aluredus, per Danos oppressus, et per Sanctum Cuthbertum in forma pauperis visitatus et confortatus, de Danis triumphans monarcha est effectus; et suo adjutori Sancto Cuthberto terram inter Tesam et Tinam, cum regalitate contulit possidendam.

Edwardus senior Rex.—2. Rex Edwardus senior, filius Aluredi, patri succedens, memor beneficii suo patri per Sanctum Cuthbertum impensi, eundem Sanctum, et suam ecclesiam, multum honoravit, et privilegiavit; plurimaque dona regalia eidem conferebat.

Ethelstanus Rex.—3. Rex Ethelstanus, filius Edwardi primi, a patre monitus, Sanctum Cuthbertum, et ipsius ecclesiam pluribus ditavit, et possessiones per Danos ablatos pro magna parte restituit, ac ecclesiam Beverlacensem in multis honoravit et privilegiavit.

Edmundus Rex.—4. Rex Edmundus, frater Ethelstani, legem Cuthberti, ut in vulgari Saxonico dicitur, Mid, Fullon, Indon, et Wreck, et Witviter, et Inner, et Sacca, et Socne, cum plenis legibus et consuetudinibus, omni terræ Sancti Cuthberti dedit, et super sepulchrum ejus obtulit.

Kanutus Rex.—5. Rex Angliæ et Danamarchiæ Kanutus, ad corpus Sancti Cuthberti Dunelmum, nudis pedibus a Garmundisway venit; ejusque servientibus monachis Staindropam cum appendiciis donavit; Scotos, Wandales, Norwagenses subjugavit; et in locis quibus pugnavit ecclesias fundavit.

Willielmus Conquestor.—6. Rex Willielmus conquestor omnes terras et libertates, quas antiqui Reges Anglorum Sancto Cuthberto dederunt, ratificavit; Houedenshire Episcopo, et Hemmingburgh monachis Dunelmensibus de novo donavit; et Billingham, quod mali homines abstulerunt, monachis restituit.

Rex Willielmus secundus.—7. Rex Willielmus secundus dedit Sancto Cuthberto et Willielmo episcopo et successoribus suis Alvertonshire, et monachis Dunelmensibus ecclesias de Alverton, Siggeston, et de Runton, et plures terras in comitatu Notingham, ac etiam antiquas libertates ecclesiæ Dunelmensis confirmavit.

Henricus primus Rex.—8. Rex Henricus primus hanc legem Sancto Cuthberto constituit; quatenus omnis terra, quæ ei data, sive de illius pecunia empta fuerit, libera et quieta, cum omnibus terris ejus, ab omnibus consuetudinibus quæ ad regis coronam pertinent, ita ut nullus jus in ea ulterius expetat, cujuscunque debiti vel servitutis ante fuisse constiterit.

Scripturæ sub imaginibus regum ad ostium chori ecclesiæ Dunelmensis ex parte boreali.

Sex Reges Northumbiæ a Trente et Mersee usque Foorth, ubi est mare Scoticum. Et duo Reges Scotiæ promotores hujus ecclesiæ, sedis episcopalis, et cœtus monachalis.

Oswaldus Rex.—Oswaldus Sanctus, fundator ecclesiæ et sedis episcopalis, ac cœtus monachalis, qui quondam erant in Lindisfarnia, nunc sunt in Dunelmo; cujus caput cum corpore Sancti Cuthberti requiescit.

Oswinus Rex.—Rex Oswin, frater Sancti Oswaldi, Pendam regem Merciorum paganum, Sancti Oswaldi occisorem, in bello superavit et occidit, et pro hac victoria, sibi a Deo concessa, plura monasteria fundavit et dotavit, quorum sex erant in Deira et sex in Bernicia.

Egfridus Rex Northumbriæ.—Egfridus Rex Northumbriæ Sanctum Cuthbertum consecrari fecit in episcopum Lindisfarnensem, et sibi dedit civitatem Lucubaliam, quæ nunc dicitur Carleil; ac manerium regium de Creak cum pertinentiis. Dedit etiam possessiones ad fundandum monasterium de Warmoth et Jarrow.

Rex Alfridus Northumbriæ.—Rex Northumbriæ Alfridus dedit monachis Lindisfarnensibus locum in Rippon, ubi fundatum erat monasterium monachorum; in quo Sanctus Cuthbertus ad receptionem hospitum deputatus angelum Domini in specie hominis recepit; dedit et Sancto Wilfrido terram juxta Stanfordiam, ubi est prioratus Sancti Leonardi.

S. Ceolwlfus Rex Northumbriæ.—Sanctus Ceolwlfus Rex Northumbriæ in scientiis divinis et humanis nobiliter instructus, in tantum quod Beda Librum de Gestis Anglorum illi misit ad examinandum, anno nono regni sui, relicta corona, factus est monachus Lindisfarnensis, cujus ossa, ut sanctæ Reliquiæ, in ecclesiam hanc sunt translata.

Guthredus Rex.—Guthredus Rex, per Sanctum Cuthbertum in regem promotus, totam terram cum jure regali inter Tine et Were eidem Sancto donavit. Adversus quem Scoti apud Mungdnigdene pugnaturi, subito terræ hiatu sunt absorpti, precibus Sancti Cuthberti et Regis Guthredi.

Edgarus Rex Scotiæ.—Edgarus Rex Scotiæ dedit Deo et Sancto Cuthberto ac monachis in ecclesia Dunelmensi servientibus regiam mansionem de Coldingham, ubi dedicari fecit ecclesiam in honore Beatæ Mariæ. Dedit et his plures villas in Lodoneyo, secundum voluntatem eorum disponendas.

David Rex Scotiæ.—David Rex Scotiæ confirmavit donationem regis Edgari super Coldingham, et aliis; cujus donationi ipse David addidit plures villas et terras cum magnis libertatibus, et quietudinibus ac franchesiis; confirmavit etiam ecclesias et villas eisdem per alios datas.

Scripturæ sub imaginibus pontificum ad ostium chori ecclesiæ Dunelmensis ad austrum.

Sanctus Cuthbertus. — Sanctus Cuthbertus monachus, episcopus Lindisfarnensis, nunc patronus ecclesiæ et civitatis ac libertatis Dunelmensis, cujus corpus, post 418 annos sepulturæ suæ, incorruptum et flexible, dormienti quam mortuo similius est inventum; et sic vitam intemeratam commendat corporis incorruptio.

Sanctus Eadbertus.—S. Eadbertus monachus, septimus episcopus Lindisfarnensis, vir, sapientia divinarum scripturarum et observantia præceptorum cælestium, ac maxime operatione eleemosynarum insignis, corpus Sancti Cuthberti, post undecim sepulturæ suæ annos, incorruptum et flexible inventum, absque læsione pannorum, quibus erat involutum, de terra jussit levari, et theca reconditum super pavimentum veneratione dignum locari, in quo sepulchro idem Eadbertus sepultus erat, sed in ultima translatione corporis Sancti Cuthberti ejus reliquiæ cum eodem corpore sunt repositæ, et in hac Dunelmensi ecclesia adhuc servatæ.

SANCTUS EADFRIDUS.—S. Eadfridus, de habitu monachali, octavus episcopus ecclesiæ Lindisfarnensis. Hujus hortatu venerabilis Beda presbyter, et monachus Giruensis, vitam Sancti Cuthberti tam in metro quam in prosâ composuit; cujus ossa in arca cum corpore Sancti Cuthberti sunt inventa, et in hac ecclesia Dunelmensi conservata.

SANCTUS ETHELWOLDUS.—S. Ethelwoldus, de habitu monachali, nonus episcopus ecclesiæ Lindisfarnensis. Hic primo religiosæ vitæ abbas et presbyter monasterij Mailrocensis, et quondam Beati Cuthberti dignus minister erat; ac episcopus consecratus, sanctissime vixit et obiit; cujus ossa cum corpore Sancti Cuthberti inventa, et in hac ecclesia in scrinio sunt reposita.

WALCHERUS EPISCOPUS.—Walcherus episcopus sextus hujus loci, Dunelmi, et de habitu seculari consecratus. Hic Walcherus, reperiens in alba ecclesia, quæ erat in loco ubi nunc est tumba Sancti Cuthberti in claustro, cum paucis monachis, clericos seculares insolenter viventes, et ritum monachorum in officio divino servantes, proposuit monachos, quibus monasterium de Wermuth et de Jarrow cum suis pertinentiis prius commiserat, secundum morem Lindisfarnensis ecclesiæ, eos, absque secularibus ministraturos, in hunc locum introducere; sed per Northumbrenses in ecclesia de Gateshead peremptus, propositum suum ad effectum non perduxit.

WILLIELMUS EPISCOPUS.—Willelmus de Sancto Karilepho septimus episcopus hujus loci, et de habitu monachali consecratus. Hic Willielmus intelligens propositum sui predecessoris Walcheri de introductione monachorum in locum, et quod quidam de clericis hujus loci causa erant necis Walcheri episcopi, fultus authoritate Apostolica, et authoritate Regia, dictos Clericos de hoc loco ad ecclesias de Awckland, et Darlington, et de Norton transtulit, et Monachos de Warmoth et Jarrow hic induxit: ac Houedenshire a Rege Willielmo primo, et Alvertonshire a Rege Willielmo secundo, et plures terras monachis hujus ecclesiæ adquisivit. Hic chorum a fundamentis construxit.

RANULPHUS EPISCOPUS.—Ranulphus octavus episcopus hujus loci, et de habitu seculari consecratus. Hic Navem hujus ecclesiæ per predecessorem suum immediatum Willielmum inchoatam ad tectum perduxit. Corpus Sancti Cuthberti de loco in alba ecclesia, ubi nunc est Tumba in claustro, post annos depositionis ejus 418, anno gratiæ 1109, incorruptum et flexibile inventum, in hanc ecclesiam, ubi nunc, transtulit. Inter hanc ecclesiam et castrum, destructis habitaculis, in planitiem redegit; Hospitale de Kepier fundavit; veterem pontem de Framwelgate in Dunelmia et castrum de Norham construxit; ac plura ornamenta huic ecclesiæ reliquit, et erat episcopus 29 annos.

Hugo de Puteaco Episcopus.—Hugo de Puteaco undecimus hujus loci episcopus Dunelmi, et de habitu seculari consecratus. Hic Hugo de sanguine regio natus, et thesaurarius Eboracensis, electus per capitulum hujus ecclesiæ, consecratus est episcopus ejusdem per summum Pontificem. Gallileam cum Feretro Sancti Bedæ composuit; Hospitale de Sherburn fundavit et dotavit; pontem de Elvet, et plura ædificia in Castello Dunelm. ac turrim validam in Northam, et ecclesiam de Darlington a fundamentis construxit; Sadbergiam, quæ de antiquo jure hujus erat ecclesiæ, de manu Regis pro undecim millibus librarum redemit; ac preciosa ornamenta huic ecclesiæ reliquit. Jura et libertates Sancti Cuthberti prudenter defendit; ac completis in episcopatu xli. annis, in Domino feliciter obdormivit, et obiit apud Houeden.

Scripturæ sub imaginibus pontificum, ad ostium chori ecclesiæ Dunelmensis, ex parte boreali.

S. Aidanus.—Sanctus Aidanus, natione Scotus, monachus monasterij de Hij, episcopus factus, per Sanctum Oswaldum vocatus, anno gratiæ 635, fundavit sedem episcopalem et monachorum congregationem in insula Lindisfarnensi; ac Gentem Berniciorum, cooperante Sancto Oswaldo, ad fidem Christi convertit. Hujus Aidani animam Sanctus Cuthbertus ab angelis in cœlum deferri conspexit, et ejus caput et ossa in hac ecclesia Dunelmensi, ut sanctæ reliquiæ, sunt servata.

Sanctus Finanus.—S. Finanus, natione Scotus, et monachus, secundus erat episcopus Lindisfarnensis; hic baptizavit Sigebertum, regem Orientalium Saxonum, et Pendam mediterraneorum Anglorum principem; ac Ceddam presbyterum et monachum ecclesiæ Lindisfarnensis ordinavit episcopum Gentis Orientalium Saxonum, et, completis in episcopatu decem annis, in Domino feliciter obdormivit.

S. Eata.—S. Eata monachus et abbas Mailrosensis, et Lindisfarnensis, fecit Sanctum Cuthbertum monachum, ac præpositum sive priorem, primo Mailrosensem, post Lindisfarnensem, et dato loco ab Alfrido rege in Rippon fundavit monasterium, ubi Sanctus Cuthbertus hospitio suscepit angelum Domini. Et episcopus factus, quintus in ordine rexit ecclesiam Lindisfarnensem, simul cum ecclesia de Hexham, cujus ossa in ecclesia de Hexham sunt canonizata.

Ecgredus.—Ecgredus, de habitu monachali, quatuordecimus episcopus Lindisfarnensis. Hic vir nobilis dedit Sancto Cuthberto ecclesiam de Northam, quam edificavit; villam quoque de Gedworth cum appendiciis; ecclesiam quoque et villam de Geynford, et quicquid ad eam pertinet.

Eardulphus.—Eardulphus, de habitu monachali, sextus decimus et ultimus episcopus ecclesiæ Lindisfarnensis. Hic vir magni meriti erat; audito adventu Danorum paganorum, ille [et] Edredus abbas, tollentes secum corpus Sancti Cuthberti ecclesiam Lindisfarnensem reliquerunt, post annos 241, ex quo sedes episcopalis cum cœtu monachali ibidem erat instituta, anno gratiæ 875, et de loco ad locum fugientes, per septennium, rabiem Danorum, tandem reportaverunt dictum corpus in Cestriam in Strata, ubi per centum et tredecim annos dictum corpus et sedes episcopalis permanserunt.

Cutheardus.—Cutheardus secundus episcopus Conkcestrensis et de habitu monachali. Hic Cutherdus de pecunia Sancti Cuthberti, ad opus ejusdem, emit Bedlington cum appendiciis; et cum miles quidam regis Reynwaldi Pagani, Onlafbal nomine, et ipse Paganus, qui terras Sancti Cuthberti usurpavit, et eidem Sancto improperavit, ut episcopum et congregationem multis injuriis vexaret, ad ostium ecclesiæ venerat, et alterum intra, alterum extra, pedem posuerat, quasi clavo confixus stetit, sicque est tortus, quod miseram animam in eodem loco reddere est compulsus Sancti Cuthberti meritis et Cutheardi precibus: Quo exemplo alii omnes conterriti, nihil quod ecclesiæ Sancti Cuthberti competebat ulterius invadere præsumebant.

Aldwinus.—Aldwinus nonus et ultimus episcopus Conkcestrensis et primus Dunelmensis, et de habitu monachali. Hic Aldwinus episcopus, vir eximiæ religionis et prosapiæ nobilis, anno gratiæ 995, cœlesti præmonitus oraculo, corpus Sancti Cuthberti in Dunelmum transportavit. Quem locum densissima undique sylva pro tunc occupaverat, nullis habitaculis ibi constructis, ubi infra breve ecclesiam et habitacula cum auxilio Comitis Northumbrorum, cui, dum necessitatem paterentur, ad tempus prestitit, quod Comites, qui ei successerunt, per violentiam detinuerunt.

EDMUNDUS.—Edmundus secundus episcopus Dunelmensis, de habitu monachali consecratus. Hic, de clericali habitu, per vocem de Feretro Sancti Cuthberti prolatam, et per sacerdotem Magnam Missam celebrantem ter auditam, nominatus est episcopus eligendus; quod et factum est; sed ille Cathedram Prædecessorum suorum, qui monachi fuerant, nullo modo se posse ascendere fatebatur, nisi illos et ipse monachico habitu indutus imitaretur. Qua propter, monachali habitu suscepto, a Wlstano Archiepiscopo Eboracensi episcopus Dunelmensis est consecratus. Et in ecclesiæ regimine valde strenuum se exhibebat; nullius potentia res vel terras hujus ecclesiæ passus est violari, vel inde auferri; pravis multum erat metuendus, ac bonis humilis amandus.

V. LIBERATURA SPECIALIS. 1510.

Magistro Johanni Underwod, 3 ulnæ.*
Magistro Scolarium, 3 uln. Item M. Cheston, ulnæ.
Et eidem hoc anno quia pro patre.
Magistro Thomæ Farn de pannario, 4.
Et domino Priori ex precepto, 4 uln.

GENEROSI.

Willielmo Bulmer, militi, 3 uln.
Johanni Rakett, 3.
Henrico Killinghar, marshall, 3 et 1¾ præter &c. stipend.
Hugo Holland, 3 et 1 ultra. Quietus in stipendio.
Radulpho Hagerston, 3 et 1 ultra. Solvit.
Roberto Langforth, cantori, 3 et 1 ultra 2s. 8d. In stipendio.
Johanni Salamond, 3, ex precepto, et 1 ultra solvit 2s. 8d.
Magistro Johanni Clerk, ex precepto Domini, scribæ, 3 et 1 ultra.
(Esset inter valectos pro officio scribæ. Quietus.)
Leonell Elmeden, kervour, 3 et 1 ultra. In stipendio.

CLERICI VALECTI.

Clerico capellæ 3.
Clerico supprioris 3.
Clerico bursarii 3.

VALECTI.

Johanni Bukley, valecto cellarii vini, 3 et 1 ultra. In stipendio.
Petro Barnard, cursori scaccarii, 3 et 1 ultra. In stipendio.
Thomæ Taylyour, popinario, 3 et 1 ultra. In stipendio.
Johanni Browell, yoman ussher, 3 et 1 ultra.
Roberto Burges, valecto stabuli, 3 et 1 ultra. In stipendio.

---

* The figures denote the number of ells of cloth *delivered* to each person.

Edwardo Swalwell, valecto Terrarii, 3 et 1 ultra.
Ricardo Person, valecto coco domini Prioris, 3.
Roberto Langforth, janitori, 3.
Johanni Salamond, provisori cator', 3.
Nicholao Brown, barbour, 3.
Christofero Wrangham, valecto refectorii, 3.
Johanni Hudspeth, valecto parvæ domus Bursarii, 3 et 1 ultra.
Georgio Scot, pistori, 3.
Willielmo Sanderson, fabro, 3.
Johanni Wynter, pandoxatori, 3.
Johanni Champnay, carpentario, 3.
Henrico Brown, carpentario, 3.
Thomas Benet, valect sclater, 3.
Thomas Thomson, sawer, 3.
Willielmo Pape, valect' carter, 3.
Willielmo Midilton, whelewright, 3.
Ballivo de Billingham, Georgio Davyson, 3.
Ballivo de Shells, Willielmo Sanderson, 3 et 1 ultra. Quietus.
Ricardo Tyndall, catori apud Newburn raw, 3.
Roberto Whitehede, catori apud Sunderlande, 3.
Edwardo Smyth, catori apud Teas, 3.
Johanni Raket, forestario de Bearparke, 3.
Relictæ Morlande, firmario de Pitington, 3.
Johanni Cowper, cowper, in officio, 3.
Johanni Nicholl, coco lardariæ carnium, 3.
Rauff Dicson, barngreiff de Billingham, 3.
Georgio Davison, barngreiff de Wolveston, 3.

Valectis Officiariorum.

Sacristæ, pro 5 valectis, 15 uln. et gratis $\frac{3}{4}$.
Hostillario, 3 valectis, 9 uln. et $\frac{3}{4}$ gratis.
Cellerario, pro 1 valecto, 3 uln.
Elemosiniario, pro 2 valectis, $3\frac{1}{2}$ uln. pro uno, et 3 uln. pro alio.
Camerario, pro uno valecto, 3 uln., et 1 uln. ultra.
   Johanni Florenc, 3 uln., ex precepto, quia non tunc serviens, et 1 ultra.   In stipendio.

Et Domino Priori, 6 uln.

Gromi.

Ric' Catlynson, gromo cameræ, 3 uln., et $\frac{1}{2}$ ultra.
Heliæ Kelsey, gromo popinæ, 3 et $\frac{1}{2}$ ultra.

Thomæ Foster, gromo aulæ, 3 et 1 ultra.
Jacobo Foster, gromo stabuli, 3 et 1 ultra.
Johanni Cotysfurth, gromo bursarii, 3 et 1 ultra.
Johanni Wryght, gromo terrarii, 3 et ½ ultra.
Thomæ Swalwell, 3, granario.
Ricardo Stobbs, 3, aledrawer.
Cuthberto Verty, 3, gromo coco.
Johanni Clerke, cater, 3.
Thomas Bowman, 3, ortulano.
Henry Bayle, 3, claustrario.
Willielmo Leigh, fyshake, 3.
Willielmo Jacson, sethar, 3.
Willielmo Robynson, cator, 3.
Roberto Busby, slawghterman, 3.
Johanni Dicson, bowter, 3.
Edwardo Brown, bowter, 3.
Ricardo Pentland, maltster, 3.
Edmundo Elison, maltster, 3.
Edwardo Withan, mylner, 3.
Ricardo Batmanson, bagman, 3.
Johanni Richardby, carter, 3.
Johannii Shoroton, carter, 3.
Antonio Thomson de Rille, 3.
Thomæ Falderley, palesser de Beaupark, 3.
Willielmo Moryson, waynman, 3.
Roberto Redeman, waynman, 3.
Roberto Sanderson, procuratori de Norham, 3.
Hostillatori, pro 3 gromis, 9 uln., et 3 uln. ultra scilicet cuilibet 1 uln.
Sacristæ, pro 5 gromis, 15 uln. et ¾ gratis.
Elemosinario, pro uno gromo, 3 uln.
Camerario, pro uno gromo, 3 uln.
Communiario, pro uno gromo, 3 uln.
Cellerario, pro 2 gromis, in singyll clothe.
Apprenticio kervour, ex precepto Domini, 3 uln.
Apprenticio lathami, ex precepto Domini, 3 uln.
Et venditæ Thomæ Kirkeman 3 uln. 5s. in stipend.
Et Domino priori 6 uln.
Domino priori ut infra 6 uln. generos. 6 uln. valect. 6 uln. gromor.

Capt. hoc anno de pannario Dunelm. Wº. Mildesley 3 pec. panni generosorum, quælibet continens 18 uln. Et de eodem, pro Magistro Scolarium et . . . . preste, 8 uln. de sad, et pro Magistro Thomæ Farn, commissario nostri Archidiaconatus,

4 uln. Summa 66 uln. viz. 2 cloths integr. et $\frac{3}{4}$ ad 53s. 4d. £7 6s. 8d.

Item de valectis 6 pece ad 18 uln. continentes, 108 ma. uln. viz. 4 cloths et $\frac{1}{2}$ ad 46s. 8d. £10 10s.

Item 10 pec. gromorum ad 18 uln.

Item 2 singill pece contin. 18 uln. dowbill.

Item 1 pec. panni strictis cont. 12 uln. singill excepto.

Et altera pecia stricti panni cont. 12 uln. singill excepto qr. Summa gromorum 193 ma. uln. viz. 8 pece integr. $\frac{1}{2}$ et $\frac{1}{4}$ et 3 uln. ad 40s. £17 15s.

Summa totalis £35 11s. 8d.

Et præter pec. 11 uln. generos. de me ex panno meo proprio.

Summa ulnarum 338 ma.

Ric. Bentley, 3.

Chr. Brown, 3.

Sand. Loksmyth sibi vend. 3.

Tho. Whitfelde, 6 uln. strict. et ultra.

VI. INDULGENTIÆ.

I.—*Indulgenciæ concessæ omnibus conferentibus de bonis suis ad Fabricam Ecclesiæ Dunelmensis.*

UNIVERSIS has literas inspecturis vel audituris Thomas Prior et Conventus Dunelmensis Ecclesiæ salutem in Domino. Quamvis ad opera misericordiæ diligenter in hâc vitâ seminanda Christiani populi tam ex Catholicæ fidei professione quam ex evangelicâ pariter et apostolicâ exhortacione teneantur astricti, ut, diem visitacionis extremæ pietatis operibus præveniendo, eternorum intuitu præmiorum seminare studeant in terris, quod, reddente Domino, cum multiplicato fructu recolligere mereantur in cœlis; volentes tamen fidelium populorum animos spiritualibus beneficiis ac cœlestibus promissis specialiter incitare, ut ad fabricam Ecclesiæ nostræ promovendam de bonis sibi a Summo Largitore collatis largas cum devotione dextras extendant; quod quidem opus esse pietatis eximium et insigne cunctis per fissuras et fracturas ipsius Ecclesiæ ex orientali sui parte prominentes ac terribilem ruinam minantes intuentibus veraciter apparet, numerositatem dierum quos quidem summus Pontifex ac quidam Episcopi tam Angliæ quam Scotiæ omnibus illis auctoritate pontificali ex injunctâ sibi penitenciâ relaxaverunt qui pias elemosinas ad opus dictæ Ecclesiæ erogare curaverint, numerum quoque missarum ac psalteriorum quæ viri religiosi omnibus fabricam supradictæ Ecclesiæ ex suis elemosinis promovere volentibus liberali magnificentiâ concesserunt, ad universorum noticiam presenti scripto inserere decrevimus. Noverit igitur universitas vestra a Domino Papa XL dies, ab Archiepiscopo Ebor. XL dies, de Hugone Episcopo Dunelm. LXXX dies, de Nicholao Episcopo Dunelm. XL. dies, ab Episcopo Karliolensi XL dies, ab Episcopo Lincoln. XL dies, de Episcopo Galwathiæ XL dies, de Episcopo Sancti Andreæ XL dies, de Episcopo Duncheldens. XL dies, de Episcopo Glascuens. XXX dies, omnibus predictæ ecclesiæ benefactoribus de injunctâ sibi penitenciâ misericorditer esse indultos. Et est summa dierum CCCC et XXX^{ta} dies. Preterea noveritis ab Abbate et Conventu Novi Monasterii DC missas et M psalteria, ab Abbate et Conventu de Alba Landa CCC missas et CCC psalteria, a Priore et Conventu Augustaldens. CCC missas et CCC psalteria, a Priore et Conventu de Brenkeburn CCC missas cum omnibus psalteriis in ecclesiâ suâ dicendis, a Priore et Conventu de Tynemuth ccc missas et cc psalteria, a Priore et Conventu de Coldingham cccc missas et cccc psalteria, a Priore et Conventu de Boulton lxxx missas, a Priore et Conventu de Finchall cccc missas et cccc psalteria, a Priore et Fratribus de Insula ccc missas et cc psalteria, a Fratribus de Banburgh c missas, a Fratribus de Jarwe ccc missas, a Fratribus de Weremuth cc missas, a Fratribus de Farn c missas et c psalteriâ, a Priorissâ et Conventu de Nesham ccc psalteria, a Priorissâ et Conventu de Lamely ccc psalteria, a Priorissâ et Conventu de Berewich lx missas & ccc psalteria, a Priorissâ et Conventu de Halistan lii missas et ccc psalteria, a Priorissâ et Conventu de Novo Castro ccc psalteria, cum ceteris bonis quæ in singulis ecclesiis prenotatis fient privatim et publicè, benefactoribus omnibus prenominatis liberaliter esse concessa. Summa vero psalteriorum iv. m. Nos autem præter missas suprascriptas facimus singulis diebus sex missas pro predictis benefactoribus in monasterio nostro celebrari. Et est summa missarum viim ccc et xxxii. Et in hujus rei testimonium sigillum nostrum presentibus literis fecimus apponi. (*Before* 1244.)

II.—H. Elyens. conferentibus ad fabricam ix altarium xl dies per septem annos. Anno m.cc.xxxv.

Omnibus hoc scriptum visuris vel audituris H. Dei gratia Eliensis Episcopus salutem in Domino. Inter præclaros Christi Confessores quorum præsentia corporalis Anglicanæ patrocinatur Ecclesiæ Beatus Cuthbertus non mediocre sanctitatis preconium dinoscitur optinere. Nec immerito laudibus humanis attollitur cujus meritis infirmi sanitatis gratiam consequuntur. Cujus caro carie carens et prorsus integrè perseverans dormientem potiusquam mortuum representare videtur. Membra namque beati viri manere penitus incorrupta non solum Venerabilis Bedæ presbiteri scriptura testatur, verum etiam probavit ipsius sanctissimi corporis translatio, sub hoc novissimo tempore celebrata. Hic itaque thesaurus super aurum et topazion preciosus apud Dunelmensem requiescit Ecclesiam, ubi supra sacrum illius sepulchrum devocio veterum lapideas erexit testudines, quæ jam nunc plenæ fissuris et rimis dissolutionem sui indicant imminere, adeoque propinquam minatur ruinam ut quicunque molem illam tam suspecte pendentem aspexerit veraciter dicere possit, quoniam terribilis et tremendus est locus ille. Cum autem venerabilis frater Dominus R. Dunelmensis Episcopus tam manifesto desiderans obviare periculo disponat, auxiliante

Domino, apud orientalem supradictæ Ecclesiæ partem novum opus extruere in quo ipsius sancti Confessoris corpus valeat tutius pariter et honestius collocari, universitatem vestram monemus et hortamur in Domino ut ad prefati operis fabricam celerius consummandam de bonis vobis a Deo collatis aliqua caritatis subsidia velitis misericorditer erogare, quatenus per hæc et alia bona quæ feceritis eterna possistis gaudia promereri. Nos vero de Dei misericordia et de gloriosæ Virginis necnon et Sancti Cuthberti omniumque sanctorum meritis confidentes omnibus qui fabricæ memoratæ pias elemosinarum largitiones impenderint, seu predictum locum per hoc septennium proxime futurum causa orationis adierint, et quorum Diocesani hanc indulgentiam nostram ratam habuerint, si de peccatis suis vero contriti fuerint et confessi, triginta dies de injunctâ sibi penitentiâ relaxamus. Data London. anno gratiæ Millesimo Ducentesimo tricesimo quinto. Septimo id. Julii.

III. INDULGENTIA quadraginta dierum concessa per Clementem permissione divina ecclesiæ Dumblanensis ministrum humilem omnibus visitantibus Majus Altare in ecclesia Dunelmensi per ipsum in honorem Sanctæ Mariæ semper virginis consecratum. Data apud Dunelm. die consecrationis predicti Altaris, scilicet nonis Junii, pontificatus anno xxx. *In dorso* 1240.

IV. INDULGENTIA quadraginta dierum concessa per Clementem permissione divina ecclesiæ Dunblanensis ministrum humilem omnibus aliquid ad reparationem fabricæ Dunelmensis ecclesiæ, quæ horribilem minatur ruinam, conferentibus. Data anno gratiæ 1243, kal. Octobris.

V. INDULGENTIA quadraginta dierum concessa per Silvestrem Dei gratia Karleolensem episcopum omnibus visitantibus &c. Data Dunelm., 16 kal. Junii, primo anno pontificatus.

VI. INDULGENTIA quadraginta dierum concessa per Gilbertum Candidæ Casæ episcopum omnibus visitantibus Feretrum Sancti Cuthberti cum orationibus et donis. Data Dunelm. vii. kal. Novembris 1248, pontificatus xiii°.

VII. INDULGENTIA quadraginta dierum concessa per Ricardum episcopum Mannensem et Insularum. Data apud Dunelm. primo anno pontificatus.

VIII. INDULGENTIA quadraginta dierum concessa per Gilbertum Dei gratia Candidæ Casæ episcopum " omnibus qui ad aliquod de quinque Altaribus in fronte Dunelmensis ecclesiæ positis, quorum fecimus dedicationem, causa devotionis advenerint." Data die dedicationis dictorum Altarium, scilicet xvi. kal. Julii, 1253, apud Dunelm.

IX. INDULGENTIA quadraginta dierum concessa conferentibus aliquid ad Feretrum Sancti Cuthberti per Ricardum Dei gratia episcopum Dunkeldensem. Data apud Dunholm. 1254.

X. INDULGENTIA quadraginta dierum concessa per Albinum permissione divina ecclesiæ Breynensis ministrum humilem omnibus visitantibus Galileam, &c. Data apud Dunelm., 1254.

XI. INDULGENTIA quadraginta dierum concessa per Abel Dei gratia episcopum Sancti Andreæ omnibus visitantibus Feretrum Sancti Cuthberti sive Galileam cum orationibus et donis. Data apud Dunelm. 4 non. Junii, 1254 primo anno pontificatus.

XII. INDULGENTIA quadraginta dierum concessa per Walterum Dei gratia Norwicensem episcopum omnibus visitantibus Feretrum Sancti Cuthberti. Data Dunelm. vi. id. Septembris, 1254. Pontificatus 10°.

XIII. INDULGENTIA quadraginta dierum concessa per Walterum episcopum Dunelmensem cum confirmatione Indulgentiæ Silvestris episcopi Karleolensis, Gilberti episcopi Candidæ Casæ datæ 7 kal. Novembriis 1248, item Indulgentiæ quadraginta dierum ab eodem singulis diebus in perpetuum ad quodlibet quinque Altarium in fronte ecclesiæ ab ipso consecratorum, anno 1253—Thomæ episcopi Egdunensis, viginti dierum— Clementis episcopi Dumblanensis, viginti dierum, anno 1253, kal. Maii—Indulgentiæ quadraginta dierum concessæ ab eodem eodem anno, non. Junii, in consecratione majoris Altaris singulis diebus in perpetuum—Ricardi Sodorensis, Mannensis, et Insularum, quadraginta dierum—Abel episcopi Sancti Andreæ, quadraginta dierum, 4 non. Junii, 1254—Willielmi episcopi Norvicensis, quadraginta dierum, 6 id. Septembris, 1256— Ricardi episcopi Dunkeldensis, quadraginta dierum, crastino S. Luciæ virginis, 1254—Roberti Rossensis, quadraginta dierum—Willielmi episcopi Catanensis, quadraginta dierum— Ysaac episcopi Connorensis, quadraginta dierum—Alani episcopi Ergadiensis, quadraginta dierum. Data apud Aukland 8 id. Aprilis, pontificatus nostri anno septimo (1255).

XIV. INDULGENTIA quadraginta dierum concessa per Alanum Dei gratia Ergadiensem episcopum omnibus visitantibus Feretrum Sancti Cuthberti sive Galileam. Data apud Dunelm. 1255.

XV. INDULGENTIA Ysaac episcopi Conorensis de quadraginta diebus concessa visitantibus Galileam sive Feretrum Sancti Cuthberti Dunelm. Data apud Dunelm. 1255.

XVI. INDULGENTIA quadraginta dierum concessa per Robertum Dei gratia Rosensem episcopum, xii. kal. Julii, 1255, pontificatus anno 6to apud Dunelm.

XVII. INDULGENTIA quadraginta dierum concessa per Willielmum Catanensis ecclesiæ episcopum omnibus visitantibus Feretrum Sancti Cuthberti sive Galileam cum donis et orationibus. Data apud Dunelm. 16 cal. Octobris, 1255, anno pontificatus 9°.

XVIII. INDULGENTIA Albini Dei gratia Breynensis episcopi concessa omnibus visitantibus quodlibet de quinque Altaribus in fronte ecclesiæ Dunelmensis. Data apud Dunelm., 4 non. Martii, 1256.

XIX. WILLIELMUS Dei gratia Connorensis episcopus concedit quadraginta dies Indulgentiæ. Data apud Dunelm. 1258. Pontificatus anno secundo.

XX. INDULGENTIA viginti dierum ad fabricam sive reparationem ecclesiæ Dunelmensis concessa per Willielmum episcopum Glasguensem. Data apud Alnecrumb, kal. Octobris, 1258.

XXI. INDULGENTIA quadraginta dierum concessa per Henricum Dei gratia Candidæ Casæ episcopum omnibus visitantibus, &c. Data Dunelm. die Sancti Leonardi, 1259.

XXII. INDULGENTIA quadraginta dierum concessa per Augustinum miseracione divina Landocensem episcopum omnibus visitantibus Feretrum Sancti Cuthberti. Data apud Dunelm. xv. kal. Decembris, 1259.

XXIII. INDULGENTIA quadraginta dierum concessa per

G. Archiepiscopum Eboracensem omnibus visitantibus Feretrum Sancti Cuthberti sive Galileam, et conferentibus, &c. Data Dunelm. xv. kal. Decembris, 1259, pontificatus anno 2º.

XXIV. INDULGENTIA triginta dierum concessa per Robertum Dei gratia Dumblenensem episcopum. Data Dunelm. pridie id. Septembris, 1260.

XXV. INDULGENTIA viginti dierum concessa per Henricum miseracione divina Londoniensem episcopum. Data London, 1260.

XXVI. INDULGENTIA viginti dierum concessa per Rogerum Dei gratia Conventrensem et Lichefeldensem episcopum. Data apud Oxon. 4 id. Martii, sexto anno pontificatus.

XXVII. INDULGENTIA quadraginta dierum concessa per Hugonem Elyensem episcopum. Data London, 3 kal. Martii, octavo anno pontificatus.

XXVIII. INDULGENTIA quadraginta dierum concessa per Archibaldum miseratione divina Moraviensem episcopum "omnibus visitantibus Feretrum Venerabilis Bedæ, presbiteri et doctoris egregii, cujus venerandæ reliquiæ in majori ecclesia Dunelmensi sunt reconditæ." Data Dunelm. vi. kal. Aprilis, 1268.

XXIX. INDULGENTIA quadraginta dierum concessa per fratrem Carbricium miseratione divina episcopum Rathbonensem, dummodo loci dyocesanus hanc indulgentiam ratam habuerit. Data Dunelm. 1273.

XXX. INDULGENTIA quadraginta dierum concessa per Petrum Dei gratia Archadiensem episcopum omnibus visitantibus Feretrum Sancti Cuthberti cum donis, &c. Data apud Dunelm. septimo kal. Januarii, 1273.

XXXI. INDULGENTIA quadraginta dierum concessa per Henricum Dei gratia Candidæ Casæ episcopum "omnibus qui ad aliquod de duobus Altaribus in fronte Dunelmensis ecclesiæ in parte australi positis, quorum fecimus dedicationem, causa devotionis advenerint, quorum unum dedicatum est in honorem Sancti Johannis Baptistæ et Sanctæ Margaretæ virginis et martyris, et aliud in honorem Sancti Andreæ et Sanctæ Mariæ Magdalenæ." Data die dedicationis dictorum Altarium, scilicet,

vii. kal. Januarii, anno Domini M.CC.LXX quarto, apud Dunelm.

XXXII. INDULGENTIA quadraginta dierum concessa per Robertum Dei gratia Dunelmensem episcopum cum confirmatione Indulgentiarum predecessorum suorum. Data apud Myddelham xiii. kal. Martii, pontificatus anno primo.

XXXIII. INDULGENTIA quadraginta dierum concessa per Walterum permissione divina Rofensem episcopum omnibus aliquid de bonis suis ad reparationem novæ fabricæ Dunelmensis ecclesiæ celerius consummandam conferentibus; " præsentibus usque ad predictæ fabricæ inchoatæ perfectionem valituris." Data apud Dunelm. xii. kal. Septembris, 1277.

XXXIV. INDULGENTIA quadraginta dierum concessa per eundem episcopum omnibus visitantibus Feretrum Sancti Cuthberti. Data eodem die.

XXXV. INDULGENTIA quadraginta dierum concessa per Willielmum Dei gratia episcopum Sancti Andreæ in Scocia. Data apud Dunelm. pridie idus Octobris, 1277.

XXXVI. INDULGENTIA quadraginta dierum per Willielmum permissione divina Norwicensem episcopum omnibus conferentibus aliquid de bonis suis ad reparacionem novæ fabricæ Dunelmensis ecclesiæ. Data apud Dunelm. nonis Martii, 1278.

XXXVII. INDULGENTIA quadraginta dierum concessa per Robertum Dei gratia Batoniensis ecclesiæ episcopum omnibus visitantibus Feretrum Sancti Cuthberti cum orationibus et donis. Data apud Dunelm. xvi. kal. Octobris, 1280.

XXXVIII. INDULGENTIA quadraginta dierum concessa per Petrum Dei gratia Conerensis ecclesiæ episcopum omnibus visitantibus Feretrum Sancti Cuthberti. Data apud Dunelm. kal. Mar. 1280.

XXXIX. INDULGENTIA quadraginta dierum concessa per Willielmum Dei gratia Dunkeldensem episcopum omnibus visitantibus Feretrum Sancti Cuthberti et aliquid conferentibus. Data apud Dunelm. xv. kal. Junii, 1285.

XL. INDULGENTIA quadraginta dierum concessa per Willielmum Dei gratia Brheyensem episcopum omnibus, &c. Data apud Dunelm. 17 kal. Septembris, 1286.

XLI. INDULGENTIA quadraginta dierum concessa per Thomam Dei gratia Candidæ Casæ ecclesiæ episcopum omnibus visitantibus Feretrum Sancti Cuthberti. Data Dunelm. nonis Septembris, 1302.

XLII. INDULGENTIA ejusdem episcopi visitantibus Altare Sanctæ Crucis, *s.a.*

XLIII. INDULGENTIA quadraginta dierum concessa per Willielmum (Lamberton) episcopum Sancti Andreæ omnibus visitantibus Altare Sanctæ Crucis de novo constructum in ecclesia Dunelm. Data apud Dunelm. 7 kal. Maii septimo anno pontificatus.

XLIV. INDULGENTIA quadraginta dierum concessa per Robertum Elyensem episcopum. Data apud Novum Castrum super Tynam, 3 non. Octobris, 1306, consecrationis quarto.

XLV. INDULGENTIA quadraginta dierum concessa per fratrem Andream permissione divina Ergadyensem episcopum omnibus visitantibus Altare Sanctæ Crucis in ecclesia Dunelmensi. Data Dunelm. xiii. kal. Decembris, 1310, pontificatus anno 13º.

XLVI. Alia ejusdem episcopi, eodem anno.

XLVII. *Antonius Patriarcha visitantibus feretrum vel reliquias* XL *d. Item idem Antonius Dunelm.* XL *d. Aº.* Mº. CCC *decimo.*

UNIVERSIS Sanctæ Matris Ecclesiæ filiis presentes litteras inspecturis Antonius permissione divinâ sanctæ Jerosolimitanæ Ecclesiæ Patriarcha et Episcopus Dunolmens. salutem in eo qui pro redempcione humani generis Jerosolimis voluit crucifigi. Gratum Deo impendere credimus obsequium ipsumque Creatorem et Dominum omnium precipue veneramur dum sanctos suos devotæ Christianorum memoriæ recommendamus, eoque prestantius quo per allectiva indulgenciarum et remissionum munera ad orationis devocionem et elemosinarum largicionem animos fidelium excitamus. De Dei igitur omnipotentis misericordiâ, gloriosæ virginis Mariæ matris ejus, sanctorum apostolorum Petri et Pauli, et beatissimi Cuthberti Confessoris omniumque sanctorum meritis et precibus confidentes; omnibus Christi fidelibus de peccatis suis vere penitentibus et confessis, qui causa devocionis et oracionis ad Cathedralem Ecclesiam nostram Dunolmensem accesserint, et Feretrum beatissimi Cuthberti Confessoris aliasque Reliquias ibidem in quacumque parte dictæ

Ecclesiæ existentes visitaverint, seu de bonis sibi a Deo collatis aliquid eidem Ecclesiæ offerendo, seu alio modo largiendo caritative contulerint, quadraginta dies auctoritate nostra Patriarchali et rursum quadraginta dies jure nostro Episcopali de injuncta sibi penitencia misericorditer in Domino relaxamus. Ratificantes insuper per presentes omnes Indulgencias a confratribus nostris Archiepiscopis et Episcopis quibuscumque ex causis premissis concessas et imposterum concedendas. In cujus rei testimonium sigillum nostrum presentibus est appensum. Data apud Eltham Roffens' Dioces' quinto die mensis Junij. Anno Domini millesimo trecentesimo decimo, Patriarchatus nostri quinto, et Consecracionis nostræ vicesimo septimo.*

XLVIII. INDULGENTIA quadraginta dierum concessa per Willielmum archiepiscopum Eboracensem omnibus visitantibus Reliquias ecclesiæ Dunelmensis. Data Dunelm. 4 non. Maii, 1311, pontificatus sexto.

XLIX. INDULGENTIA quadraginta dierum concessa per Willielmum Archiepiscopum Eboracensem omnibus visitantibus Feretrum Sancti Cuthberti et aliquid de bonis suis conferentibus. Data Dunelm. iv. non. Maii, 1311, pontificatus vi^{to}.

L. INDULGENTIA quadraginta dierum concessa per Johannem episcopum Conerensem omnibus visitantibus Feretrum Sancti Cuthberti vel locum Reliquiarum cum donis. 3 id. Aprilis, 1319, pontificatus anno 25º.

LI. INDULGENTIA quadraginta dierum concessa per Johannem Dei gratia Karliolensem episcopum. Data apud manerium nostrum de Bello Loco, xvi. kal. Novembris, 1333, et consecrationis secundo.

LII. INDULGENTIA Ricardi Dunelmensis episcopi conferentibus ad fabricam Ecclesiæ vel ad Feretrum Sancti Cuthberti cum ratificatione omnium Indulgentiarum precedentium.
UNIVERSIS—Ricardus, permissione divina episcopus Dunelmensis, salutem — Cum, ad promerenda sempiterna gaudia Sanctorum, sint nobis suffragia plurimum opportuna, loca Sanctorum omnium pia sunt devotione fidelium veneranda; ut, dum Dei veneramur amicos, ipsi nos amicabiles Deo reddant, et illorum quodammodo vendicando patrocinium apud Deum,

---

* Seal engraved in Surtees's History of Durham,—Seals, plate v. No. 1.

quod merita nostra non obtinent eorum mereamur intercessionibus obtinere. Cupientes, igitur, ut ecclesia Dunelmensis, in qua venerabilis patris nostri Cuthberti incorruptum corpus honorifice collocatur, congruis honoribus et crebris populorum accessibus frequentetur, omnibus vere pœnitentibus quadraginta dies, &c. Data Dunelm. 7 Junii, 1334, pontificatus primo.

LIII. INDULGENTIA quadraginta dierum concessa per Willielmum Archiepiscopum Eboracensem omnibus visitantibus locum Reliquiarum in ecclesia Sancti Cuthberti Dunelm. Data Dunelm. nonis Junii, 1334, pontificatus xvij°.

LIV. INDULGENTIA quinquaginta dierum concessa per Johannem Archiepiscopum Cantuariensem omnibus visitantibus Reliquias ecclesiæ Dunelmensis. Data Novi Castri super Tynam x. kal. Januarii, 1335, translationis 2°.

LV. INDULGENTIA triginta dierum concessa per Thomam Dei gratia Enhegdunensem episcopum. Data Dunelm. 4 non. Aprilis.

LVI. INDULGENTIA quadraginta dierum concessa per Rogerum episcopum Rossensem omnibus visitantibus Altare Sanctæ Crucis in ecclesia cathedrali Dunelmensi de novo constructum. Data Dunelm. 13 . ., consecrationis 4to.

INDEX.

A.

Abbey gates, 84, 88.
——— yard, 53.
Aidan, St. his picture in glass, 41.
——— image for processions, 89.
Aldunus or Aldwinus, bishop, 41, 47, 56, 60, 61, 62, 63.
Allerton, hospital, 63.
Almeries, 1, 4, 11, 28, 38.
Almery, children of, 15, 44, 45, 54, 77.
Altars, Nine, or front of the church, 1, 2, 3.
——— Indulgences for building this part of the church, 129—138.
——— five in the Nine Altars, Indulgences for visiting, 132—138.
Altar of St. Aidan and St. Helen, 2.
——— of St. Andrew and Mary Magdalen, 1, 134.
——— of St. Bede, 1, 38, 39.
——— of St. Benedict, 19.
——— of Bound Rood, 35, 136, 138.
——— of St. Cuthbert, 1.
——————— in the Feretory, 3, 4.
——— of St. Gregory, 19.
——— The High, 6, 9, 12, 14, 15, 16, 131.
——— of St. Jerome and St. Benedict, Inscriptions, 105—117.
——— of Jesus, 28, 34, 87.
——— of St. John the Baptist and St. Margaret, 1, 134.
——— of St. Nicholas and St. Giles, 20, 25.
——— of Neville, 34.
——— of our Lady of Boulton, 26.
——————— of Houghall, 26.
——————— of Pity, 33.
——— of our Lady of Pity in the Galilee, 37, 38.
——— of St. Laurence and St. Oswald, 1.
——— of St. Martin, 2.
——— of St. Michael, 2.
——— in Porch, 16.
——— of St. Peter, and St. Paul, 2.
——— of St. Saviour, 33.
——— of Bishop Skirlaw, 17, 81.
——— of St. Thomas and St. Fides, 26.

Altar of St. Thomas of Canterbury and St. Catharine, 1.
——— in Vestry, 17.
Altars, Keys of, 82.
——— Chalices, robes, &c. belonging to each, 82.
Altar Screen or Reredose, 5, 6.
Alured, King, 36, 43.
Anchoridge, the, 15.
Andrew's, St. 48.
Awkeland, John, prior of Durham, 30, 46.
Aydanus, bishop, 47.

B.

Bailey, South, 88.
Baites Baytes, George, Clerk of the Feretory, &c., 67, 69.
Banner of St. Cuthbert, 20—23, 88—90.
——— of King of Scots, 6, 80.
——— of Lord Neville, 5.
Barber, the 44.
Barnes, Jo. 53.
Basins, for the High Altar, 8, 12.
Basin and Ewer in the Frater House, 69.
Beake Beeke, Anthony, Bishop of Durham, 2, 50.
Bearparke, or Beaurepaire, 25.
Bede, The Venerable, 63.
——— his bowl, 68.
——— his picture in glass, 41.
——— his shrine, 38, 39, 80.
——————— carried in procession, 88, 89.
——————— defaced, 87.
——————— Indulgences to visitors of, 134, &c.
Bello Monte, L. bishop of Durham, 12, 13, 14, 51.
Bells, 33, 34, 35.
——— in Lantern, 19.
——— ringers, 19.
Benefactors, prayers for, 82.
Bennett Robert, Bowcer or Bursar, and his duties, 82, 83, 84.
Berrington, Robert, prior of Durham, 19, 46.

INDEX.

Bishop of Durham—mode of burial of, 49, 50.
———————— place of burial of, 46, 47, 48.
———————— seat in quire, 16.
Black Rood of Scotland, 16, 21, 22.
Blythman, Master, 85, 86.
Boisil, Abbot of Melrose, 55.
Bonnie, Master, prebendary of Durham, 84.
Book of Benefactors, 14, 15.
Books in the Cloister, 71.
Book of the Gospels, 60.
Book of Relics, 15.
Bough or Bowe Church, 61, 88.
Bowling Allie for the Monks, 75.
Branxton or Flodden, battle of, 79, 80.
Brewen, a fellow so called, 12.
Brimley, John, master of the Song School, 37.
Browne, Henry, master of the Common House and his duties, 84.
Bruce, David, king of Scotland, 21, 22.
Burnbie, Burnby, John prior of Durham, his burial place, 30, 46.
Bursar, the, and his duties, 82, 83, 85.
Bury, Richard de, bishop of Durham, his burial place, 2.
Buttery or great cellar, 74.

C.

Candlesticks, 5, 8, 9.
Canopy for the Sacrament, 7.
Carilepho, William de, bishop of Durham, 62, 63.
Carrells in the Cloister, 70, 71.
Castell, Thomas, prior of Durham, 27, 29, 46, 68.
Castro Bernardi, Ricardus de, 39.
Cathedral and see of Durham founded, 61.
Cedda, bishop, picture of in glass, 43.
Cellar, 69, 73, 74.
——— door, 78.
——— yeoman of, 78.
Cellarer and his duties, 83.
——— his chamber, 83.
Censers, 8.
Centry or cemetery garth, 1, 44, 45, 51, 52, 64, 74.
——— vault in, 51.
——— song school in, 54.
——— destruction of tombs in, 52, 53.
Chalices for the High Altar, 8.
Chamber of Church keeper, 34, 35.
Chamberlains, 81.
Chamberlain and his duties, 84.
Chapel of St. Andrew, 44, 45.
——— of Virgin at the east end of the church, 37.

Chapel of wands, 57.
Chapter House, 44, 45, 46, 47, 48, 49, 82.
——— masse, 82.
——— seal, 71.
——— stone seat in, 48.
Charles king of England, his progress to Scotland, 81.
Chester le Street, 56, 61.
Children, poor, 77.
Choir door, Inscriptions upon the screen, 118—124, see Quire.
Choristers, 54.
Clark, Robert, porter of the Prior, 77.
Clock, 26, 27, 66.
——— near the Altar of Jesus, 29.
Cloisters, 54—56.
——— Almerie in, 67.
——— armorial bearings in ceiling, 65.
——— bench of stone, 67.
——— doors and door-keeper, or porter, 67, 78.
——— East Alley of, 64, 65.
——— South Alley of, 67—70.
——— North Alley of, 70, 71.
——— West Alley, 71, 72.
——— Tomb of St. Cuthbert in, 58, 59.
Colegarth, the, 83.
Colleine, three kings of, 40.
Common House, 75.
——— Hall, 84.
Communer and his duties, 84.
Conduit, the, 53, 84.
Consistory Court in Galilee, 63.
Convent, clerk of, 77.
Corporax cloth of St. Cuthbert, 20, 79.
Corpus Christi day, Procession on, 89, 90.
——— shrine in St. Nicholas Church, 59, 90.
Crake Minster, 56, 60.
Crosbie, Richard, master of the Novices and his duties, 81.
Crosses for Processions, 8, 88.
Cross of blue marble in the Nave, 30.
——— at North Chilton Pool on the Mayde's Bower, 25.
Cross-week, processions in, 87, 88.
Crucifix of Gold for the Passion, 9, 10.
Cruetts for the High Altar, 8.
Covey or Pantry, 77, 78.
Cuthbert, Saint—*passim*.
———————, accusation against him by the daughter of the king of the Picts, 30.
———————, his banner, 79, 80.
———————, his feast in Lent, 69.
———————, his history, 54, 59, 65.
———————, his image and tomb in the Cloister Garth, 58, 59, 63, 64.
———————, his picture in glass—*passim*.

Cryers, an organ so called, 14.

D.

Danes, invasion of, 55, 56, 60.
Darlington, church of, 63.
David, king of Scotland, 16.
Dead man's chamber, 44, 45.
Dean's buttrie, 53.
——— hall, 85.
——— kitchen, 53.
——— lodging, 66.
Doctors, the four, 14.
Domus Infirmorum, 44, 45.
Dorter, or Dormitory, 72, 73, 82, 84, 85.
———————, monks' chamber in, 78.
Dove Cote in cloister, 70.
Draxe, Wm., prior of Coldingham, 98.
Dunholme and the Milk Maid, 57, 61.
Dunbar, battle of, 12, 50.

E.

Eadmundus, bishop, 41, 47.
Eadredus, bishop, 47, 60.
Eagle of brass (a lectern), 12.
Eardulf, bishop, 55, 60.
Eata, St., 41, 55.
Ebchester, Robert, prior of Durham, 26, 46.
——————, William, ———————, 26, 46.
Edrede, abbot of Lindisfarne, 55.
Egelwyn, bishop, 48.
Egfrid, bishop, 43.
Elfride, king, 43.
Elfridus, priest, 39.
Elmden, Mr., his monument, 52.
Elvet Bridge, 63.
Epistoler, the, 7.
Ethelwold, bishop, 43.
Evidences and Records, 71.
Exchequer of Bursar, 82.
——————— of Cellarer, 83.
——————— of Communer, 84.
——————— of Master of the Garners, 84.
——————— of Prior's Chaplain, 85.
——————— of Sacrist, 82.
——————— of Terrar, 83.

F.

Farne Island, 36.
Farnham, Nicholas, bishop of Durham, 48, 62.
Fawden (folding) gates, 78, 83.
Feretory, or shrine of St. Cuthbert, 3—6, 37, 58, 62, 63, 67, 85, 86.

Feretory, master of, 78, 79.
———, clerk of, 79.
———, Indulgences to visitors of, 131 —138.
Fermery, 44, 45, 75, 76.
———, Bursar's Chamber in, 83.
———, school, 77.
———, without the Abbey gates, 77, 78.
———, ———————, chapel in, 78.
Finchale Priory, 63.
Flambard, Ralph, bishop of Durham, 47, 62.
Form in Cloister, 66.
Font for holy water, 11.
——— in the Galilee, 40.
Fossour, John, prior of Durham, 20, 25, 46.
Foster, William, keeper of the garners and his duties, 84.
Frater House, 4, 5, 68.
——————— door, 78.
———————, ambrie in, 68, 69.
———————, picture in, 68.

G.

Galilee, the, 36—43, 63, 80, 87.
———, Indulgences to visitors of, 133, &c.
——— bell, 35.
——— sermon, 33.
——— steeple, 33.
Garden, the, 75.
Garners, the, 84.
———, keeper of, and his duties, 84.
Gaufridus, bishop of Durham, 47.
Glass, painted, 27, 36, 40—43, 49, 65, 91—102.
Godric, St., 63.
Gospels, Book of, 56, 58.
Gospeller, the, 7.
Grace cup in the Frater House, 68.
Grammar School, 38.
Great Hall in the Guest Hall, 83.
Great Kyrke, 57, 58.
Greatham Hospital, 66, 67.
Guest Hall, 76, 77, 83.
——— Chamber, 83.
Guthrid, king, 36, 43.

H.

Halden, king of the Danes, 55.
Hall door of Prior, 76.
Harvy, Dr. 59, 90.
Haselrige, Sir Arthur, 12.

Hartburne, Sir Robert, schoolmaster, 77.
Hatfield, Thomas, bishop of Durham, 16, 51.
Hemmyngbrowghe, John, prior of Durham, 26, 46.
Henly, Dr. 85, 86.
Henry VI. letter from, 103.
——— king, picture of, 42.
Hexham, Thomas, 95.
Holy Island, 54, 59, 60.
Holy Rood House, 16, 21.
Holy Thursday, procession on, 88.
Holy Water Stones, 30, 32, 33, 35, 52, 53.
Horne, Robert, Dean of Durham, 46.
Hundredus, 56.

I.

Image of St. Cuthbert in the Cloister, 58, 59.
——— and crucifix at the altar of our Lady of Boulton, 26.
Inscriptions upon the screen of the choir, 118—124.
——— near the altar of St. Jerome and St. Benedict, 105—117.
Insula, Robert de, bishop of Durham, 48.
Ireland, kings of, 55.

J.

Jarrow, monks of, 58, 62.
——— monastery of, 39.
Jesse window, 36, 49.
Judas's cup in the refectory, 68.

K.

Kellowe, Richard de, bishop of Durham, 48.
Kilne, the, 84.
Kimblesworth church, 77.
King's chamber in the Guest Hall, 76.
Kirkham, Walter de, bishop of Durham, 48.
Kitchen, the Great, 69, 73, 76, 82, 83.
——— expenses, 83.

L.

Lambeth, 51.
Lamb's shop on Framwellgate bridge, 53.
Langley, Thomas, bishop of Durham, 37, 38, 51, 65, 92, 99.
——————— his picture in glass, 42.

Lantern, or Middle Tower, called the New Work, 17, 18, 19.
——————— North Alley of, 19, 20.
——————————— description of windows in, 93, 94.
——————————— South Alley of, 26, 27.
——————————— description of windows in, 94, 95.
——————————— Bells, 34.
Laver in cloister, 70.
Lecterns, 11, 12, 14.
Lee, Dr. 85, 86.
Lent, austerities of, 84.
Library, the, 26.
Livery, the names of those who received livery in the church of Durham, in 1510, with their offices, 125—128.
Loft, the, 69, 73, 74, 78.
——— at the Altar of Jesus, 29.
——— at the north side of the abbey gates, 77.
Lyegate, 88.
Lynghouse, the, 75.

M.

Mailrose, abbey of, 55.
Magdalen's Chapel, 77.
Malcolm, king of Scotland, 47, 48, 62.
Margaret, St. 48.
——————— St. Margaret's ward, 81.
——————— St. Margaret's cross, 89.
——————— St. Margaret's church, 88.
Marley, Mr. Stephen, superior and master of the Fratry, his duties, 78.
————————————— his lodgings, 77.
Marisco, Richard de, bishop of Durham, 48.
Mark, St. procession on his day, 87.
Master of choristers, the, 54.
Matthew, Tobias, dean of Durham, 67, 68.
Maunday Thursday, 9.
——————— ceremonies on, 66, 67.
Mazers in the Frater House, 69.
Melsonby, Thomas, prior of Durham, 62.
Milk maid and her cow, image of, 63.
Monks, clothing of, 84.
——— wages, 81.
——— burial place and mode of burial, 43—45, 51.
Muriardach, father of St. Cuthbert, 55.
Myers, Ambrose, 53.

N.

Nave or body of the church, from the Lantern to the Galilee, 28—32.
——————— North Alley of, 32.

INDEX. 143

Nave or body of the church, South Alley of, 34, 35, 36, 50.
—————— description of the windows in the North Alley of, 91, 92.
—————— description of the windows in the South Alley of, 92, 93.
Neville, John, Lord, 21—25.
—————— his monument, 50.
—————— Ralph, Lord, 21—25.
—————— his monument, 50.
—————— Robert, bishop of Durham, 34, 51.
—————— monuments, defacing of, 50.
—————— tomb, 87.
—————— porch, 34.
—————— windows, 92, 93.
Neville's Cross, battle of, 20—25, 50.
—————— erection of, 23, 24.
Newcastle, 12.
Nicholas, St. church of, 59, 88, 90.
Nine altars, 1—6.
—————— description of windows in, 99—102.
North Bailey, 53.
Novices, the, 69, 70, 71, 81.
—————— master of, 71, 72, 77, 81.
—————— school of, 71, 72.
—————— table of, 77.
—————— clothing of, 84.

O.

Officers of the church at the Dissolution, 78—85.
—————— in 1510, 125—128.
Organs, 14, 54.
O Sapientia, Feast of, 75, 85.
Oswald, King and Saint, pictures of, 42, 88, 89.
—————— St. Oswald's church, 87.

P.

Pantry, the, 77, 78.
Parlour, the, 44, 59.
Pascal, the, 8, 9, 15.
Passion, the, 9, 10.
Pattinson, Edward, keeper of the Cloister, 67.
Pax, the, 7.
Pelican of silver, 7.
Peter, the maker of Bede's shrine, 39.
Pews in the Cloister, 70, 71.
Pictavia, Philip de, bishop of Durham, 48.
Pilkington, Master, 84.
Pix at the High Altar, 7.
Place Green, 38, 89, 90.
Porch in the North Aisle, 16.
Poor children, 77.
Porters, 67, 76.

Porter, alias Smythe, John, Sacrist, and his duties, 81.
Priors, mode of burial and burial place of, 45, 52.
Prior's apparel, 85.
—————— chamber, 85.
—————— chaplain, and his duties 44, 85.
—————— gentlemen, 54.
—————— hall, 54, 55, 56.
—————— hospitality, 76.
—————— officers and servants, 85.
—————— plate, 85.
—————— seat in the nave, 34.
—————— table, 83.
Prison for monks, 48.
Privies, 72, 73.
Processions, 11, 32, 87—90.
Pudsey, Hugh, bishop of Durham, 37, 38, 39, 47, 63.
Pulpit of iron in the Galilee, 40.

Q.

Quire, the, 6—15.
—————— North Alley of, 15, 16.
—————— Description of windows in, 96, 97.
—————— South Alley, 16.
—————— Description of windons in, 97, 98.

R.

Rackett, Mr. his burial place and monument, 52.
Readhills or Neville's Cross, battle of, 20—25.
Records and evidences of the Church, 66, 67.
Registry and register's office, 64, 66, 67, 79.
Relics in the shrine, indulgences to visitors of, 137, 138.
Resurrection, ceremony of, 10, 11.
Revestry, see Vestry.
Richard, king of England, his parliamentary robe, 89.
Richardson, Jo. 53.
Ripon, 56, 60.
Rood doors, 28.
—————— over altar of Jesus, 28, 29.

S.

Sabina, mother of St. Cuthbert, 55.
Sacrist, the, 1.
——————, his office and duties, 81, 82.

144 INDEX.

Sadberge, 63.
Sanctuary, the, 35, 36.
——— cross, the, 36.
——— grate, the, 35, 36.
——— men, 35, 36.
Scotch prisoners, 34.
Screen of quire door, 17.
——— pictures upon, 17, 18, 19.
Seaton, W., sub-prior, his picture, 94.
Seggerstonhewgh, 81.
Sepulchre in Passion week, 10, 11.
Sermon in Galilee, 40.
Sherburn Hospital, 63.
Ships of silver for incense, 8.
Shrine of St. Cuthbert, *see* Feretory.
——————————— defaced, 85, 86.
Skirlaw Walter, bishop of Durham, 15, 16, 51, 64.
Smyth, Robert, prior's porter, 76.
Song school, 16, 54.
———, Sacrist's Exchequer converted into, 81.
——————— in cloister, 81.
Sparke, Thomas, suffragan bishop, 34.
——————— Chamberlayne and his duties, 84.
Stephen, king of England, 47.
Stichell, Robert, bishop of Durham, 48.
Stone for cressetts, 19.
Subprior's chamber, 73, 78.
——— his office, 78.
Swalwell, Dr. 16.

T.

Table at the Altar of Jesus, 28.
Te Deum Window, 27, 66.
Terrar, 76.
Terrar's chamber, 83.
Tinmouth, haven of, 55.
Todde, Dr. 83.
Toll booth, 89.
Tomb of St. Cuthbert in the Cloister, 58, 59.
Treasure house, 71.
Trellis door in the north alley of the Nave, 32.
Trinity Sunday procession, 89.
Tunstall, Cuthbert, bishop of Durham, 51.

Turgot, Prior of Durham, 47, 48, 57, 62.

U.

Usher door, the, 66.
Uthred, Earl of Northumberland, 51, 61.

V.

Vestry, or Revestry, 7, 17.
——— Description of windows in, 98, 99.
Visitation of Bishop in the Chapter House, 48.

W.

Walcherus, bishop of Durham, 47.
Ward Lawe, 56, 61.
Washington, or Weshington, John, Prior of Durham, 19, 46.
Watson, Roger, Terrar, and his duties, 83.
——— alias Wylome, William, Prior's chaplain, and his duties, 78, 79, 85.
Wearmouth, Monks of, 58, 62.
Whitby, Dr. 59, 90.
White Chapel or Kirke, 57, 61.
Whithead, Hugh, the last Prior, 46, 77.
Whitsunday Processions, 88, 89.
Whittingham, William Dean of Durham, 33, 34, 52, 53, 64, 69.
——————— Katherine, 23, 52, 53.
Wilfrid, bishop, picture of, 42.
William, bishop of Durham, 47, 57, 58.
Window of St. Catharine, 2, 6.
——— St. Cuthbert, 3.
——— the four Doctors, 27.
——— Joseph, 3.
Wine for the monks, 85.
Women, why prevented from entering beyond the cross, 30, 31, 32.
Wryght, Roger, Cellarer, and his duties, 83.
Wyndshole gate, 90.

Y.

York, Organ at, 14.

J. B. Nichols and J. G. Nichols, 25, Parliament Street, Westminster.

Also published by Llanerch:

A HISTORY OF THE CHURCH OF DURHAM
Simeon of Durham
(the story of the monks of St. Cuthbert)
translated from latin by Joseph Stevenson

A HISTORY OF THE KINGS OF ENGLAND
Simeon of Durham
translated from latin by Joseph Stevenson

NORTHUMBRIAN MINSTRELSY
Bruce and Stokoe

A CORNER IN THE NORTH
Hastins M. Neville

NORTHANHYMBRE SAGA
John Marsden
A History of the Anglo-Saxon Kings of Northumbria

LIVES OF THE BRITISH SAINTS
Baring-Gould and Fisher
An eight volume set

ROMANO-BRITISH PERIOD AND CELTIC
MONUMENTS
by J Romilly Allen

For a complete list of c. 250 titles, small-press
editions and facsimile reprints
of Llanerch Press Ltd
publications, please visit our website:
www.llanerchpress.com
or alternatively write to:
Llanerch Press Ltd, Little Court, 48 Rectory Road
Burnham-on-Sea, Somerset. TA8 2BZ

It is v. diff for anyone to stand in D today & visualise as it was. The vast solidity of the structure gives a false expression that the bldg has not changed — this is how it is 'meant to be'. Yet for the most part, the Cathdl has taken its current form ex internal layout through historical accident rather than design. Some of the key focal points — St Cuthbert's golden shrine; the Rood Screen — have been destroyed, and others replaced or obscured. As a result the building cannot easily 'talk for itself'

Galilee portal space, worship, lieu ferrule devotion.

May now enclose chples — daily div. ser. — lastly Lishn — worshp pasnakes, opns up